Fractured Families and Rebel Maidservants

Fractured Families and Rebel Maidservants

THE BIBLICAL HAGAR
IN SEVENTEENTH-CENTURY
DUTCH ART AND LITERATURE

CHRISTINE PETRA SELLIN

continuum

NEW YORK • LONDON

T & T Clark International,
80 Maiden Lane, New York, NY 10038
T & T Clark International, The Tower Building,
11 York Road, London SE1 7NX
T & T Clark International is a Continuum imprint.

Unless otherwise indicated, biblical quotations are from the New Revised
Standard Version Bible, copyright 1989, Division of Christian Education of the
National Council of the Churches of Christ in the United States of America.
Used by permission. All rights reserved.

Biblical quotations marked KJV are from the King James Version.

Cover art: Caspar Netscher. *Sarah Leading Hagar to Abraham*, signed and
dated 1673. Canvas, 58 x 49 cm. Collection of Sol Sardinsky, Philadelphia.
Cover design: Brenda Klinger

Library of Congress Cataloging-in-Publication Data

Sellin, Christine Petra, 1961–
    Fractured families and rebel maidservants: the Biblical Hagar in seventeenth
century Dutch art and literature / Christine Petra Sellin.
        p.   cm.
    Includes bibliographical references and index.
    ISBN 0-567-02891-7 (hardcover : alk. paper) — ISBN 0-567-02901-8 (pbk.
: alk. paper)
    1. Hagar (Biblical figure)—Art.   2. Hagar (Biblical figure)—In literature.
3. Ishmael (Biblical figure)—Art.   4. Ishmael (Biblical figure)—In literature.
5. Arts, Dutch—17th century.   I. Title.
NX652.H32S45   2006
700.4'8251—dc22

                                                                2005025252

Printed in Malaysia

06 07 08 09 10 11   10 9 8 7 6 5 4 3 2 1

Voor Ake, Paul, Ans,
Karel, Rita, en Arie

✝
CONTENTS

✝
ILLUSTRATIONS

Fig. 1: Matthaeus Merian. *CEDAT SERVA DOMINAE, LEX GRATIA.* Designed by M. Merian, engraving by P. H. Schut. From *Bybel printen, vertoonende de voornaamste historien der Heylige Schrifture.* Amsterdam: N. Visscher, before 1674. Universiteitsbibliotheek, Amsterdam.

Fig. 2: Henrik Goltzius. *Dissidence in the Church,* from the series *The Allegories of Faith,* ca. 1594. Engraving, 240 x 185 mm. Printroom of Leiden University, Leiden, the Netherlands.

Fig. 3: Jacob Matham (after Abraham Bloemaert). *The Expulsion of Hagar and Ishmael,* 1603. Engraving, 431 x 354 mm, signed at the bottom. Collection: Museum Boijmans Van Beuningen, Rotterdam, the Netherlands.

Fig. 4: Georg Pencz. *Sarah Presenting Hagar to Abraham,* from the series *The Story of Abraham,* ca. 1543. Engraving, 50 x 82 mm, only state, signed with monogram at lower left. Rijksprentenkabinet, Rijksmuseum, Amsterdam.

Fig. 5: Georg Pencz. *Abraham and Agar,* 1548. Engraving, 114 x 77 mm. Department of Prints and Drawings, British Museum, London.

Fig. 6: Crispijn van der Passe I. *Longing for Posterity, Abraham's Concubine Agar,* 1616. Engraving published in *Liber Genesis,* 1616, XXX. Universiteitsbibliotheek, Amsterdam.

Fig. 7: Mathais Stomer. *Sarah Bringing Hagar to Abraham,* no date. Oil on canvas, 112.5 x 168 cm, inv. no. 2146. Photo: Joerg P. Anders. Gemäldegalerie, Staatliche Museen zu Berlin, Berlin, Germany. Photo credit: Bildarchiv Preussischer Kulturbesitz/Art Resource, NY.

Fig. 8: Dirck van Baburen. *The Procuress,* signed and dated 1622. Oil on canvas, 101.6 x 107.6. M. Theresa B. Hopkins Fund, Museum of Fine Arts, Boston. Photo © 2006 Museum of Fine Arts, Boston.

Fig. 9: Mathais Stomer. *Sarah Brings Hagar to Abraham*, ca. 1640s. Canvas, 81.5 x 100 cm. Göteborgs konstmuseum, Göteborg, Sweden. Photograph © Göteborgs konstmuseum.

Fig. 10: Salomon de Bray. *Sarah Presenting Hagar to Abraham*, signed and dated 1650. Oil on panel, 12.5 x 9.75 in. Collection of Dr. Alfred Bader, Milwaukee. Photo: Rijksbureau voor Kunsthistorische Documentatie, Den Haag.

Fig. 11: Caspar Netscher. *Sarah Leading Hagar to Abraham*, signed and dated 1673. Oil on canvas, 58 x 49 cm. Collection of Sol Sardinksy, Philadelphia.

Fig. 12: Willem van Mieris. *Sarah Bringing Hagar to Abraham*, ca. 1685–90, signed upper right: "W. van Mieris." Oil on panel, 44.2 x 36.3 cm. Private collection. Photograph © Jack Kilgore & Company, Inc., New York.

Fig. 13: Adriaen van der Werff, *Sarah Presents Hagar to Abraham*, signed and dated 1699. Oil on canvas, 76.3 x 61.2 cm. Bayerische Staatsgemäldesammlungen, Alte Pinakothek, Munich. Photo: Arthotek, Germany.

Fig. 14: Tobias Stimmer. *Neue Künstliche Figuren Biblischer Historien*, gruntlich von Tobias Stimmer gerissen / und zu gottsforchtiger—ergetzung andachtiger hertzen mit artigen Reimen begriffen durch J;F;S;W. Woodcut. Basle: Thomas Gwarin, 1576, no. 13.

Fig. 15: Pieter Paul Rubens. *Hagar Leaves the House of Abraham*, 1615. Oil on panel, 62.8 x 76 cm, inv. no. GE-475. The State Hermitage Museum, St. Petersburg.

Fig. 16: Bartholomeus Breenbergh. *The Angel Commands Hagar to Return to Sarah*, signed and dated 1632. Copper, 38 x 32 cm. Private collection. Photograph © Sotheby's, New York, January 30, 1997, lot no. 32.

Fig. 17: Attributed to Carel Fabritius. *Hagar and the Angel*, ca. 1643–45. Oil on canvas, 157.5 x 136 cm. Collection of Schönborn-Buchheim, Residenzgalerie, Salzburg. Photo: Fotostudio Ulrich Ghezzi, Oberalm.

Fig. 18: Attributed to Jan Linsen (with figures by Salomon de Bray?). *Hagar and the Angel*, ca. 1640s–50s? Oil on canvas, 106 x 132 cm. Collection of Dr. Alfred Bader, Milwaukee.

Fig. 19: Lucas van Leyden. *Abraham Dismissing Hagar*, ca. 1506. Engraving, 27.5 x 21.7 cm. Rijksprentenkabinet, Rijksmuseum, Amsterdam.

Fig. 20: Cornelis Engelbrechtsz. *The Expulsion of Hagar*, ca. 1500. Oil on panel, 34.5 x 47 cm, inv. no. GG 6820. Kunsthistorisches Museum, Vienna.

Fig. 21: Jan Mostaert. *The Expulsion of Hagar and Ishmael*, ca. 1525

(1527?). Oil on oak, 94 x 131 cm. Collection of Thyssen-Bornemisza. Copyright © Museo Thyssen-Bornemisza, Madrid.

Fig. 22: Pieter Lastman. *The Expulsion of Hagar and Ishmael*, 1612, signed and dated "Anno 1612 Lastman fecit." Oil on canvas, 49 x 71 cm, inv. 91. Photo: Elke Walford. Hamburger Kunsthalle. Photo Credit: Bildarchiv Preussischer Kulturbesitz/Art Resource, NY.

Fig. 23: Rembrandt van Rijn. *Abraham Casting Out Hagar and Ishmael*, 1637. Etching and drypoint, only state, 125 x 95 mm. Collection of Rembrandt House Museum, Amsterdam. Photograph © Rembrandt House Museum.

Fig. 24. Georg Pencz. *The Expulsion of Hagar and Ishmael*, from the series *The Story of Abraham*, ca. 1543, signed with monogram at lower left. Engraving, 50 x 82 mm, only state. Rijksprentenkabinet, Rijksmuseum, Amsterdam.

Fig. 25: Francesco Ruschi. *The Expulsion of Hagar*, ca. 1644–45. Oil on canvas, 55 x 75 in. Collection of Bob Jones University.

Fig. 26: Salomon de Bray. *The Expulsion of Hagar*, 1662. Oil on panel, 21^1/4 x 18^5/8 in. (54.0 x 47.3 cm). Norton Simon Art Foundation, Gift of Mr. Norton Simon.

Fig. 27: Gabriel Metsu. *The Expulsion of Hagar*, ca. 1650–55, signed "Gmetsu." Oil on canvas, 115 x 89 cm, inv. no. S 2209. Collection of Stedelijk Museum De Lakenhal, Leiden, the Netherlands. Photograph © Stedelijk Museum De Lakenhal, Leiden.

Fig. 28: Jan Steen. *The Expulsion of Hagar*, ca. 1660, signed in full on the cornerstone of the archway. Oil on canvas, 54 x 43.5 in. Gemäldegalerie Alte Meister, Staatliche Kunstsammlungen, Dresden.

Fig. 29: Nicolaes Maes. *Abraham Dismissing Hagar and Ishmael*, 1653, signed and dated. Oil on canvas, 34.5 x 27.5 in. All rights reserved, Metropolitan Museum of Art, New York.

Fig. 30: Artist unknown. *The Expulsion of Hagar and Ishmael*, early 1600s?. Dimensions, present location unknown. Photo: Rijksbureau voor Kunsthistorische Documentatie, Den Haag. RKD note below image: "Collection of C. E. Schlyter, Stockholm; photograph Karl Schultz, Stockholm; collection of Sonja Ahlklo, Lidmg 1974" [sic].

Fig. 31: Jan Pynas. *The Departure of Hagar*, signed and dated 1614. Oil on panel, 78 x 106 cm. Private collection, the Netherlands. Photo courtesy of Rijksbureau voor Kunsthistorische Documentatie, Den Haag.

Fig. 32: Abraham Bloemaert. *The Expulsion of Hagar and Ishmael*, signed and dated 1638. Oil on canvas, 57.75 x 71 in. The J. Paul Getty Museum, Los Angeles. Photo © The J. Paul Getty Museum.

Fig. 33: Philip van Dyck. *Abraham Expels Hagar and Ishmael*, late seventeenth century. Oil on copper, 40 x 50 cm. Louvre, Paris, France. Photo Credit: Réunion des Musées Nationaux/Art Resource, NY.

Fig. 34: Pieter Lastman. *Hagar and the Angel*, 1614. Oil on panel, 20 x $26^{7}/8$ in. (50.8 x 68.3 cm), M.85.117. Los Angeles County Museum of Art, purchased with funds provided by the Ahmanson Foundation, Mr. and Mrs. Stewart Resnick, Anna Bing Arnold, Dr. Armand Hammer, and Edward Carter in honor of Kenneth Donahue. Photo © 2005 by Museum Associates/LACMA.

Fig. 35: Matthaeus Merian. *Hagar's Rescue*, in *Icones biblicae praecipuas Sacrae Scripturae historias eleganter et graphice repraesentantes. Biblische Figuren etc. mit Versen und Reymen in dreyen Sprachen*. Strassburg: Zetzner, 1625, vol. 1; 1627, vol. 2; 1630, vol. 3; 1629, vol. 4.

Fig. 36: Johannes Voorhout. *Hagar and Ishmael in the Wilderness*, ca. 1700, signed by the artist. Canvas, 112 x 84 cm. Collectie Centraal Museum, Utrecht. Photo © Centraal Museum, Utrecht.

Fig. 37: Karel du Jardin. *Hagar and Ishmael in the Wilderness*, ca. 1662. Oil on canvas, $73^{3}/4$ x $56^{1}/4$ in., SN 270. Bequest of John Ringling, Collection of the John and Mable Ringling Museum of Art, State Art Museum of Florida, Florida State University.

Fig. 38: Gerard de Lairesse. *Hagar in the Wilderness*, ca. 1675–80, signed at the right "G. Lairesse f." Oil on canvas, 74 x 60 cm, inv. no. GE-622. The State Hermitage Museum, St. Petersburg.

Fig. 39: Herman van der Myn. *Hagar in the Desert*, signed and dated "H. Van Der Myn 1718." Oak panel, 47.5 x 38.5 cm, inv. no. 212. Collection of the Budapest Museum of Fine Arts. Photo © The Budapest Museum of Fine Arts.

† PREFACE

Whoever works with the textual and pictorial interpretations of the Bible from the late medieval and early modern periods will be confronted with the fact that the history of exegeses has not been systematically studied. Certainly, a number of short studies address specific questions, while longer investigations offer overviews. However, we lack comprehensive studies that clarify how those questions and topoi passed down in exegeses from early church fathers developed across a range of media. And we also lack how confessional differences or medium-specific conditions led to many variations in the interpretation of biblical stories.

For centuries, the same exegetical models could be used, but alternative interpretative modes evolved in a variety of expressive media—commentaries, sermons, meditations, bible histories, theatrical plays, spiritual poetry, song (hymns), picture bibles, graphic arts, paintings, and even political literature—and in the process of conversion, encouraged new and divergent forms. Of course, these alternative interpretations were aimed at a particular denomination or constituency, but, as was more often the case, popular modes of interpretation tended to mute denominational distinctions in favor of a broader, multi-confessional appeal.

Thus, alongside the established interpretations handed down by theologians—such as the interpretation of Old Testament stories as a set of "typologies" or a series of divine occurrences foreshadowing events in the New Testament—new interpretive strategies emerged. Popular literature and visual imagery, for example, sought to make connections between the persons and events in the Bible and their counterparts in contemporary life.

Certainly, traditional interpretations from theological works must not be confused with those perspectives which poets, opera composers and painters imposed upon biblical narratives. Here, in artistic interpretations, one encounters the greatest deviations. This is why it is so important to examine the breadth of interpretations from an Old Testament theme, using a single biblical figure to flesh out the differences, in order to demonstrate how interpretation evolves across media.

In broad strokes, one can outline the general characteristics of the historical developments in the interpretation of Old Testament stories. In the Middle Ages, Old Testament stories in the Bibles of the Poor and related works were viewed as prefigurations of the salvation events of the New Testament. Transcendance of the typology first occurs among lay piety and theologians influenced by Rabbinical exegeses. In history bibles, scriptural passages were retold in literal terms. Finally, the translation of the Bible into native tongues, intended for those who had little or no Latin, must have led to a new understanding of scripture among a broad readership. Old Testament stories were understood as historical accounts of Israel; chapter headings summarized historical synopses and their meanings. The Reformation—in this way, a child of Humanism—restored the dominant role of *sola scriptura* (scripture alone) to the individual theological disciplines. Luther, like Calvin, determined that the properly understood, historical meaning of the Bible, which is directed at Christ, is the actual content of the stories.

This led to a new understanding of the Old Testament. Old Testament stories could be interpreted as moral examples. The narratives showed men who obeyed the Laws of Moses and those who did not, resulting in reward or punishment accordingly. Not only were moving, thrilling, or positive events from the stories sought out for their didactic value, but scandalous or lascivious transgressions were also considered instructive and represented by writers and artists in compelling terms. The stories showed, according to Luther, how faith justified by good works fails. Nevertheless, even from such negative stories, as Luther saw it, one could gain an understanding of human nature and strengthen a sense of appropriate conduct. This new understanding of Bible stories is reflected in the development of Bible illustrations.

Increasingly, the Bible, or specific books from the Bible, were illustrated in their entirety as narrative sequences. The histories of biblical

heroes, such as Abraham, Lot, or Noah, were treated in illustrated narrative sequences. These illustrations, which favored portrayals from the Old
Testament, were turned into picture bibles, or existing illustrations from
earlier picture bibles could be reworked. The illustrated biblical series had
a decisive effect on sixteenth- and seventeenth-century artists. For instance,
by 1526, almost all the scenes of the story of Abraham, Sarah and Hagar
were depicted in a series of illustrations from the book of Genesis. In the
next century, artists found many of these existing scenes worthy of reproduction, since the same scenes are repeated in seventeenth-century texts.

Placed in chronological order, with inscriptions only synopsizing the
historical content of the narrative, the illustration sequences superceded
the typological system of the late Middle Ages. Consequently, the biblical
illustrations became an important source of inspiration for painters in the
sixteenth and seventeenth centuries. In some books, the title page includes
a sentence directly addressing artists: painters, goldsmiths, and sculptors
were encouraged to use it.

The painters of the Golden Age, such as Rubens, copied the picture
bibles as apprentices or students. Later, they could refer back to the compositions and themes they had found there. It is interesting that even a theologically knowledgeable artist like Rubens does not, when discussing a
painted biblical narrative with an interested collector, emphasize its typological meaning, although Rubens' composition is based on a sixteenth-
century bible print which included the typology in an inscription (chapter
4). Instead, Rubens sees it as a common human conflict and refers to it in a
letter as a "galanteria." For them, the interpretation of the Old Testament
in terms of the New Testament (the typological) has vanished. This also
holds true for poets, for whom the triangle of Abraham, Sarah and Hagar
was a story rich with human conflict. They show Sarah beginning to doubt
the promise of God and, in a very human manner, attempting to force
God's promise by foolishly giving her maidservant to Abraham as a second
wife. What Sarah had not foreseen were her own feelings of disappoint-
ment, nor had she anticipated that Hagar would become arrogant because
of her dual, conflicting role as maidservant and wife. Pressured by Sarah,
commanded by God, Abraham must sacrifice his beloved son and the
attractive Hagar. By banishing Hagar and Ishmael, Abraham successfully
passes his first test of faith. In the end, Hagar and Ishmael are rescued in
the wilderness. The ways in which Hagar was treated in literature and the

various associations she had or values she modeled in the Dutch Golden Age resulted in a variety of portrayals. Christine Sellin has been able to look into the question of Hagar in this book to give us a rich picture of the variety of interpretations and the freedom of the artists. This expands our knowledge of exegetical history greatly. We need more such studies on other biblical themes.

Dr. Christian Tümpel
Professor Emeritus
Radbout Universiteit
Nijmegen, the Netherlands

ACKNOWLEDGMENTS

This book began as a doctoral dissertation. Both the book and the dissertation owe an enormous debt to several institutions and individuals. Dissertation fieldwork was supported by a grant from the International Studies and Overseas Program at UCLA, a travel stipend from the UCLA Women's Studies Center, and a housing stipend from Utrecht University, the Netherlands. Thereafter, the UCLA Department of Art History provided funds from the Carter and Edward E. Dickson Fellowships for the writing of the dissertation. In spring 2005, Woodbury University contributed a faculty development award to secure illustrations.

A number of individuals at UCLA deserve specific appreciation. First and foremost, I thank David Kunzle, principal advisor, mentor, and friend. He first suggested I investigate the topic of Hagar and, without him, this book would not have been written. I have had the privilege to work closely with Joanna Woods-Marsden, whose interest and support extended far beyond the dissertation. I benefited from the illuminating studies of John L. Thompson of Fuller Theological Seminary, also a dissertation advisor. I owe a special debt of gratitude to advisors Margaret C. Jacob and Wijnand Mijnhardt. They established the distinguished UCLA-Utrecht University research and exchange program in which I was fortunate to participate as its first fellow.

I am deeply grateful for generous help from several scholars. In the Netherlands, specialists Christian Tümpel, Albert Blankert, and Yvonne Bleyerveld contributed valuable criticism. Dr. Tümpel, in particular, devoted much time and thought to this project. J. Nieuwstraten, Gee van der Meer, and Rudolf Dekker provided further insights and support. In the United States, fresh encouragement and criticism came from David R.

Smith. Ruth Mellinkoff offered marvelous ideas and friendship. I am indebted to Paul R. Sellin for his literary and historical expertise and to Ake Sellin-Weststrate for her cultural knowledge and for passing on the gift of language. I am fortunate to have been able to consult German language specialists Douglas J. Cremer, Christopher Stevens, and Peter Tokofsky for the translation of Dr. Tümpel's preface into English.

In addition, I gratefully acknowledge publisher and editor Henry Carrigan at T&T Clark for his direction and expertise. He made the publishing process a true pleasure. I warmly thank senior managing editor Amy Wagner, also at T&T Clark. At Woodbury, Kris Christ prepared illustrations for press. Galina Kraus also offered assistance.

Finally, for their moral support, I wish to thank my friend Phillip G. Richards and two colleagues at Woodbury University: Elisabeth L. Sandberg and Edward M. Clift.

Introduction

Troublemaker. Sinner. Rebel. Pagan. Jew. Heretic. Infidel. These were among the most common terms early Christian fathers used to characterize Abraham's slave and concubine Hagar. Mentioned only briefly in the Old Testament, the lowly maidservant was conventionally cast as a reprobate, reflecting the patriarchal biases and prejudices of the Bible and its interpreters. Hagar might have been passed over by church fathers altogether had it not been for St. Paul. Instead, the apostle's allegorical reading in Galatians 4—Hagar as a kind of enemy of the Christian Church—assured her ignominy.[1]

Hagar's tale is among the more disturbing, complex accounts of a female figure in the Old Testament, a tragic story of servitude and heir-making surrogacy followed by expulsion and exile. Genesis 16 and 21 briefly tell of the Egyptian slave who, at the suggestion of her barren mistress, Sarah, became Abraham's concubine, the mother of his firstborn son, Ishmael. Strife between mistress, maidservant, and siblings ensues. Later, at Sarah's behest, Hagar and Ishmael are banished from the household. On the verge of perishing from thirst in the wilderness, the outcasts are miraculously rescued by an angel who guides them to water. They go on to live in exile there. It is the nature of Hagar's ordeal and her "outsider" status in Abraham's household that encourages most modern readers to pass her by or to side with St. Paul in denouncing her. Only a few scholars, specifically feminist critics in the last few decades, have raised Hagar out of her relative anonymity to reconstruct her as a historical figure in her own right and to recognize her value as a symbol of the oppressed.[2]

While Hagar was ignored or rejected by modern commentators until feminist critics came along, she was a major preoccupation in the seventeenth-century Dutch Golden Age, as the many iterations of her story in literature and art demonstrate. By the 1630s, her story became a favorite subject in Dutch painting and prints, which treated her with an unprecedented degree of sympathy, mercy, and dignity. The Dutch transformed the outcast into a symbol of redemption and a model of maternity. Hagar's story was interpreted as a didactic domestic drama, touching on topics as relevant to households then as now. These included family breakups, extramarital sex, rivalry between women over men, feuding stepsiblings, and struggles between husbands and wives and masters and servants.

Hagar's story fired up the imagination because it offered Dutch artists the storytelling possibilities of something approaching the equivalent of a modern-day family soap opera. But it also revealed what mattered most to the Dutch and perhaps lay at the heart of the fledgling Republic's success and survival. This included the primacy of the family, an emphasis on domestic well-being, and the maintenance of ideal civic order. For the Dutch, the most highly urbanized culture in Europe, the events that left Hagar and her son homeless were especially troubling, and they made a place for her in their hearts. As the imagery reflects, the Dutch develop a tenderness, understanding, and compassion for Hagar that the world had never seen before. Exiled in scripture, cast off by Paul, Hagar came to find refuge among the burghers of the Dutch Republic and given pride of place on the walls of their homes.

Seventeenth-Century Dutch Painting and Hagar

About 140 paintings of the Hagar narrative survive—probably far exceeding any other comparable biblical subject—many by well-known Dutch artists. Combined with a group of drawings, prints, etchings, and engravings, these paintings suggest that the theme was a peculiarly northern Netherlandish preoccupation, and not just a subject of interest concentrated in Rembrandt's "circle," as has been supposed.[3]

This study concentrates on the portrayal of the story of Hagar and Ishmael in seventeenth-century Netherlandish painting and also considers seventeenth-century Dutch literature on the subject. Artists tended to portray four of the most compelling incidents from the narrative: the moment when Sarah leads Hagar to Abraham's bed (Gen 16:2–4); the moment when an angel appears to the runaway maidservant to command her to return to her mistress, foretelling Ishmael's birth (Gen 16:7–12); the moment when Abraham ejects Hagar and Ishmael from his household (Gen 21:14); and the moment when the angel miraculously intervenes to rescue Hagar and Ishmael in the wilderness (Gen 21:17).[4]

The popularity of the theme, the expulsion scene in particular, simply has no match anywhere else in Europe at this time, not even in the southern Netherlands. For northern Netherlanders, the expulsion scene seems to have held the most fascination: some seventy-five paintings of this scene survive, forming the core of this study. In addition, I count forty extant paintings of the wilderness-rescue scene. Less commonly rendered was the runaway Hagar scene, of which some fifteen paintings survive; the presentation of Hagar scenes are rarer still.[5] The popularity of the Hagar-themed paintings culminated from 1640 to 1660, despite the fact that demand for Old Testament subjects appears to have declined after 1640.[6]

In Amsterdam alone, inventories from surviving estate records show that some forty-two Hagar-themed paintings were owned by the Amsterdam elite, including merchants, ministers, artisans, civic leaders, and members from Regent families, among others. Typically small in size and intended for residential use, these works hung in the more important living spaces, most often in the "voorkamer" (main room or parlor) or "op de Sael" (the large reception hall in the home).[7] For example, an inventory of 1664 noted that "a painting of Hagar" hung in the reception hall in the home of one of Amsterdam's most powerful Calvinist ministers, Otto Badius; it was placed in the most "public" space of what must have been an extremely socially active household.[8] In one well-to-do Haarlem household, a painting described as the "story of Hagar" hung in the kitchen.[9] The subject also held currency among the Dutch nobility. A painting by Gerard Honthorst of Sarah leading Hagar to Abraham's bed, probably painted for stadtholder Frederik Hendrik,[10] hung in the audience hall at Honselaarsdijk, according to a 1707 palace inventory.

Part of the difficulty in approaching the Dutch Hagar-themed paintings has been establishing meaning for the pictorial subject matter. The theological and literary interpretations of the story are varied and complex, and shift depending on context. As a result, much of the historical scholarship on Dutch art has sidestepped the theme's significance or underestimated its importance in seventeenth-century Dutch culture. The few studies on the subject tend to be restricted in scope or concerned with questions of style or attribution. Hagar was a complex, multivalent figure in seventeenth-century Dutch culture, and perhaps for this reason she has been lightly passed over by modern Dutch scholarship; yet it is precisely this complexity that makes the study of her story so fascinating. By considering both art and literature, we gain a better understanding of the subject's significance in Dutch culture and we develop a greater appreciation for the paintings themselves. Moreover, this approach enables us to examine the parallels and discontinuities between religious art and literature.

Earlier Christian theology saw Hagar and Ishmael merely as typological reprobates, as Paul's epistle prescribed (Gal 4:21–31).[11] Hagar and Sarah were allegories for the old and new covenants, respectively; Hagar represented the old Jerusalem on earth, while Sarah stood for the heavenly Jerusalem, or salvation through belief in Christ. Hagar was in bondage with her son, Ishmael, a child born of "the flesh," while Sarah, the "free woman," bore Isaac, a child of "the promise," God's chosen seed. Most medieval depictions of Sarah and Hagar present the maidservant in neutral terms, part of the larger biblical pictorial narrative, but sometimes Hagar may appear as a symbol for the false Christian, the unbeliever, or the Synagoga discredited by Ecclesia (Sarah).[12] Not surprisingly, in these "emblematic, judgment-like scenes," Sarah is favored over Hagar with the Lord's blessing or embrace.[13]

However, seventeenth-century Dutch painting appears to have ignored the traditional Pauline stereotype: Hagar and Ishmael are rarely seen as archetypal wrongdoers. Instead, the pictorial Hagar is almost always shown as a remarkably sympathetic figure.[14] Increasingly, she comes to occupy a central place in the composition, upstaging Abraham. By mid-century, she appears as a peasant beauty and, toward the later part of the century, takes on the classical attributes of a mythological goddess. Meanwhile, Abraham appears as a kindhearted patriarch caught in the throes of a familial tragedy. Why?

Early modern literary developments, rooted in the Reformation, had implications for the story's broad appeal and visual form. Beginning in the sixteenth century, Hagar underwent renewed scrutiny and attracted the attention—and even the praise—of theologians, most notably, sixteenth-century Reformers. Revised attitudes toward Hagar coincided with the development of new, pietistic literature forged by Protestant writers.[15] Grounded in scripture, a new "literature of the heart" developed—inward, psychological, and lyrical—that encouraged the believer to find connections between providentially ordained events in the Bible and his own experiences.[16] As theological positions shifted, biblical stories were recast and "Protestant poetics" flourished—in the form of biblical commentaries, rhetorical handbooks, poetic paraphrasing of scripture, emblem books, and manuals on meditation and preaching—designed to help the individual chart the spiritual stages of his or her own life.[17] The many print books that appeared also reflected this shift in attitude: graphic illustrations of biblical narratives incorporated inscriptions that emphasized the psychological dimension or human experience of an episode.[18] Dramatic renditions of Old Testament narratives had particular appeal, and the flood of compositions and motifs developed in this century would greatly influence painters in the next.[19]

Thus, seventeenth-century Dutch thought and literature—following in the footsteps of Luther and nourished by this new "language of the heart"—could not see Hagar and Ishmael solely as allegorical outcasts or typological foils. The Pauline typology did not always suffice and was set aside to reconcile the complex ancient story with contemporary concerns and values, part of a broader humanizing trend so characteristic of the baroque period. As we shall see, a range of remarkably sympathetic attitudes toward Hagar sprouted up alongside the traditional allegorical interpretations. Dutch reformers and moralists sometimes appropriated the story in Christian conduct books, sermons, prayers, and commentaries to further the special aims and needs of the young, struggling Dutch Republic. There is some evidence that the war-torn, isolated Netherlanders may have even felt a special affinity with the plight of the biblical exiles. Some writers used Hagar's story to enforce the primacy of the Christian family and order in domestic life, which was always at the core of Calvinist and Lutheran social theory.[20] All this and more boosted the special appeal and applicability of Hagar's story in Netherlandish culture.

Something analogous is also at work in seventeenth-century Dutch paintings of Hagar's story. For painters, the revised theological and literary attitudes toward the rebel maidservant meant that a variety of interpretations, influences, and concerns quintessentially Dutch could be brought to bear in paintings of the theme. More specifically, the theological and literary reappraisal of Hagar's significance left artists freer to make the maidservant sympathetic and to tell the story in terms of fundamentally human values and emotions. Painters recognized the dramatic appeal of a beautiful young woman caught in a terrible bind with a well-meaning, God-fearing Abraham. Like their literary counterparts, Dutch artists sympathized with the concubine; however, after mid-century, painters, perhaps feeling the pressure in a competitive art market, responded by portraying her with increasing erotic allure. Thus, after mid-century, "art" takes over, as the religious meaning of the story recedes. On a fundamental level, this study becomes an investigation of the intersection between art, theology, and literature.

Summary of Art History Scholarship

Most art history studies on the subject have concerned themselves with the seventeenth-century Dutch expulsion scene. The principal art history study is Richard Hamann's 1936 survey of seventeenth-century Dutch expulsion scenes, which concentrates on drawings and paintings from Rembrandt's circle. Beginning with Lucas van Leyden and Pieter Lastman, he traces the stylistic development and, as he shows, much of the imagery through the 1670s draws on the 1637 etching by Rembrandt and a 1612 painting by Lastman (reviewed below in chapter 5). Hamann, counting more than one hundred drawings of the expulsion scene, suggests that the subject was used for study by Rembrandt's students: the master may have favored the theme because the story offered rich emotional possibilities, ideal for study. Rembrandt, as Hamann points out, helped popularize the subject. However, Hamann's investigation is primarily concerned with style and attribution of works within Rembrandt's artistic circle and as such is limited. Hagar's story appears to have been part of a larger cultural trend. Moreover, although many expulsion scenes were created in Amsterdam, as Hamann says, these may have been proportionate to the magnitude of its art market. Expulsion scenes were also produced in Haarlem, Utrecht, Delft, Leiden, Rotterdam, and Dordrecht. Most of the datable Hagar paintings fall between the 1620s and 1660s.

In a comprehensive summary of Old Testament subjects in Dutch art, Christian Tümpel theorized that the expulsion scene was prevalent in painting because the story gave expression to familiar human emotions, such as jealousy, love, and strife.[21] In her study about biblical women in sixteenth-century Dutch literature and art, Bleyerveld reviewed several sixteenth-century images of the expulsion scene and arrives at a similar conclusion.[22] Van der Coelen's investigation concentrating on Dutch sixteenth- and seventeenth-century prints of the expulsion and wilderness-rescue scenes compares traditional renderings to underscore the artistry of Rembrandt's 1637 expulsion etching. Various literary references, which van der Coelen outlines, leave us unable to pinpoint exact meaning for the pictorial theme: the story's meaning would have varied widely, depending on context and viewer.[23] Tümpel, Bleyerveld, and van der Coelen make important points, and their studies offer valuable visual and literary sources. Nevertheless, closer scrutiny of the expulsion episode in art and literature yields greater insights, clarity, and patterns.

Van de Waal investigated the significance of the runaway Hagar and the angel and wilderness-rescue episodes, predicated on several drawings by Rembrandt and others from his circle. He posited that both episodes, set in the wilderness, naturally lend themselves to pastoral scenes, and thus might account for their popularity in Dutch art, since there "certainly did not seem to be any theological basis" for Dutch interest in the pictorial theme.[24] However, the episodes are best considered in the larger context of developments in art and literature on the episode. As we shall see, the varying emphases artists placed on the visual moment suggest a heightened awareness of Hagar's theological significance and the scriptural episode, paralleling literary trends.

An increasing number of art history studies dedicated to biblical women, an area that has traditionally suffered from scholarly neglect, have appeared over the last two decades. Nevertheless, Hagar has been passed over, despite her standing as one of the most popular Old Testament female figures in Dutch art, perhaps second only to the chaste Susannah.[25] This may be partly because, as we shall see, she cannot be made to fit neatly within the traditional rubrics of villainess or heroine, Eve or Maria, whore or virgin.

Summary of Modern Biblical Scholarship and Christian Exegeses

Until the last few decades, modern biblical scholarship and Christian exegeses have overlooked the Egyptian maidservant figure, reflecting the longstanding patriarchal biases of the Bible and its commentators. Fortunately, this study benefited from the recent exegetical investigations by Thompson, as well as from several feminist studies in biblical scholarship focusing on Old Testament women.[26] Thompson's survey of Hagar's portrayal in ancient, medieval, and early to mid-sixteenth-century exegeses was particularly valuable to this study. The literary framework I develop for seventeenth-century Dutch attitudes stems largely from his findings.

This book is divided into six chapters. Chapter I surveys the rich literary development of the theme by ancient, patristic, medieval, and sixteenth-century commentaries of Hagar's story; these inform and resurface in seventeenth-century Dutch views. Chapter 2 reviews Dutch literary attitudes in religious tracts, Christian conduct books, sermons, prayer books, poetry, and a theatrical play, among other texts. This literary overview clarifies meaning, traces thematic patterns, and establishes a cultural context for the paintings. In chapters 3 through 6, we examine the paintings in narrative sequence: first, the presentation of the Hagar episode, followed by the runaway Hagar and the angel, expulsion, and wilderness-rescue scenes. Scriptural passages are from the King James Version of the Bible. Unless otherwise noted, all translations are my own.

Notes

1. For a survey of views, see Thompson 2001, 17–99.

2. Bailey 1994; Bellis 1994; Teubal 1990; Emmerson 1989; Weems 1988; Trible 1984. Outside academic circles, however, Hagar's story had been hallowed since the early nineteenth century for its parallels to the African-American experience of slavery and abuse (Thompson 1997, 213. See also Williams 1993).

3. Hamann 1936, 471–580; Van de Waal 1974; Van der Coelen 1997, 272–82.

4. For the complete story in scriptural text and its allegorical reading by Paul, see the appendix.

5. The number of paintings is derived from referencing various sources and libraries: Pigler 1974; *Marburger Index*, Bildarchiv Foto Marburg, 1976; Van de Waal's *Iconoclass*, 1973–83; Roberts 1987; Korwin 1981; Havlice 1977; Schweers 1994; Wright 1992; the Getty Provenance Index, 1996; Rijksbureau voor Kunsthistorische Documentatie, The Hague; Warburg Institute Library, University of London; Witt Library, Courtauld Institute of Art, London.

6. Montias 1991, 350.

7. Getty Provenance Index Cumulative Edition (GPI 1996), compiled by J. Montias and M. J. Bok.

8. GPI 1996, no. N-2040.

9. GPI 1996, no. N-5319.

10. Albert Blankert, communication with author, August 19, 2003. The painting is now lost. Inventory Honselaarsdijk, 1707, no. 31: "Abraham daer Sara hem met Hagar te bedt legt van Honthorst" (Judson and Ekkart 1999, 50, cata. no. 2).

11. Thompson 1997, 230.

12. Mellinkoff 1998, 38–49, fig. 5; Cahn 2001, 104–5, fig. 8.

13. Cahn 2001, 104.

14. Van der Coelen 1997, 281; Mellinkoff 1998, 49.

15. David Smith, letter to author, July 24, 2003.

16. Arshagouni 1988, 12.

17. Lewalski 1979, 13–21.

18. Christian Tümpel, letter to author, May 17, 2005.

19. C. Tümpel 1974, 142–43; for more on the sixteenth-century northern Netherlandish biblical print tradition, see van der Coelen 1997. For the Hagar theme in sixteenth- and seventeenth-century Netherlandish graphic art specifically, see van der Coelen 1997, 274–82.

20. Durantini 1983, 72.

21. C. Tümpel 1991, 30.

22. Bleyerveld 1991, 117–24.

23. Van der Coelen 1997, 274–82.

24. Van de Waal 1974.

25. Montias 1991, 339, 359.

26. Thompson 1992, 1994, 1997, 2000, 2001; Trible 1984; Bailey 1994; Bellis 1994; Williams 1993; Emmerson 1989.

CHAPTER ONE

✝

The Story of Hagar and Ishmael in Traditional Christian Literature

ANCIENT, PATRISTIC, MEDIEVAL, AND SIXTEENTH-CENTURY INTERPRETATIONS

To establish meaning and context for Dutch paintings depicting the biblical story of Hagar and Ishmael, we must first understand the story's significance in traditional Christian theology and literature, as well as in seventeenth-century Dutch literature. Up until the Reformation, most commentary interpreted the story primarily in terms of its typological significance. Of all the stories in the Bible, the story of Hagar and Ishmael is the only one to receive an allegorical interpretation that became, in effect, "canonical"—an interpretation provided by St. Paul in the New Testament (Gal 4:21–31). Early Christian commentators relied on the apostle's allegorical reading to reconcile this disconcerting, complex story—of two rival pairs of mothers and sons, two promises, one inheritance, and an ambivalent patriarch—with exile as its outcome.[1]

The Pauline Typology in Ancient, Patristic, and Medieval Commentary

Following Paul's reading, early Christian commentators portrayed Sarah and Hagar as "types." For Christians, Hagar and Sarah became allegories for the Old and New Testaments or the old and new covenants. Sarah and the legitimate Isaac stood for the new covenant of Christianity as renewed through Christ. According to Paul, "And if you are Christ's, then you are Abraham's offspring, heirs according to the promise" (Gal 3:29). "But what does scripture say?" Paul asks and then answers: "'Cast out the slave and her son [Ishmael]; for the son of the slave shall not inherit with the son [Isaac] of the free woman.' So, brethren, we are not children of the slave, but of the free woman" (Gal 4:30–31).

Traditional interpretations also read the story as "a parable of law and gospel"[2] or law and grace. Hagar was in bondage with her illegitimate son, Ishmael, a child born of "the flesh," while Sarah, the "free woman," bore Isaac, a child of "the promise" (Gal 4:22–23). The rivalry between the pairs of mothers and sons, then, represented man's dual nature, symbolizing the conflict between the "flesh" and the "spirit." Hagar and Ishmael signified the carnal nature of human beings, while Sarah and Isaac connoted the spirit or grace. The banishment of the former (Hagar), then, made way for the attainment of true virtue (Sarah), clearing the path to salvation.

Hagar also personified the old Jerusalem on earth, the synagogue, while Sarah represented the heavenly Jerusalem, the church of Christ (or salvation).[3] According to the Apostle Paul, "For this Agar is mount Sinai in Arabia, and answereth to Jerusalem which now is, and is in bondage with her children. But Jerusalem which is above is free, which is the mother of us all" (Gal 4:25–26, KJV). Thus, the expulsion came to be seen as the prefiguration of the separation between the Synagogue (the slave or concubine) and the Church (the free wife):[4] "the Synagogue would be rejected by God and wander the desert."[5]

Some early Christian commentaries perpetuated the polemical aspects of the Pauline allegory "in order to underscore the continuing inferiority of the Synagogue to the Church," of Jews to Christians.[6] The biblical repudiation could be used to justify Christian anti-Judaic attitudes: so long as the Jews continued in their beliefs that "mocked' or betrayed Christ (and Christians), so too they should endure exile, punishment, and suffering. The expulsion of Hagar and Ishmael was sometimes seen as a prefiguration of the Jewish Diaspora.[7]

Not only did Hagar represent the Jews; she and her son also came to signify "all those whose relationship with the Church was irregular" or heterodox, including schismatics, non-Christians, unbelievers, or heretics.[8] Already by the end of the seventh century, Ishmael stood for the Muslims, who were considered Christendom's greatest enemies; Ishmaelites were thought to be the ancestor of the homeless Saracens.[9] Fears of Islam and slurs against non-Christians occasionally appeared in medieval and Reformation writings.[10] Traditionally, the story was used to rationalize the strife between peoples, to account for different belief systems, or to assert political righteousness and religious orthodoxy.

Certain medieval accounts singled out Ishmael as particularly evil, especially when discussing the enigmatic scriptural passage that describes Sarah observing Ishmael at "play" with his younger half brother. This "play" takes place during a feast celebrating the weaning of Isaac (Gen 21:8–9) and precedes the banishment. What exactly had Ishmael done? Interpreters debated the underlying connotations of the word "play": for some, "play" could connote simple mockery, but for others, such as the Franciscan exegete Nicolas of Lyra, the word incriminated Ishmael for the sins of idolatry, murder, and licentiousness.[11]

In *Jewish Antiquities*, the ancient Jewish exegete and historian Flavius Josephus roughly paraphrases Gen 16 and 21.[12] Since his writings recount the history of the Jewish people to win the sympathies of his readers, both Hellenized Jews and pagan Greeks, the biblical account is glossed— and Hagar is used as a foil—to bring out the moral excellence and virtues of Abraham, founder of the faith, and his family.[13] Genesis 16:6 tells us only that a fearful Hagar fled to the wilderness to escape a wrathful Sarah, but Josephus interprets this in a way that avoids placing Sarah in anything other than a favorable light, to Hagar's detriment. According to Josephus, insolent Hagar, after "abusing" her mistress, "resolved to fly" to the wilderness rather than endure the "humiliations" of "chastisement" she had earned at home. There, she "entreat[s] God to take pity on her."[14] Josephus emphasizes that Sarah truly "cherished" Ishmael as "her own son"; only after Isaac's birth did she begin to worry about sibling rivalry over inheritance and urge Abraham to "settle [Hagar and Ishmael] elsewhere." When it comes to the expulsion episode itself, Josephus enhances our sense of Abraham's reluctance to be so cruel. In this way, Josephus avoids any unfavorable reflections on Abraham. Thus, Josephus's Hagar is "wrong" rather than "wronged."[15]

So traditionally, Hagar and Ishmael were used as typological foils for Sarah and Isaac and often underwent excoriation. Occasionally sympathetic portrayals of Hagar also surfaced.[16] The ancient Jewish exegete Philo portrayed Hagar in relatively positive terms, interpreting the allegorical strife between mistress and maidservant not as a rivalry or conflict, but as two parts of one struggle necessary to achieve spiritual enlightenment. Sarah represented virtue or heavenly wisdom, while Hagar represented philosophy or earthly learning. According to Philo, the "soul [was] barren with respect to virtue or wisdom [Sarah], until it [had] been trained in preparatory studies [Hagar]."[17] Thus, preliminary studies [Hagar] necessarily served as "handmaiden" to virtue [Sarah].[18] But Philo's sympathetic reading was an exception to the rule: most ancient and medieval interpretations disapproved of Hagar and Ishmael. To sum up the interpretations in ancient, patristic, and medieval times, the Pauline typology comprised several binary sets of allegorical meaning:[19]

Hagar / Ishmael	*Sarah / Isaac*
Slave (in bondage)	Free wife (redemption, salvation)
Illegitimate son	"Promised" ("chosen," legitimate) son
Body, flesh (carnal)	The spirit (grace)
Old covenant (law; Old Testament)	New covenant (grace, gospel; New Testament)
Wilderness, exile, Mount Sinai	Abraham's house
Earthly Jerusalem	Heavenly Jerusalem (salvation, forgiveness of sins through Christ)
The "heterodox": Jews, Muslims, Saracens, unbelievers, schismatics, etc.	Christians (God's "chosen" people, "children of Israel," the "true heirs")
The Synagogue	The Church
Earthly philosophy/preparatory studies	Heavenly wisdom/virtue

The Reformation:
The Pauline Typology Recedes, Sympathetic Portraits of Hagar and Ishmael Gain Currency

In the early modern period, the traditional Pauline typology receded as sympathetic portraits of Hagar and Ishmael gained some currency, boosted by popularized Christian teachings and the invention of movable type. During the Reformation, a spirit of scriptural enquiry took hold and attitudes toward Hagar and Ishmael underwent further reconsideration. Certainly, the traditional Pauline typologies persisted in early modern European Christian thought, just as they do into the present day; but beginning in the early sixteenth century, a change of heart took hold. Other, more sympathetic or historically minded portraits of the slave and her son began to take root and grow alongside the Pauline typology. The castigated, suffering mother "not only attracted the attention and sympathy of Protestant Reformers," she was extolled as a model of penitence and even, in one instance, was referred to as a saint.

A brief summary of principal Protestant reappraisals of Gen 16 and 21 is useful here, because these laid the foundation for seventeenth-century Dutch theological attitudes: many of these same Reformation tenets resurface in Dutch seventeenth-century Christian literature, as we shall see. This helps establish meaning and provide context for the paintings.

Zwingli, Pellikan, Musculus, Vermigli[20]

The more Hagar's story was scrutinized, the more compassion and even admiration the maidservant seemed to attract from Protestant Reformers such as Ulrich Zwingli, Conrad Pellikan, Wolfgang Musculus, Peter Martyr Vermigli, and, most outspokenly, Martin Luther. These and other exegetes began their commentaries by condemning Hagar in the traditional manner for her pride, presumption, and servile, womanish behavior in Abraham's household. But when these commentators reach the point in the story when Hagar seeks the wilderness as refuge (Gen 16) or is punished by exile there (Gen 21), "they make a surprising turnabout: Hagar is now praised for her repentance, faith, endurance, and piety."[21] She personifies the model of contrition, especially in Gen 21. That God heard the cries of mother and son—the name Ishmael means "God hears"—afforded the pair higher esteem in Reformation thought.

Zwingli interpreted Gen 16 as an example of how one should bear the castigation of one's superiors: as the runaway maidservant who returns to her mistress when the angel commands it, Hagar offered a lesson in obedience, humility, and faith. Vermigli and Pellikan favored Hagar for her "confession of error which merits forgiveness, consolation or grace" and for her self-control in not blaming or accusing her mistress or master for her troubles. Musculus deemed Hagar the model of "a convicted conscience," "sincere confession," and contrition. [22]

In the Reformers' commentary on Gen 21, the views are even more sanguine. "No one is born without vices," writes Musculus; under duress,

Hagar shows herself to be as much an exemplar of obedience as Abraham. Musculus even compares Hagar's sufferings to those of Christ on the cross. Zwingli offers a more reserved endorsement. For him, Hagar is simultaneously a type of "carnal Israel" and an instance of "how God rescues the pious who hope in him." Pellikan admitted that Hagar is "not perfect," but nevertheless considers her a "member of the faithful": "[Hagar and Ishmael] were a type of the gentiles who would come to believe." Like Pellikan, Vermigli saw the ordeal as transforming: although punished with exile for his pride and presumption, Ishmael's despair gave rise to his new-found faith; thus, when mother and son called out, God heard them.[23]

Not only Protestants praised Hagar. In 1539, the Catholic theologian Thomas de Vio, Cardinal Cajetan, affirmed the portrait of Hagar as the runaway maidservant brought to true repentance. In Gen 16, Cajetan saw Hagar's experience as a kind of epiphany, drawing parallels between Hagar and the Virgin: each "having been greeted by the angel, pondered the nature of that greeting." For Cajetan, Hagar's response was joyful and her repentance sincere. In Gen 21, the divine rescue of Hagar and Ishmael, Cajetan sidesteps the Pauline allegory to consider the story in literal terms: here "he sees the 'literal' blessing of God" at work in the lives of mother and son.[24] This reassessment of Hagar and Ishmael meant that Cajetan had to consider the implications of Abraham's actions in the banishment: how could he send mother and son away with such slender provisions, dooming them to certain death? Was this not unconscionable, even cruel? The apparent brutality was at odds with traditional notions of Abraham as a wise and decent patriarch. Cajetan took pains to reconstruct the biblical text by understanding the specified provisions of "bread and water" given to Hagar and Ishmael as literally meaning "all kinds of provisions [*omnia victualia*]," carried by pack animals and attendants.[25]

Martin Luther

But the most sympathetic, heartfelt account of the story of Hagar and Ishmael in the early modern period comes from Luther. For him, Hagar is an ideal example of the sinner who repents. "Most of us are like Hagar," Luther said, because we too exhibit arrogance and pride toward others, but, like her, we have been "guided to faith and repentance." In Gen 16, Luther says, the "saintly Hagar" was engaged in an act of "true worship." The moment when the rebellious, runaway slave names God "is a confession of faith" and represents "the hymn of the whole church": "And she called the name of the LORD that spake unto her, Thou God seest me . . ." (Gen 16:13, KJV).

However, Luther's commentary on Gen 21 is even more remarkable. The wilderness ordeal humbled Hagar and Ishmael; they learned to set aside "carnal prestige" and trust only in God's grace. As a result, they were changed and rewarded: Ishmael is called a "true son of promise," reconciled with father and church. Hagar, transformed by the Holy Spirit, becomes a "mother of the church," teaching her descendants the importance of humility. Luther's "radical rehabilitation" of Hagar and Ishmael makes for a happier ending than events hitherto had promised.[26]

Endorsing Hagar meant that Luther, like Cajetan, had to grapple with Abraham's problematic conduct in the scriptural passage. Despite their faults, Luther wondered how Abraham could send away not only the mother, but also his firstborn son: "Where is [Abraham's] fatherly heart?" In the end, Luther, echoing Cajetan, maintained that an obedient Abraham sacrificed his eldest son in accordance with God's wishes.[27] Later, of course, Abraham would also prepare to sacrifice Isaac.

John Calvin

And what were John Calvin's views? Publishing his commentaries on Genesis in 1554, Calvin remained unmoved by the story: for Calvin, Hagar and Ishmael remain "reprobates." In Gen 16, Calvin holds that Hagar, who was "always wild and rebellious," only repents because she breaks down under hardship. Ishmael fares no better. In Calvin's view, Ishmael's derision of the chosen Isaac is equivalent to blasphemy of God's grace and word.[28] But, as we shall see shortly, Abraham and Sarah also share in Calvin's censure.

In Gen 21, things are bleaker still—neither mother nor son is deserving of God's mercy. Their banishment, Calvin explains, is divine punishment for the pride and ingratitude shown by Hagar and Ishmael: "God willed that the banishment of Ishmael should be so harsh and sorrowful, so that his example might strike terror into the proud, who . . . trample under foot the very grace to which they are indebted for all things . . ."[29]

Whether they were brought to repentance, as other commentators asserted, remains at best "an uncertain conjecture for Calvin": the pair were rescued, Calvin says, despite Hagar's "sloth and stupor."[30]

Calvin and Luther: Genesis 21 as Political Metaphor in the Time of Religious Troubles, Persecution

Calvin's singular "hard-heartedness" is surprising. In general, in Calvin's writings, Hagar and Ishmael do not always appear as their "historical selves" but are "emblematic of Protestantism's elder 'half-brother,' Roman Catholicism"; "arrogant and tyrannical, the villainous [Hagar and Ishmael were] emblematic of the 'papists' who were tormenting Calvin's evangelical brothers and sisters in France and elsewhere." Calvin was not the first to use the story to vilify his enemies: in the fifth century, Augustine used the "insolent Hagar" to attack the Donatists, enemies of the Church.[31] And in the eleventh century, Pope Urban II "rallied Christendom for the first crusade against 'the impious Saracens [descendants of Hagar and Ishmael],' by invoking the cry from St. Paul, 'Cast out the slave woman and her son!'"[32]

But the role of victim and persecutor in this biblical tale could be interchanged, if necessary, by portraying the wrathful Sarah as villain and Hagar as a victim. In a surprising typological twist, Luther portrayed himself as Hagar, analogizing his own excommunication by the pope with the life-threatening exile the maidservant faces because of Sarah's persecution.[33] In this context, Luther identified with Hagar the victim.

When necessary, then, both Calvin and Luther used the story as a metaphor to attack political foes, rally support, or express notions of persecution. Such patterns of usage, as we have seen, can be traced back to patristic and medieval thinkers.

Setting Pauline Allegory Aside to Address Dissidence in the Household

However, in the early modern era, it appears that Luther, Calvin, and others found new applications for the biblical story that would come to have a special significance in Dutch seventeenth-century thought. Setting the allegorical typologies aside, reformers used the story to address a more fundamental form of dissidence: strife in the family household.

Calvin used Hagar's story to talk about household management and the proper conduct of masters and domestic servants, emphasizing Hagar's punishment at the hands of Sarah and warning husbands to set store by their wives. Here, Abraham, Sarah, and Hagar each receive their fair share of Calvin's censure. Sarah is blamed for instigating Abraham's polygamy and for her "womanish jealousy and intemperance . . . [and] despite displaying greater equanimity, Abraham . . . is upbraided . . . for the fickleness of his affection for Hagar [by throwing Hagar out]."[34] In this context, Calvin valued the passage because it demonstrates that "even the most orderly homes are not sometimes without quarrel," and he reiterates the need for harmony in the household: domestic strife was sinful.[35]

For Calvin, then, the story of Hagar mirrored the difficulties associated with household life. On the one hand, he specifically applies it to discuss the management of subordinates, reinforcing domestic hierarchy and, with that, harmony; but on the other hand, he also insists that masters respect the well-being of their servants:

> God shows [in the scriptural text on Hagar] . . . with this word *chambermaid* or *servant*, that he approves of the political order . . . he does not draw servants away from the subjection and power of their masters, nor does he deprive masters of the service they pay to them, but he commands only that one treat [servants] with gentleness and generosity.[36]

Luther too employed the biblical passage to discuss the difficulties of domestic life. He used the story to address the principles of marriage and to promote understanding between husband and wife, calling it a useful account "for spouses, in order that they may not think it strange if disputes arise among even the most affectionate and saintliest people." According to Luther, for those managing a household, the biblical passage was valuable because one "can learn from [this example] that in wedlock there is far severer training in faith, hope, love, patience, and prayer, than there is in all the monasteries."[37]

Like Calvin, Luther equated the biblical Hagar with domestic servants in contemporary life, advocating subservience among servants and responsible management among masters. This passage is from one of a series of lectures he gave on the stories from Genesis beginning in 1535:

> The angel undoubtedly calls that an affliction which Hagar felt to be an affliction, namely the fact that she was a slave . . . it is as if [God] were saying, "do not resent being a maidservant. God loves maidservants and free women alike . . ." Therefore bear this: be subject to your mistress. . . . The circumstances of this life differ greatly. . . . [t]his inequality . . . agitates hearts so much that people change their situations by sinning. But one should hold fast . . . and think: "behold, I am a man servant, a maidservant, one who is stricken with poverty and overburdened by works, etc., so be it! But let this be my comfort, that my God regards all alike . . . God hears all alike—you in your menial state and another in his free state . . ."[38]

Thus, the story of Hagar—the runaway Hagar and expulsion episodes specifically (Gen 16 and 21)—was recognized for its didactic value and employed to enforce the primacy of the Christian family, obedience, and order in domestic life, values at the core of Calvinist and Lutheran social theory.[39] Both Calvin and Luther regarded family government as the paradigm for all other government; family order was a reflection of divine order, emblematic of respect for the social hierarchy necessary to maintain a stable and peaceful society.[40] At one point in his lecture, Luther draws on Gen 21 to make the analogy between family and commonwealth explicit:

> Why does the Holy Spirit mention these quarrels? . . . In this historical account, the Holy Spirit depicts the source of all dangers that arise not only in the *household, but also in the state and church.* . . . In the household, quarrels and disputes arise between husband and wife. [The expulsion] is an admonishment to those who want to be *husbands or rulers of state* without having any troubles. . . . [I]f you are a husband, it is impossible for you not to have a Hagar in your home. . . . [T]herefore, let us remember this example, and let us too, together with the faithful Abraham, trust in God, and as much as possible preserve the harmony . . .[41]

Like Calvin and Luther, the sixteenth-century Dutch humanist Desiderius Erasmus recognized the Hagar story for its didactic value in domestic life, using it to improve relations between and to clarify the roles of husband and wife. At one point in his *Institutio Matrimonii Christiani* (Institution of Christian Matrimony), published in 1526, Erasmus urges husbands to listen to their wives, just as Abraham responded to Sarah's wishes by sending Hagar and Ishmael away.[42] Here, Erasmus sidesteps the traditional exegetical problems associated with this moment, that is, the perceived impropriety of Abraham's being bossed around by his wife (Gen 21:9–10).[43] Sarah was not only criticized for her jealous, typically "womanish" behavior overall, but commentators traditionally found Sarah's bossy behavior problematic here, since she stepped outside the boundaries of acceptable female conduct.[44] In this scriptural instance, interpreters pointed out, Sarah could not serve as a role model for women, and they used this "misstep" to reinforce proper marital roles: husbands give orders; wives obey them.

Luther, Calvin, and Early Church Fathers: Wrestling with the Question of Abraham's "Polygamy"

As we have seen, Hagar's story received greater scrutiny during the Reformation when new Protestant attitudes developed. But the additional scrutiny also meant that one aspect of the story became increasingly worrisome: was Abraham's coupling with Hagar immoral behavior on Abraham's part? Was it polygamy?

Biblical patriarchs were, generally speaking, heroes and role models for Christians, and yet here, church fathers capitulated, one should not follow in Abraham's footsteps. Interpreters were faced with reconciling saintly precedent with contemporary morality and civic law, a task that became increasingly difficult with the advent of the Reformation and dramatic changes in Protestant thinking about marriage.[45] Other Old Testament pillars such as King David (adultery), Lot (incest), and Jacob (bigamy) also came under fire.

Patristic and medieval writers, followed by Renaissance and Reformation exegetes, found a variety of excuses to justify Abraham's immoral behavior. Abraham was "divinely obliged to polygamy in order to increase the chosen people," one line of argument ran.[46] Another claimed that Abraham and other Old Testament fathers had divine permission for their actions and thus were heroic exceptions—a dispensation, it was carefully pointed out, that the common man did not have. Others skirted the whole matter altogether by asserting that the story was not literal history, but that Abraham's actions were typological: his union with Hagar was divinely ordained in order to prefigure the two covenants. Another allegorical tack argued that the taking of multiple wives should actually be understood as the taking of multiple virtues—each wife representing a particular virtue. Yet another strategy was to cite the laws and customs of the time: since the taking of multiple wives and concubines was customary during Abraham's time, his actions were therefore lawful and not sinful. Another approach attempted to exonerate Abraham by claiming his action was born from a necessary desire for progeny—as Luther explained it, the elderly couple was eager to obtain the "promised seed," the Messiah; since Abraham's conduct was not driven by lust, he could be excused.[47] Then the blame often shifted to Sarah as instigator of the polygamy.[48] Like the scriptural text, exegetes did not mention Hagar's view of the matter.

Still, aside from this trend excusing Abraham, a handful of commentaries that called the "polygamy" of Abraham into question also appeared in the first half of the sixteenth century. "Occasionally in Luther, and more frequently in the writings of Musculus and Vermigli," such "stirrings of reaction" can be detected, as Thompson observes. They appear in the comments of Calvin by the late 1530s more firmly and consistently.

According to Calvin, polygamy was never permitted in Old Testament law: from the beginning, monogamy was a natural law in the Bible, "for God did not give Adam three Eves."[49] Although Abraham and other Old Testament patriarchs committed polygamy, says Calvin, "it was never lawful."[50] For Calvin, Abraham committed a sin and becomes an example, despite his longstanding faith and stamina, of "how even the most faithful must pray daily to avoid temptation."[51] Calvin assigned the principal blame, however, to Sarah: she showed impatience, faithlessness, and presumption in reinterpreting the divine prophecy—God had already promised her the birth of a son—in her own terms by instigating Abraham's polygamy to secure the promised heir.[52]

More than theoretical exercises, however, exegetical interpretations had significant practical applications: patriarchal precedents were consulted to establish legal precedents.[53] In the 1530s, the story of Abraham's polygamy would come to have a special relevance. In this decade, three major political events—causing international controversy and affecting the course of the Reformation—forced authorities to reconsider this aspect of patriarchal precedence. They involved England's Henry VIII, the German landgrave Philip of Hesse, and the infamous incident of "enforced polygamy" in the radical Anabaptist city of Münster.[54]

Some counseled polygamy as an alternative to divorce in the cases of Henry in the early 1530s and Philip in the mid-1530s.[55] In the end, however, Henry broke from the Roman Catholic Church to bring about his own annulment in 1533, while Philip entered into a bigamous marriage in 1540.[56] The latter obtained the covert approval of both Luther and Philip Melanchthon, drawing them into the quicksand of a messy affair, scandalizing their allies, and delighting their Catholic opponents. No less embarrassing to Luther and Melancthon was the alacrity with which several Protestant ministers, following their lead, "expatiated further from the pulpit in favor of polygamy, leading to publications of ephemeral writings, both pro and con."[57]

However, pan-European condemnation was the response to events in Münster, northwest Germany, when a radical Anabaptist sect took control of the city in 1534. Led by a Dutchman known as John of Leyden, they proclaimed polygamy as the ideal form of marriage, divinely revealed in the Old Testament. At the time, it was estimated that three times as many women as men lived in Münster, and the revolutionary authorities, scrambling to keep civil order and to stop rampant adultery, sought to live by the book.[58] This situation lasted some eleven months before the sect could be overthrown and its leaders promptly tortured and executed.[59]

Thus, at a time when legal divorce was "all but impossible and bigamy biblical," marital traditions would continue to be called into question, and a number of prominent personages, when faced with predicaments not unlike those of Henry VIII and Philip of Hesse, considered dual marriage as an alternative. When Luther broke his monastic vows or Henry seceded from the papacy, marital conventions were reexamined, particularly in Protestant regions. These and other developments coincided with the European realization that polygamy was customary in other parts of the world, as reports by explorers and missionaries about ruling elites in Asia, Africa, and the Americas explained. This revelation was brought even closer to home by the Ottoman Turks, who threatened Christian Europe.[60]

The fact remained that nowhere in the Old or New Testaments was there an explicit condemnation of plural marriage, and many leading theologians and legal authorities, Protestants and Catholics alike, wavered in doubt.[61] Not until the Council of Trent (1545–1563) was a definitive decision against plural marriage decreed, and this, "[Cardinal] Bellarmine tells us, was to a considerable degree motivated as a direct shaft against Luther."[62]

After the mid-1560s, no known western European writer argued publicly in favor of polygamy until the mid-seventeenth century, although writings against plural marriage continued.[63] Nevertheless, throughout the end of the sixteenth century, while advocates for polygamy remained a small minority, they would continue to surface, particularly in radical religious groups and in the retinues of sovereigns.[64] And, just like Philip of Hesse or John of Leyden, those in favor of polygamy could lay claim to Abraham's example.[65] Questions concerning Abraham's apparent polygamy would resurface in the seventeenth century, as we shall see in chapter 2.

We have reviewed early commentaries in order to trace the exegetical and theological development of Hagar's story in ancient, patristic, medieval, and sixteenth-century European thought. We can now turn to seventeenth-century Dutch literature on the subject, which takes up many of these early attitudes, particularly those of the sixteenth-century Reformers.

Notes

1. Thompson 2000, 94.

2. Thompson 2001, 94.

3. The rivalry between Hagar and Sarah takes on characteristics of the rivalry between the female stereotypes of Synagoga and Ecclesia in medieval thought, as van Lier observes. In Gothic cathedral imagery, these appear as paired icons (e.g., the portal carvings at Chartres): Synagoga appeared as an unhappy, blindfolded woman (blind to the salvation of Christ); her attributes included a broken staff, a crown falling from her head, and the tablets of law slipping from her hands. Conversely, Ecclesia is shown as a proud woman wearing a crown and holding a cross, the symbol of Christ's crucifixion and triumph (van Lier 1995, 35–36).

4. Bede interpreted Ishmael and Isaac as symbols of the two covenants. "Hagar with Ishmael in the desert signified the Synagogue and its people expelled from its land, without a priesthood and ignoring the path of Christ" (Schapiro 1963, 353, f. 28).

5. Thompson 2001, 62, summarizing Deutz, Comestor, and Hugh of St. Cher, twelfth to fifteenth centuries.

6. Thompson 2001, 96.

7. Van der Coelen 1997, 279.

8. Thompson 2001, 36, cites Ambrose and Augustine. In contrast, in Jewish and Muslim tradition, Ishmael came to be regarded as the ancestor of the Saracens (desert-dwelling tribes, a pre-Islamic, nomadic people of the Syrian-Arabian deserts). Arabs venerate Ishmael as their ancestor and, according to Muslim tradition, he and Hagar are buried in the sacred Ka'aba in Mecca (Myers 1987, 534).

9. Schapiro 1963, 353. Bede, among others, linked Ishmael with the Saracens.

10. Thompson 2001, 63.

11. Nicolas of Lyre (ca. 1270–1349). Both Christian and rabbinical sources reflected these views. In certain Christian and rabbinical sources, it was reported that Ishmael grew up to become a brigand or highwayman (Mellinkoff 1998, 42; Kirsch 1997, 49; Thompson 1997, 218).

12. Flavius Josephus (ca. 37–100), a Palestine native honored with Roman citizenship (ca. 69) by the emperor Vespasian (Thompson 2001, 24, 27–28).

13. Ibid.

14. From Josephus's *Jewish Antiquities* 4.188–89, ca. 94 (Thackeray, LCL).

15. Thompson 2001, 24, 27–28, citing Josephus, *Jewish Antiquities* 4.215.

16. The first glimmers of theological appreciation for Hagar appear in the Middle Ages, as Thompson's recent exegetical study shows, citing interpretations by Isidore, archbishop of Seville (560–636); the Venerable Bede (673–735); and Raban Maur, abbot of Fulda and archbishop of Mainz (ca. 780–856). See Thompson 2001, 227, 238.

17. Thompson 2001, 24–25. Philo (ca. 20 BC to AD 50) was thought to be the most important figure and thinker among Hellenistic Jews of his age. Thompson's discussion is drawn primarily from Philo's *De congressu quaerendae eruditionis gratia* (*On the Preliminary Studies*), but also three treatises written in sequence, *De fuga et inventione*, *De mutatione nominum*, and *De Abrahamo* (*On Flight and Finding, On the Change of Names, On the Life of Abraham*).

18. Thompson 2001, 25.

19. I am adapting and expanding on a basic outline first proposed by van Lier 1995, 34.

20. Protestant theologian and Christian Hebraist Conrad Pellikan of Zurich (1478–1556); Swiss reformer Ulrich Zwingli (1484–1531); former Benedictine monk Wolfgang Musculus (1497–1563) took up Protestantism, working in Bern and Augsburg; Florentine-born Augustinian monk Peter Martyr Vermigli (1499–1562) fled to Zurich after embracing Protestant beliefs.

21. Thompson 2001, 238.

22. Ibid., 75–83.

23. Ibid.

24. Thompson 1997, 216–17, 219, citing Cajetan's exegetical writings on the Old Testament (Gen 16:8 and 21:15) in *Commentarii illustres . . . in Quinque Mosaicos libros* (Paris: Guillaume Bossozel, 1539), 80, 99.

25. Ibid.

26. Thompson 2001, 89–92.

27. *Luther's Works* (Pelikan 1955), 3:37.

28. Thompson 2001, 84, citing Calvin's commentaries on Gen 21:14: "Agar quae semper ferox et rebellis fuerat . . ."

29. Thompson 2001, 85–86, citing Calvin, *Comm. Gen. 21:14*, ". . . tam dura et tristis . . ."

30. Ibid.

31. Thompson observes that in the anti-Donatist treaty *De baptismo contra Donatistas* 1.10.14 (fifth century), "Augustine reiterates the ominous ejection formula in Gen. 21:10, implying that the Donatists (like Ishmael) have no part in the inheritance of Abraham. . . . Hagar . . . is [used as] a hammer against his foes." However, in another treatise, Augustine likens "the Church's persecution of the anti-Donatists to Sarah's persecution of Hagar in Gen. 16.6" (Thompson 2001, 36, 86).

32. Thompson, 2001, 63, citing Urban II, *Oratio II in Concilio Claromontano. Habitae De Expeditione Hierosolymitana* (PL 151:569).

33. From Luther's lectures on Gen 16. Luther's main point is that although Hagar misbehaved, Sarah was still not justified in condemning her to exile—essentially, in condemning her to death: two wrongs don't make a right: ". . . thus I am bearing the excommunication of the pope and the hatred of the entire

world, but I do not for this reason approve or praise the pope as though he were doing what is right when he opposes the true doctrine and condemns and murders the members of Christ solely for the purpose of maintaining his rule. . . ." Luther, on Gen 16:6, in Pelikan 1955, 3:57.

34. Thompson 2001, 83, citing Calvin's commentaries on Gen 16:1, 16:6, 21:10.

35. Calvin, *Commentaires de Jean Calvin sur L'Ancien Testament* (Malet 1978), 247.

36. My italics. Luther, *Lectures on Genesis* (Pelikan 1955), 3:53–55.

37. Pelikan 1955, 4:22, 3:43, 4:21. Luther gave his lectures from Genesis beginning in spring 1535, in Wittenberg (Pelikan 1955), 3:ix, 59–60.

38. Ibid., 3:64.

39. This theological emphasis on the family and on relationships may fit in with what some argue is a positive shift in tone on the subject of women and the household during the sixteenth century; a growing emphasis on the family seemed to follow, suggested by the volume of Dutch domestic conduct literature that appears at the turn of the century.

40. Durantini 1983, 72.

41. My italics. Luther, *Lectures on Genesis* (Pelikan 1955), 3:53–55.

42. Cited by Bleyerveld 1991, 124.

43. Thompson 2001, 72.

44. Thompson 1997, 219.

45. Thompson 1994, 5.

46. Ibid.

47. Ibid., 9.

48. Ibid., 9–11.

49. Thompson citing Calvin's sermon on I Tim 3:2. The maxim "for God did not give Adam three Eves" is not original; it is also found in Zwingli and probably in others (Thompson 1994, 13).

50. Ibid., 15, citing Calvin's sermon on I Tim 6.

51. Thompson 2000, 44.

52. Thompson 1992, 167–68.

53. Thompson 1994, 7.

54. For more, see Cairncross 1974: ". . . For Puritan polygamy never took root in Italy, nor indeed in any Catholic country. It is a specifically Protestant phenomenon . . ." (Cairncross 1974, 65).

55. Various viewpoints circulated. Remarkably, Luther privately expressed to Robert Barnes in a letter dated September 3, 1531, that he would rather see Henry take a second wife than divorce Catherine of Aragon (Thompson 1994, 9).

56. Ibid., 7–8; Cairncross 1974, 44–45, 57–59.

57. L. Miller 1974, 22.

58. Ibid., 45–47.

59. Cairncross 1974, 26–28.

60. L. Miller 1974, 49–54.

61. Ibid., 7, 26, 37.

62. Ibid., 36.

63. Ibid., 49; Cairncross 1974, 65–75.

64. ". . . there were a few exegetes who denied that polygamy was necessarily limited to the patriarchs or to the Old Testament era, and this minority opinion was not always universally condemned. . . . Sixteenth-century commentators who espoused this position included Cajetan, Luther, Philip Melanchthon, Martin Bucer, and (perhaps) Vermigli—Catholic, Lutheran, and Reformed" (Thompson 1994, 8–9,11). "Currents of pro-polygamous thought" cropped up in France and in Italy sporadically, according to Cairncross 1974, 73n1.

65. One of Philip's own arguments used Abraham's precedent as justification: "How can [Philip] be pilloried for following the example . . . [of] the pious Abraham?" John of Leyden mainly rested his case on Old Testament fathers who had practiced polygamy uncensored (Cairncross 1974, 26, 44–45).

✝

CHAPTER TWO

Of Households and Thresholds
SEVENTEENTH-CENTURY DUTCH CHRISTIAN LITERATURE AND THE STORY OF HAGAR

Acknowledging that Hagar's story could be adapted in many ways to serve a variety of purposes in Dutch literature, a pattern of literary usage nevertheless emerges. The story was used, more or less, in three different ways: theologically, allegorically, and as a practical homily on domestic life. A review of these forms of usage helps establish an immediate context and meaning for the biblical story in Dutch art.

Theological and Allegorical Uses: The Traditional Pauline Typology Persists

Certainly, the Pauline typology persists in seventeenth-century Dutch culture. In many writings, Hagar and Sarah appear as personifications of the old covenant of the law (Old Testament) and the new covenant of the gospel or grace (New Testament). For example, in Hugo Grotius's commentary in Latin in the 1640s (Dutch edition, 1693), the author clarifies the Pauline allegory in Gal 4 for readers: Isaac represents the "chosen" (the spirit), while Ishmael (the flesh) does not.[1]

As another example, the names of Hagar and Sarah could be invoked when examining theological questions of the old and new covenant. Several theological disputations, published in a bound set, relied on the familiar Pauline typology of the rival wives as useful headings under which to house the complex arguments that follow. *Disputatio Theologica-quinta Sara & Agar, hoc est, De Numero A Naturâ foederum Dei cum hominibus* (Five Theological Disputations on Sarah and Hagar, that is, on the Extent, Number, and Nature of the Covenant of God with Man) was published under the auspices of Leiden University in 1668. These volumes comprised formal, extended arguments submitted by Protestant theology students at Leiden for their final examinations.[2] The theses explored scripture to define and propose what exactly the new covenant entailed in order to achieve salvation.

A third example of the traditional Pauline typology appears in a theological tract titled *Hagars Dienst onder de Vrye Sara* (Hagar's Service under the Free Sarah), officially approved by the province of Friesland in 1673.[3] The introduction indicates that Hagar represents earthly philosophy, while Sarah signifies divine wisdom (hearkening back to Philo's interpretation of the Pauline allegory). The tract goes on to distinguish between the earthly and the heavenly Jerusalem, or law and grace, for example, to promulgate religious faith.

Like their theological forefathers, Netherlanders held that the Jews, Islamic Turks, Arabs, Saracens, as well as the gypsies were descendants of Ishmael. In certain writings, Hagar and Ishmael could also represent unbelievers generally.[4] Seventeenth-century Dutch Christian literature reiterates the traditional associations with the Jews, and on one unique occasion includes an anti-Judaic slur inscribed on an engraving, as we shall see shortly. This reminds us that the Reformation was capable of ugly forms of polemics against its enemies. Still, while the Dutch draw upon the traditional associations between the outcast Hagar and the Jews, several writings do so in more "tolerant" terms, relatively speaking—tolerant, at least, in an age when the persecution of Jews was conventional elsewhere in Europe. For example, one Dutch minister used Hagar's story to temper the traditional anti-Judaic Pauline allegory as argument that they should not "cause [the outcast Jews] additional suffering, as so many others [peoples] do." Instead, they should pray—by raising their voice to God like Hagar did for Ishmael—for the Jews' salvation.[5] He went on to say that Christians should seek the conversion of the Jews through prayer and eschew violence, since violent acts only thwarted the Jews from finding the path to salvation voluntarily.[6]

Ishmael and Isaac, a Tale of Two Brothers, or Hagar and Sarah, a Tale of Two Churches

Predictably, the Dutch also make use of the traditional Pauline allegory for religious or political polemics. Ishmael's supposed bullying of Isaac

and the familiar Pauline typology were occasionally appropriated for political purposes, which sometimes surface in literature and on at least two
occasions in the inscriptions in Dutch Christian bible prints and engravings. Thus, we find that the Pauline typology—of two wives and two sons
in a struggle over "true inheritance," "the chosen seed"—could function
as a patriotic allegory, appropriate at the time. The antagonism between
the biblical Sarah and Hagar was analogized with the hostilities between
the northern Netherlands and Spain in at least one literary instance. In
the 1616 play *Hagar's vlucht ende weder-komst* (Hagar's Flight and Return) by
Abraham de Koningh, a celebrated playwright, poet, publisher, and book
and art dealer in Amsterdam, the biblical story is adapted to mirror aspects
of contemporary Dutch domestic life, about which more will be said
shortly. Of interest here is the point in the play, at the end of act two,
scene three, when Sarah gets very angry with Hagar. The chorus intervenes
with a song that parallels the antagonism between Sarah and Hagar to the
hostilities between the Netherlands and Spain:

> The Egyptian, foreign, arrogant woman (i.e., Spain)
> Is the (cause of) strife in our lands.
> Sarah is true to her husband (God, or the Christian Faith),
> Through the pure hands of bonds of faiths:
> But Hagar means, through her master's love,
> And holding within the fruit of the Lord
> Which plagues her mistress,
> To be victorious here.
> Defy Sarah, go ahead, as long as you (Hagar) will
> (oh, foreign Christians) with your pitiful stratagems:
> The Lord is (Sarah's) reward and shield.
> If you mistakenly think that, with all your fighting
> In the hopes that you will live
> Here as wife (regain sovereignty);
> You (Spain) will, with Hagar,
> Nevertheless flee far and wide
> Just as we show (in this play).[7]

Hagar is described as the "Egyptian foreign, arrogant woman," the
cause behind turmoil in "our lands." Here, Hagar represents Spain, and
Sarah the United Provinces. Just as the Dutch were forced to split off
from the "Christian family" by repudiating the Catholic Church (to return

to a "pristine church"), so Sarah was forced to reject Hagar. On one level, then, the biblical story of the expulsion could be adapted to justify this historic moment of political-religious division, marking the emergence of the new, reformed church. In his play, de Koningh's typology serves patriotic and religious prejudice; it helps to justify Sarah's anger as necessary for the preservation of faith and fatherland.

The Expulsion Episode as Polemical Tool: Inscriptions on Dutch Bible Prints and Engravings Reflect Pauline Thought

De Koningh's political adaptation of the story is not unique in seventeenth-century Dutch culture. Several other Dutch writings—inscriptions that appear on Bible prints and engravings in four instances—confirm that Hagar's story, the expulsion scene in particular, could be made to harness the familiar Pauline typology for polemical purposes. From this, we not only glean a better understanding of the significance of the Pauline typology in Dutch culture and the ways it was put to use, but, more importantly, the inscriptions help us to establish one level of meaning—the theological or allegorical (Pauline typology)—for Hagar's story in Dutch visual culture.

Claes Jan Visscher's Merian Bible of 1659: "Law" Yields to "Grace"

A print from Claes Jan Visscher's Merian Bible of 1659 shows a tearful Hagar with a tiny Ishmael, whose back is turned to us, heading away from the house (fig. 1).[8] Abraham points to the distance. Sarah and Isaac appear in the doorway. Below the image, a Latin inscription reads:

> As a servant girl yields to
> her mistress, so law ought to
> yield to grace.[9]

Hagar and Sarah function as the traditional personifications of the old covenant of the law and the new covenant of the gospel or grace, respectively. The expulsion scene is made to reiterate that, like Abraham and Sarah, one should keep one's "spiritual house" in order: "Law" (Hagar) should humbly submit to or make way for its mistress "Grace" (Sarah). In short, the expulsion scene is used to promote the true religion.

CEDAT SERVA DOMINÆ, LEX GRATIÆ.

FIG. I: Matthaeus Merian. *CEDAT SERVA DOMINAE, LEX GRATIA*. Designed by M. Merian, engraving by P. H. Schut. From *Bybel printen, vertoonende de voornaamste historien der Heylige Schrifture*. Amsterdam: N. Visscher, before 1674. Universiteitsbibliotheek, Amsterdam.

Churchmen and moralists held that the Dutch family and household were the locus of Christian teaching, discipline, and religiosity. Using the household as the visual "site" for the cultivation of virtue, faith, and obedience was an especially apt visual metaphor for the Dutch, who were very domestically minded. A copy of this expulsion image and the same inscription reappeared in a later publication of biblical prints called *Bybel printen, vertoonende de voornaemste historien der Heylige Schrifture* (Bible Prints, Showing the Principal Histories of the Holy Scripture), published by Nicolaes Visscher sometime around 1660.[10] Below the expulsion image, the publisher added an explanation and a poem of rhyming quatrains in Dutch, which also reinforces notions of the rivalry between Law (Hagar) and Grace (Sarah).[11]

Schabaelje's 1654 *The Great Sacred Emblemata* and the Expulsion Episode: A Tale of Two Churches

In a few images, the expulsion scene was put to polemical use to allude to political or religious divisiveness, as it was in literature. In *De Grooten Emblem Sacrae* (The Great Sacred Emblemata), a collection of Bible illustrations with didactic text published by J. P. Schabaelje in 1654, an expulsion scene, a reprint of a 1588 etching by the Dutch artist Peter van der Borcht, is included. The scene is predominately a pretty landscape traversed by winding roads and a river, dotted with dwellings, and bordered by craggy mountains.[12] In the left foreground, a small-scale expulsion unfolds in front of a manor, with Abraham expelling Hagar and Ishmael. Sarah and Isaac are not included. The text spells out the meaning of the expulsion scene for the reader in Dutch.[13] Building upon the Pauline typology, the author used the image and text to illustrate one of the principal notions behind the Reformation itself. Abraham's repudiation of Hagar and Ishmael signifies the Protestant return to a "pristine church" (or, Abraham, Sarah, and Isaac): the expulsion symbolizes the purgation of the church service from all priestly accretions or rituals not supported by scripture (Hagar and Ishmael). The author harnessed his text to the sixteenth-century expulsion scene to rationalize the painful split in the Christian Church "family." Simultaneously, the author reasserts Protestant bias. Although van der Borcht may have originally used Hagar's expulsion as a pretext to show a pretty landscape, seventy-five years later, Schabaelje returns to a Pauline interpretation of the scene for polemical purposes.

Goltzius and Fraternal Violence: Divisiveness and Persecution in the Christian Church

As we have seen in traditional literature and in certain prints, the Pauline typology could be used as a polemical tool to hammer one's foes or to express political or religious divisiveness. One Dutch depiction uses the fraternal rivalry to mirror contemporary religious strife, a reflection of turbulent times. In Henrik Goltzius's 1594 print *Dissidence in the Church*, a vignette of a fighting Ishmael and Isaac are included along with other Old Testament instances of fraternal violence taking place in a church interior (fig. 2). The print is one of twelve allegories of the Christian creed in a series titled *The Allegories of Faith*, modeled after Antwerp graphic traditions.[14]

In *Dissidence in the Church*, we see biblical instances of fraternal strife: Cain beating a prostrate Abel; to the right, Ishmael is poised to strike a

FIG. 2: Henrik Goltzius. *Dissidence in the Church,* from the series *The Allegories of Faith,* ca. 1594. Engraving, 240 x 185 mm. Printroom of Leiden University, Leiden, the Netherlands.

younger Isaac over a game of ninepins; on the left, Joseph's jealous brothers are throwing him into the pit; and behind Ishmael, Saul takes aim at David with a javelin, among other incidents. The scene is bordered by scriptural verse in Latin numerically linked to the vignettes so that each can be identified. The principal inscription, three lines in the lower margin, is from the New Testament books of John and Galatians (KJV):

> THE THIEF COMETH NOT, BUT FOR TO STEAL AND TO KILL AND TO
> DESTROY. JOHN 10:10.[15] BUT AS THEN HE THAT WAS BORN AFTER THE
> FLESH [ISHMAEL], PERSECUTED HIM THAT WAS BORN AFTER THE SPIRIT
> [ISAAC], EVEN SO IT IS NOW. GALATIANS 4:29. YEA, THE TIME COMETH,
> THAT WHOSOEVER KILLETH YOU WILL THINK THAT HE DOETH GOD'S
> SERVICE. JOHN 16:2.

Using the figures of Ishmael and Isaac among others, the print expresses the persecution and divisiveness in the Christian Church. More specifically, Kunzle argues that the architecture in the central panel—the right wall is decorated with statues and painted altarpieces, while the left wall has been left bare, "Calvinist-style"—symbolizes the struggle for control of Haarlem's St. Bavo Church, the town's chief place of worship, which was subjected to iconographic cleansing in the 1570s.[16]

The Pauline Typology and Visual Instances of a "Heterodox" Hagar and Ishmael

In traditional Pauline commentary, Hagar and Ishmael came to represent the Jews, Islamic Turks, Arabs, Saracens, gypsies, and the heterodox in general, as noted earlier.[17] In this respect, Netherlanderish writers followed the example of their Christian predecessors. Do we come across these types of Pauline associations in any inscriptions on prints and engravings? Or, in other words, can we point to any visual trace of the pejorative Pauline attitude toward a "heterodox" Hagar and Ishmael that we confronted in traditional literature? Almost never, except in one extremely rare instance: a 1603 engraving by Jacob Matham after a drawing by Abraham Bloemaert is explicit in this regard (fig. 3).[18]

The composition presents a farmhouse in a rural setting. The eye lingers on numerous details: the rustic house, the hedge, the wheelbarrow, and lovely plant life. Small figures are in various parts of the house, but it is not clear how they are connected with the unfolding expulsion. Abraham points into the distance, a broken-down Hagar weeps, and Ishmael

FIG. 3: Jacob Matham (after Abraham Bloemaert). *The Expulsion of Hagar and Ishmael*, 1603. Engraving, 431 x 354 mm, signed at the bottom. Collection: Museum Boijmans Van Beuningen, Rotterdam, the Netherlands.

hangs on to his mother's skirt. It is not clear whether the woman figure in the lower window is Sarah.[19] At the bottom of the engraving, an epigram has been added:

WHILE THE PETULANT LADY [OF THE HOUSE, I.E., SARAH]
FEARS NOT TO HUMILIATE [HAGAR],

THE SERVANT WAS DRIVEN AWAY WITH HER SON;
THUS, WHILE THEY VIE TO MOCK CHRIST AND CHRIST'S FLOCK,
LIKE [EQUAL] PUNISHMENT ALSO DESERVEDLY WEIGHS UPON THE
JEWS.[20]

What was Bloemaert's expulsion scene appropriated to express here exactly? In 1703, the French collector Florent Le Comte, an enthusiast of Dutch art, inventoried this engraving as follows: "The large, enigmatic piece about the true religion removed from the Jews and bestowed on the gentiles. A landscape in which Hagar is driven out by Abraham."[21]

Although it finds the work enigmatic for reasons not explained, Le Comte's interpretation does not reflect a "confused" or "strained" viewpoint, as has been assumed, but rather enlarges on a traditional Christian anti-Judaic viewpoint.[22]

The Significance of the Pauline Allegory in Seventeenth-Century Dutch Literature

Thus, Netherlanders—these self-proclaimed "children of Israel"—saw themselves as the "children of promise" whom the Pauline allegory specified. Siding with Abraham, Sarah, and Isaac, they were obliged to "cast out the bondwoman and her son," as St. Paul prescribed.[23] In short, on a traditional, theological level, the story, the expulsion episode in particular, reenacted this biblical, historical moment of division and, for many Netherlanders, could mark the emergence of a purified faith, a redemptive covenant, or a reformed "church." We may conclude that many Dutch viewers would have been familiar with the traditional Pauline associations when viewing illustrations of Hagar's story, the expulsion episode in particular. The expulsion scene could simply be used as a reminder of the true faith, but it could also be appropriated to assert religious or political superiority, or epitomize the Republic's struggle for independence.

Moreover, we must remember that Netherlanders keenly identified with the line of faith leading from Abraham, Sarah, and Isaac. The Dutch Republic, or *de Neerlands Israël* (Netherlandish Israel), often compared itself to ancient Israel. Such comparisons helped form the basis for the Reformed Church's conceptions of nationhood. With Abraham, "father of faith" and founder of the House of Israel, and Sarah, "mother of Israel"[24] and "founder of the first spiritual house," the expulsion story expressed, via the family, analogies to notions of nationhood and the identity of the young "family" of the United Provinces, often divided and in civil turmoil and facing tremendous martial odds. Furthermore, the new covenant of salvation made by God with Abraham established ancient Israel as a nation (Gen 17). This covenant was often compared with the pact the Reformed churches made with God in the Netherlands; it too was viewed as crucial to the Provinces' formation as a country.[25]

Of course, the Dutch were all too familiar with the tremendous sacrifice caused by the painful "split" in the Christian family. By the end of the sixteenth century, following the Dutch revolt, the Lowlands were torn apart, divided into the "Republic" (the northern Netherlands, which comprised the Seven United Provinces) and "Flanders" (the Spanish Netherlands), which remained under Hapsburg rule. The tragic tale of expulsion and exile may have been particularly significant to religious refugees who fled from the south to the north: families were broken apart, homelands left behind, and possessions and inheritances lost. The irrevocable split between the Republic and the Spanish Netherlands, roughly coinciding with the present-day territories of the Netherlands and Belgium, would be lamented well into the next century and beyond.

From this vantage point, we can better grasp the traditional significance of the theme—and all that the Pauline associations implied—in Dutch culture. Fundamentally, in Pauline terms, the expulsion episode in Dutch culture could help the struggling United Provinces to form, justify, and maintain concepts of nationhood. When it came to the building of a nation and the need for family solidarity, the fledgling Republic claimed Abraham, Sarah, and Isaac for its own.

The Traditional Pauline Typology in Decline; Sympathetic, "Historical" Portraits of Hagar and Ishmael Emerge

So far, we have reviewed a number of examples of how and when Dutch authors, drawing upon Hagar's story, harnessed the familiar Pauline typology, sometimes for polemical use. But when did they depart from the Pauline allegory to consider Hagar and Ishmael as sympathetic or "historical" figures in their own right?

Echoing sixteenth-century attitudes that gained currency during the Reformation, seventeenth-century Dutch interpretations took on expressions of more fundamental human values and emotions: these could be voiced as sympathy for an errant Hagar, criticism of Sarah's vindictiveness, justifications to explain Abraham's apparent cruelty, or compassion for a mother distraught over a dying child.

Despite Calvin, the Dutch generally could not renounce mother and son, especially when it came to the wilderness-rescue scene (Gen 21). Some Dutch Christian literature analogized the hardships of a distraught Hagar and her dying son to those that contemporary Netherlanders might face. In several instances, the rescue episode is used as reassurance of divine mercy: the story, as one sermon summed it up at the end of the seventeenth century, "assures us that there is a higher [source] of help."[26]

Given the religious and political persecution the Dutch suffered—initially existing as a rebel state in a kind of exile from the Catholic Church, and suffering a painful split in the "Christian family"—did Netherlanders identify themselves with the exiled, victimized Hagar, as Luther once did? Nothing in the literature specifies this. Still, enough writers set the traditional theological typologies aside to offer strikingly sympathetic portraits of Hagar. As we shall see, this has its parallels in seventeenth-century Dutch painting, which also tended to portray Hagar and Ishmael as sympathetic types.

The Polysemic Hagar and the Dutch Experience

The Dutch developed a curiously ambivalent attitude toward Hagar's story. Theologically, these "children of Israel" obviously identified with the line of faith leading from Abraham, Sarah, and Isaac. At the same time, the war-torn, isolated Netherlanders, including a great number of Catholic refugees, may have felt an affinity for the biblical exiles' plight and despair.[27] In several Dutch exegeses, the name "Hagar" was translated from the ancient Hebrew and Greek as "foreigner" (*vreemdelinghe*) or "fugitive."[28] Netherlanders must have seen their own experiences mirrored in Hagar's exile, hardships, and miraculous rescue.[29] Moreover, the unique conditions that formed the new Republic meant that Netherlanders developed a special regard for foreigners: refugees and immigrants from the southern Netherlands and elsewhere had contributed significantly to the Republic's liberation and economic success.

What did seventeenth-century Netherlanders write about Hagar's story? How or when do authors depart from the Pauline tradition? As we answer these questions, we stand to gain a sharper sense of what aspects of the story mattered to the Dutch most. We can then comprehensively consider the biblical story's counterpart in Dutch art.

The Wilderness-Rescue Episode:
Hagar as a Model of Contrition in Gen 21

Not surprisingly, the most sympathetic, heartfelt accounts seem to occur when authors confront the wilderness-rescue episode. In some works, Hagar is held up as an example of contrition or penitence—one Dutch biblical concordance noted that the name "Hagar" means "pilgrim"[30]—although the Dutch would never go so far as to call her a "saint," as Luther did. Despite their offenses, the lowly slave woman and her son are worthy of God's mercy and protection: the Dutch were keenly aware that Ishmael was the "first man in the world, whose name was given him of God."[31] Not just the patriarchs received God's help in times of need, as one late-seventeenth-century Dutch minister observed, but also the "less pious," such as Hagar and Ishmael.[32] All this gave hope to sinners and unbelievers. A brief review of several literary reactions confirms Dutch sentiments.

A prayer book titled *Schriftmetige Gebeden op deerste Boeck Moysi Genesis* (Scriptural Prayers on Genesis, the First Book of Moses) by Jan Fruytiers, published in 1573 in Emden, offers two prayers predicated on the story of Hagar and Ishmael. The first relies on Gen 21, specifically on the expulsion and wilderness-rescue episodes. While the first portion of the prayer adapts the expulsion episode to advocate good household management, which I will discuss later in this chapter,[33] the second portion concentrates on the rescue scene to praise God's mercy and the comfort he brings to the distraught mother. The prayer ends by asking God to provide not only the material necessities for survival, but also the "spiritual tools" to overcome trials—as represented by Hagar, who is guided to the source of water—by giving "man wisdom and the ability to best use [this wisdom]."[34] Here, Hagar is held up as an exemplar of contrition: regardless of her sins and immoralities, she was brought to true repentance and enlightened.

Similar notions of mercy and grace in connection with the rescue appear in a popular Christian conduct book, *Voetpat der Eenvoudiger Mensen* (Footpath for Simple People, or the Royal Road to Heaven), published in several editions during the course of the seventeenth century. The 1640 edition was revised under the auspices of the powerful Calvinist minister Otto Badius of Amsterdam, to whom the book is also dedicated. It included the episode of Hagar's miraculous rescue as evidence of God's protection and benevolence. The passage appears in a chapter that deals with concepts of poverty, greed, and charity:

What I would like to emphasize is the remarkable manner in which God took care of and provided for Hagar and her child, who were in great crisis and difficulty: because both would otherwise have died from hunger and thirst; does not God [give] hope (as he customarily does), when all hope appears to be lost? Genes. 21: vers. 17. Did not the angel of the Lord call out to her from the heaven and give her nourishment and comfort? I also want to say how God, in an extraordinary and singular manner, has provided for his church in the wilderness, and furnished all necessary subsistence . . .[35]

No matter the difficulties, the text says, even dire poverty, God will prevail. Drawing on ideas we've seen before, the *Voetpat* uses the wilderness-rescue scene to reiterate that a merciful God rescues those who put their trust in him, as Hagar did. The chapter concludes with an appeal to readers to show charity to those in less fortunate circumstances. Here, too, the ordeal of Hagar and Ishmael is compared to difficulties contemporary Netherlanders might face.

This passage from *Voetpat* is especially significant, since Badius himself owned a painting of Hagar ("een schilderij van Hagar") that hung in the entry hall and reception area of his residence.[36] Badius was one of the most powerful ministers in Amsterdam and his career there spanned forty years.[37] Besides the Hagar painting, Badius also left behind portraits of stadtholder Prince Frederik Hendrik and his wife Amalia van Solms, a painting of Badius's coat of arms, a painting of "de princetocht nae Breda" (the Prince [of Orange's] expedition to Breda), one painting of the city of Cologne, another of Antwerp, and a painting of a "little white horse." It is striking that the Hagar picture is the only religious image in his collection and that it was placed in the reception area, the most "public" space in what must have been an exceptionally socially active household.

In *Voetpat* and in other Dutch writings about the wilderness-rescue episode, the themes of wilderness and Hagar's thirst are sometimes used as metaphors for a state of moral chaos and spiritual impoverishment, respectively, ideas found elsewhere in Dutch Christian literature.[38]

The concept of the wilderness or desert—in Dutch, the term *woestijn* meant both a wilderness or a desert, as it does today[39]—signified a place where men could "goe astray, or wander as Hagar did."[40] It could connote a place of uncertainty and deprivation. Yet it was also a place where God was encountered, where transformations occurred, and where community, or the "church in the wilderness," as the *Voetpat* calls it, could be formed.

Of course, the wilderness as moral proving ground and site of repentance or transformation is a centuries-old symbol in Christian thought: Old and New Testament figures journeyed there—Christ and Moses, among others—and underwent crises and transformations.

The well, also of special significance in traditional Christian thought, was a symbol of God's life-giving power or a metaphor for the cleansing of sins and the purification of the soul. The well offered salvation, redemption, communion, and baptism. For seventeenth-century Netherlanders, numerous Christian writings emphasize the well of life (*levensbron*) that could be found through faith in Christ.[41]

The Story of Hagar and Ishmael as a Practical, Domestic Homily in Dutch Literature

Hagar and the wilderness-rescue scene were used to articulate Christian concepts of contrition, divine mercy, and grace. The runaway Hagar (Gen 16) and expulsion episode (Gen 21), however, were used to illustrate other ideas. For example, poet and dramatist Joost van den Vondel, the greatest writer of the Dutch Golden Age, includes the expulsion episode in the poem "Abraham, the faithful father," from a 1620 series of portraits lauding Old Testament heroes. Here, as Abraham explains in the first person, the ejection of "my Hagar" and Ishmael is recounted as a preliminary test of faith for the more difficult trial that follows, the sacrifice of Isaac.[42] The biblical episode is used to reinforce Abraham as the "father of faith" and a model of obedience: he sacrifices not one, but both sons.

However, the runaway Hagar and expulsion scenes were most often adapted to talk about the more practical, immediate concerns of daily life. Like Erasmus, Luther, and Calvin, the Dutch often used the story as a pretext to comment on familial relations and the household. For the Dutch, a culture fixated on "domesticity"—as the flood of domestic conduct literature from this period and countless domestic genre paintings attest[43]—the biblical story of a divided household and the expulsion that leaves Hagar and Ishmael homeless must have held special significance.

Using the biblical familial conflict as example and the expulsion episode specifically, Dutch clergy, reformers, moralists, playwrights, and poets warned against domestic strife (*twist*) or misconduct, and outlined proper relations between masters and servants, husbands and wives, parents and children, and even siblings and stepsiblings. Authors knew what

the Old Testament story so effectively illustrated: familial hostility, individual pride and arrogance, sibling rivalry, conflicts over matters of inheritance, and even extramarital sexuality were followed by separation, danger,
sorrow, and punishment. Using the biblical tragedy as a foil, authors could
better impress upon Netherlanders the key domestic virtues of harmony,
obedience, humility, and diligence, as we shall see in the literary examples
to follow. Simply put, the biblical tragedy was principally used to warn
against contemporary domestic ruptures.

Household Management: Marriage, Parents and Children

To review an early example of this usage, we must return to Fruytiers's
prayer book of 1573, in which two prayers, predicated on Gen 16 and 21,
promote familial well-being. Fruytiers's second prayer, centered on the
expulsion episode, intends "to apply God's words to maintain order, to
[avoid] misery, to [raise] God-fearing children, and to [promote] wise
household management."[44] Drawing upon the conflicts that arose between
Abraham, Sarah, Isaac, Hagar, and Ishmael, the prayer asks for God's help
in eliminating strife between husband and wife, servants or siblings. As we
shall see shortly, the second half of Fruytiers's Gen 21 prayer even uses
the expulsion scene as an appeal for civic order, specifically to address relations between masters and servants.

Another example appears in the renowned moralist Jacob Cats's 1658
poem praising the state of marriage, *Proef-steen van den Trou-ringh* (Touchstone
of the Wedding Ring); Cats references the story to illustrate the biblical
maxim "the two flesh shall be as one" (Eph 5:31). The popular "Father
Cats," as he was then already known to his readers, points out that the house
of Abraham comes under pressure because Abraham slept with "sour fruit"
and because Sarah, desperate for an heir, initiated this misdeed. This leads to
many arguments in the household, Cats warns, and Ishmael's troublesome
behavior only makes a bad situation even worse. Arguably the Netherlands'
leading proponent of the primacy of the family, Cats identifies the worst
part of this situation: Abraham suffers the loss of his first son (Ishmael).[45]
Cats, then, like Fruytiers, uses this biblical tragedy of a broken family to
warn readers of its equivalent in contemporary domestic life.

Dutch parents were urged to provide children with a Christian
upbringing in the home, and here too the Old Testament figures show up.
In a book of sermons titled *De verkore Godsdienst Binnens Huys geoeffent: en
d'Opvoeding der Kinderen in de Selve* (The Chosen Ministry Practiced in the

Home: Including the Rearing of Children in Religion), published in Utrecht in 1695, the author asks, Do you care about your child?[46] Then he outlines methods to guide children toward the "proper path." Since all children are "born of the maidservant" (*geboren van de dienstmaagd*) parents must pray for their children as Abraham did for his sons: as a result, Ishmael was allowed to live and his offspring, as God foretold to Abraham, were likewise favored. Since children inherit their parents' sins—the text implies that each child comes into the world as the carnal Ishmael, and only through proper training can become the spiritual Isaac—parents must guide their offspring to God. A good upbringing, the author concludes, leads to the "best inheritance" (*de beste erfenis*), salvation.

Predicating a sermon on the story of Hagar and Ishmael, at the end of the seventeenth century, the Rotterdam minister Adrian Kattenburch offered listeners practical advice. Even in the most ideal marriages, misunderstandings arise, Kattenburch says, especially when children from second marriages are involved. Parents would be wise to treat children and stepchildren equally, he cautions: "Use this [story of Hagar and Ishmael] from the past as a lesson so that, after your death, no strife will arise over inheritance between 'children from different beds' (*kinderen van verscheidene bedden*)."[47]

When the sermon arrives at the moment that Hagar and Ishmael are in peril in the wilderness, Kattenburch appeals to all mothers to put themselves in Hagar's shoes.[48] Here Kattenburch admires Hagar for the maternal love she shows for her dying son by crying out for help: in that moment, she would have willingly given her life that Ishmael might live.[49] Like his sixteenth-century predecessors, the Dutch minister imagines and admires a contrite mother who appeals to the heavens on behalf of her child. Transformed by her ordeal, the servant realizes that her pride is to blame and puts her trust in God.

Kattenburch's sermon is especially interesting since he begins by reiterating traditional Pauline allegories—Hagar and Sarah as representatives of the Old and New Testament, the Christians and the Jews, and so forth—but he reserves the majority of the sermon for discussion of matters of family life. Thus, the biblical story functioned for him on two levels, as theological allegory and as a practical, domestic homily. In effect, Kattenburch's sermon summarizes most of the various forms the story could take in Dutch literature. In this sense, it functions not unlike a compendium of Dutch Christian thought, except in one respect. We shall return to Kattenburch's sermon later in this chapter.

Franciscus Ridderus: Like Sarah, Women Should Ensure Theirs Is a Virtuous Household and Cast Out Hagar

Up until now, we have restricted our review of Dutch literature to interpretations that concentrate on Hagar and Ishmael. However, one must keep in mind that the biblical Sarah was a figure of importance in many assertions of Dutch domestic values. For Netherlanders, Sarah was one of several female Old Testament figures held up as a role model for women beginning in the sixteenth century. A century later, she is still presented as a paragon of domesticity for Rotterdam housewives in a book by Franciscus Ridderus entitled *Onlangs Godtsaelighe, en nu Zalige Sara, voorgestelt aan de dochteren Zions van Rotterdam* ([In honor of] the formerly pious and now heavenly blessed Sara, presented to the daughters of Zion in Rotterdam), published in 1657.[50] The book was dedicated to the author's wife, recently deceased, whose name was Sarah, like her biblical counterpart. The writer advises women ("daughters of Sarah") to concentrate on the spiritual aspects of domestic life and avoid vanities. In doing so, women could then be referred to in more positive terms, rather than negative ones: "man's shipwreck" (*een schipbreuk voor de man*), "a hindrance of peace" (*een verhinderinge van ruste*), "a lifelong jail sentence" (*een gevanckenisse des Levens*), "a daily punishment" (*een dagelijcxse strafe*), "a domestic pet" (*een Huys-beest*), "an ornamental dog" (*een vercierde Hont*), and "a necessary evil" (*een Noodsaeckelick quaet*).

Women's domestic concerns, the author continues, should be about more than needlework, ironing, and linen:[51] mistresses should ensure that their household is "een Geestelijck Godts-huys" (a spiritual house of God),[52] like Sarah's, achieved through the practice of faith. Remarkably, the author asserts that it is Sarah who founded the first spiritual house (*geestelijck gebouw*), and that she was as morally righteous as Abraham. While this text focuses on Sarah as a positive role model for housewives, Hagar does make an entrance, albeit a brief one, in the poem that follows and concludes the text. Simply put, the author writes, Hagar must go and Sarah, the legitimate wife, remain.[53] Thus, the author implies that worldliness/the material realm (Hagar) must be rejected in order to make way for virtue/the spiritual (Sarah). Here, Ridderus adapts the well-worn Pauline typology to rest his case.

Poet Guillaume de Saluste and Criticism of Sarah

But reconsideration of Hagar's story and the decline of the Pauline allegory meant that traditional notions about the virtuous Sarah also underwent reappraisal, as we encountered among her harsher critics like Calvin. Criticism of Sarah's behavior continued to be periodically voiced in the seventeenth century. For example, the well-known French Calvinist poet Guillaume de Saluste, Sieur du Bartas, in a 1605 poem available in Dutch, clearly faults Sarah for her hysterical outbursts against the poor maid: he rails against "jeloux Sara's curst and threatfull crying," which prevailed and resulted in the expulsion of Hagar and Ishmael.[54] Critical attitudes toward Sarah like this are not only reflected in Dutch literature, but also in Dutch painting, as we shall see. The poem goes on to imagine what is omitted in the Bible: Abraham's paternal "joy" and tearful relief when he learns that his son Ishmael is, against all odds, alive and safe following the banishment and wilderness ordeal. Abraham fares much better here than in Calvin: de Saluste's biblical patriarch is paternal, caring, familial. This "compassionate Abraham" also surfaces in Dutch painting, as we shall see.

Jacob Cats's *Hagar* and the Proper Behavior for Wives, Young Women

We must return to the beloved moralist "Father Cats," since he refers to Hagar's story many times throughout his voluminous writings. In all cases, he uses the story to reinforce proper conduct in the household or familial domain. Clearly, to Cats and other writers, Hagar's story was of value when it came to discussing the problems associated with familial and domestic matters. But, for Cats in particular, it appears that the story may have been considered of particular didactic value for female readers, especially young women, as two specific examples suggest:

For example, in the popular *Houwelijck* (Marriage), a domestic conduct book for women that outlined proper behavior and first appeared in 1625, the story is used in the chapter titled "Vrouw" (Wife) to show that the "weaker sex" does have some say in the household: Sarah wanted to drive Hagar out and, "many words later," Abraham acquiesced. Even though modern wives cannot be as assertive, Cats assures us, they can still be heard and have positive impact on the household.[55] However, obedience was still the rule: in the same chapter, "Father Cats" writes that women should "bend" to the rule of their husbands, and daughters submit to their mothers and fathers; it is foolishness to be "hard" like Hagar and run away instead of submitting to the will of another. To avoid conflicts, Cats says, one should act according to one's rank. Among the many conduct books of the age, Cats's *Houwelijck* was addressed specifically to a female audience; it was immensely sought after and new editions were printed well into the eighteenth century. We may assume that Cats's writings reflected common values and ideals of the Dutch upper and middle class.

A second poem by Cats, published in a collection titled *Klagende Maeghden, ende Raet voor de Selve* (Lamentations of Maidens and Advice for Them), focuses exclusively on the Egyptian maidservant. Several tragic biblical maidens, such as Hagar, Thamar, and Jepthah's daughter among others, share the harsh lessons they have learned in rhyming quatrains.

In "Klaegh-Liedt van Hagar. Abrahams Maeght" (Hagar's Lamentation. Abraham's Maidservant), Hagar tells her story in the first person, serving as an example and warning to marriageable women. She laments the loss of her innocence (virginity). Just before the moment of the expulsion, Abraham tells her she must go because "he wants no more trouble around his marriage bed," and that he is tired of the quarreling between the two women. Certainly, this stanza warns of the troubles brought about by extramarital sex. Toward the end of the soliloquy, Hagar says it was her pride that brought about her fall: "Siet dus soo komt den hooghmoet voor den val" (so see how pride comes before the fall).[56]

The poem closes with a repentant Hagar being thankful for her "education": her new understanding of God's laws and the powers of salvation are a blessing in themselves.[57] Hagar's trial is thus portrayed more as a corrective measure than as a punishment. In Cats's first edition of 1633, an image of an expulsion scene was included, a sixteenth-century engraving by the German artist George Pencz (discussed in chapter 5).[58]

Most striking is the pity Cats invites us to feel for the concubine. Hagar is more than an emblem of foolish or errant female behavior: she is now repentant and God-fearing. Far more like Luther's Hagar than Calvin's, Cats's Hagar is corrigible and, by example, teaches humility, obedience, diligence, and chastity. This was in keeping with the overall aims of the publication, specifically intended for the moral education of young, marriageable women. Since a large number of marriageable women worked as live-in maidservants, were Cats's teachings also meant for those whose own experiences in contemporary Dutch society may have been similar to Hagar's?

Following in Luther's and Calvin's Footsteps: The Biblical Hagar, Contemporary Dutch Maidservants, and Domestic Order

Like Luther and Calvin, Dutch authors drew analogies between the biblical maidservant and problems associated with contemporary domestic ser-

vants. Before we review this set of writings, we must first briefly look at
how servants figured in contemporary domestic life.

The common assumption has been that servants were treated relatively
well in the Netherlands, but recent studies suggest there were significant
problems.[59] Witness the large body of moralistic literature and folklore
characterizing female domestic servants in both negative and positive
terms. It has been estimated that live-in domestic help averaged between
10 and 20 percent of the total Netherlandish population in urban and
rural areas during the seventeenth century,[60] the majority being female, a
good portion of them probably immigrants.[61] While foreigners were
astonished at how democratically servants could be treated in the Netherlands, and while there were some relatively progressive laws in place
embodied in service contracts and rules about termination, servants often
got a raw deal and could be shown the door at any moment. It was not
uncommon, moreover, for female servants to be sexually victimized by
their employers. Abortion occurred relatively often among this group;[62]
eviction was the common outcome.[63] Therefore, the subject of domestic
servants figured prominently in Dutch cultural life.

The parallels between Hagar's troubles and those associated with contemporary Dutch domestic servants are made explicit in some Dutch Christian and didactic literature, poetry, and even a theatrical play. Fruytiers's prayer
book of 1573 offered a second prayer predicated on Hagar's story. This one
is specifically addressed to masters and servants; it not only aims to promote
domestic harmony, but also serves as an appeal for civic order.[64] The prayer
meditates on Gen 16, when the angel instructs the runaway Hagar to return
to her mistress, in an effort to encourage faith in "downtrodden hearts and
to right minds" as well as to ensure that servants and masters function in
their appropriate roles.[65] The prayer acknowledges that human beings, like
Hagar, try to flee from their own sins and flaws. It asks that God "lay his
merciful eyes" on each one and show the same (undeserved) mercy as he did
with Hagar and direct one to "turn back" when one has gone astray. Echoing
Luther, it points out that God sees everyone alike, each person's failings,
hopes, and aspirations.[66] In the name of Hagar, it beseeches God to maintain civic order and to "comfort the oppressed" (servants):[67]

> . . . That [God] by these means maintain civic order: so we pray that you
> will strengthen the hearts of all (domestic) servants, that they will not
> shirk the yoke of your hand, but remain truly steadfast in their calling.

Will you also strengthen masters and mistresses that they will not behave unreasonably to their servants nor lay hands upon them, since they will ultimately be held accountable for this. And if it pleases your Goodness, to comfort the oppressed, this from a God in whom all solace can be found, as [demonstrated] in the example of Hagar . . .[68]

As in Luther, Fruytiers's prayer uses Hagar's story to make this connection between good household management and civic order explicit. This idea also ties in with Israel's observation that the Dutch attitude toward servants was

> a manifestation of a general cultural disposition in which civic freedom and safety were closely connected with the order and discipline that characterized urban life. . . . Much of the population lived in closely regulated towns, and the freedom and safety that its inhabitants enjoyed was rooted in the preponderance of cities and a high level of social discipline and control. Harmony between masters and servants was, on one level, symbolic of the civic liberty, order, and safety enjoyed by all.[69]

Given the Dutch mindset, one can see why the ancient biblical story—that of a rebellious, arrogant maidservant who, guided by faith, returns to the household (Gen 16), or, following her castigation, personifies contrition, humility, and obedience (Gen 21)—would have been symbolic, on some level, of Dutch civic order, social control, and domestic well-being.

Abraham de Koningh's Hagar: The Errant Contemporary Maidservant as Contrite, Humble, Obedient

Touching on similar notions, playwright Abraham de Koningh adapted the biblical story and featured Hagar as the central character to reinforce the domestic virtues of humility, obedience, diligence, and contrition in *Hagars vluchte ende weder-komste* (Hagar's Flight and Return) of 1616. The play portrays Hagar as a servant in a contemporary Dutch household, and touches on many aspects of domestic management. The adaptation is based on the earlier episode of Hagar's voluntary flight to the wilderness, the encounter with an angel, and her return to her mistress Sarah (Gen 16), and not the final expulsion (Gen 21).[70]

Although adapted from the Old Testament, *Hagar's vlucht ende weder-komste* includes allegorical personages and comic dialogue. Initially characterized as diligent and compliant, Hagar becomes irritated by her mistress Sarah's nagging, and then, encouraged by other servants to use her pregnancy to raise her household status, becomes arrogant. Sarah and Hagar quarrel; Hagar flees to the woods. An angel of the Lord appears to Hagar and entreats her to return home; then, the allegorical personages of Ambition and Pride try to thwart Hagar's return; after they argue unsuccessfully with Obedience, a contrite Hagar begins her return journey as the play ends, her faith restored. In short, this is a morality play whose main message is aptly summarized in one stanza from the chorus's final song:

> This is the old way of the world,
> Whenever fortune shines upon us,
> One becomes proud and haughty;
> Virtuous humility one wants to discard;
> Scarcely does one know oneself then,
> Let alone the goodly goodness of God.[71]

While Hagar is clearly to blame for her troubles, de Koningh portrays her as a sympathetic protagonist. In comparison with fellow servants "Lisjen Messy Pants" (*Lisjen klonterpels*) and "little Jannet Blabbermouth" (*Klappige jannetjen*), who serve as foils and provide comic relief, Hagar appears more conscientious and ethical, and her dissolution all the more regrettable. In sum, Hagar is portrayed as a lowly Dutch maidservant caught up in the struggle for status, a universal theme. De Koningh shows that it is Hagar's wish for a better life—her pride—that gets the better of her. Eventually, her mistakes are righted by a renewal of faith, the restoration of reason, and the acceptance (obedience) of her lot in life.

Like Luther's, Kattenburch's, and Cats's Hagars, de Koningh's arrogant maidservant has been chastened and rehabilitated. Clearly, the play's central message is to reiterate the favorite Dutch virtues of humility, diligence, obedience, and contrition. Like Cats's poem, de Koningh's plot depends on Hagar bearing her afflictions "successfully," that is, that she emerges from her ordeal newly humbled, repentant, and submissive to God.

In de Koningh's adaptation, issues of legitimacy or inheritance in connection with Hagar's pregnancy are not mentioned. What de Koningh does emphasize is Hagar's low social status as a maidservant; that she is a foreigner is also perceived as a shortcoming. Thus, doubly disadvantaged, Hagar feels motivated with sudden ambition to rise from her servile position, and she becomes insubordinate. Wrong as this is, she never appears callous or self-indulgent like the other servants in the play, amplifying the viewer's sympathy for her.

The unmistakable tone of understanding and sympathy for the Hagar character complies with Calvinist notions of social tolerance. The repeated references to her immigrant status resonated with contemporary events—de Koningh himself was a religious refugee from Flanders—when urban centers were confronted with absorbing an extraordinary influx of foreigners, triggering a range of reactions, the most hostile aimed at the immigrant poor. The playwright clearly amplifies aspects of the biblical narrative that touched on the topical issues of domestic servants, immigration, and social status, uniting them in the figure of a remarkably sympathetic, three-dimensional Hagar.

The only surviving manuscript of de Koningh's play is written in a formal, elegant hand by the artist, poet, and intellectual Anna Roemer Visscher, which suggests the play was read, at least in private, and may have been circulated, but only portions of it appear to have been printed.[72] De Koningh used Visscher as scribe on another play he authored in the same year, *Tspel van de 5 wijse ende 5 dwase Maeghden* (The Play of the Five Wise and Five Foolish Maidens). Both plays center on the foibles of young, unmarried Old Testament females who suffer the consequences of their vainglory.

Visscher was a member of P. C. Hooft's celebrated literary circle and praised as an exemplary female role model.[73] Given that de Koningh's works received high praise from luminaries Joost van den Vondel and G. A. Bredero,[74] we can assume that his play reflected a generally accepted point of view.

Jan Goeree's Poem of 1735: A Dutch Master Gets His Maidservant Pregnant, Cites the Story of Hagar as Justification

Painter, printmaker, and poet Jan Goeree is another writer who associated the biblical story with contemporary problems between masters and maidservants in a poem published in 1735. We have jumped forward in time, but the poem shows how these parallels persisted in Dutch thought. Dedicated to the misconduct of a certain "Gerrit M.," the poem refers to a "schr{\i}ftuurlyke lootgieter" (scriptural plumber) who gets a "dienstmeisje" (servant girl) pregnant for the second time. In self-defense, the "loodgieter" (is "plumber" meant as a sexual pun here?) cites the story of Abraham and Hagar:

> When Gerrit had dirtily bred his girl for the first time,
> He justified this continually using the Bible
> And said that Abraham had done the same

With Hagar his maid, just as it is written:
He was right, the proof is good, it happened so:
But one time is no time, as the old saying goes:
Still, now he has made his girl accidentally pregnant
    a second time,
And that Abraham did not do.[75]

Goeree holds "Gerrit M." responsible, but records of the court of first instance in Amsterdam show that female servants were all too often blamed and expelled from households by incensed wives or masters.[76]

Jacob Cats: Upholding Marriage

As we have seen, Goeree and other authors used the story of Hagar to condemn extramarital sexuality and to reinforce proper marital conduct and monogamy. Moralist Jacob Cats does this as well in his work *Self-Strijt, dat is de krachtige beweginge van vleesch en geest* (Inner Conflict, That Is the Powerful Movements Between Flesh and Spirit). First published in 1620, the work is comprised of a lengthy, moralizing debate about adultery between Potiphar's wife and Joseph, adapted from the Old Testament story in Gen 39. In rhyming couplets, wily "Sephyra" uses every possible argument to exhort Joseph to have sex with her.[77] A steadfast, chaste Joseph counters her at every turn with a stream of pithy, pious statements. Both draw on Abraham's relationship with Hagar to strengthen their opposing viewpoints, but Cats makes sure Joseph gets the last word.[78]

Petrus Dathenus and Upholding Marriage:
Reinforcing Monogamy, Husbands and Wives, Maidservants

Likewise, the renowned Calvinist theologian Petrus Dathenus makes a direct comparison between the biblical Hagar and contemporary Dutch maidservants when addressing the issue of marriage and monogamy. Intended for housewives and young women, *Een Christelijke Samenspreking uit Gods Woord* (A Christian Dialog Comprised of God's Word),[79] published in 1624, clarifies common misinterpretations of scripture, including the matter of Abraham's concubinage. Here, Dathenus seeks to correct the common misperception and justification that Abraham's concubinage was not a sin, since the Old Testament figure's actions preceded the laws of monogamy established in the New Testament.[80] He reminds the reader that it was indeed a sin by drawing a direct analogy between the biblical Hagar and contemporary Dutch maidservants: "As an example, could you, if you were barren, give your maidservant to your husband without [this action] being sinful, and would he be able to accept this in good conscience?" By placing the ancient tale in a domestic context, Dathenus appeals to the reader's common sense. He goes on to say that the law of monogamy has been in place since the beginning of mankind, as the first chapter of Genesis prescribes: when God created man, he created only one man and one woman with the words "and these two shall be joined of one flesh."[81]

The Faithful Abraham as "Polygamist"?

That Dathenus and Cats used Hagar's story to reinforce the concept of monogamy and decry adultery brings us back to the question of Abraham and polygamy, which, as we have seen, had begun to trouble sixteenth-century thinkers. How did seventeenth-century Dutch literature address this aspect of the story and what censure, if any, did Abraham receive?

First, a brief summary of developments elsewhere in contemporary Europe is relevant. As we saw in chapter 1, from the 1560s to the early 1640s, no western European writer wrote publicly in favor of polygamy. Nevertheless, throughout the remainder of the century and into the next, a number of legal treatises and theological tracts found it necessary to take a stand against polygamy.[82]

At mid-century, however, the subject of polygamy received renewed literary impetus when considered in the context of divorce. In 1643, the English Revolutionaries' poet and controversialist John Milton published a series of books urging the reform of marriage law.[83] Milton's works aroused heated discussion in England and attracted interest across the Continent, particularly in the Reformed Protestant circles of the Netherlands. A Dutch-language edition of Milton's arguments was reportedly published in 1655 to satisfy demand there.[84]

After mid-century, there appears to have been a limited support for plural marriage. A pro-polygamous booklet, *Dialogue of Polygamy*, by an anonymous author, appeared in London in 1657.[85] And *The Treatise of Christian Doctrine*, also by an unknown author, written between the mid-1650s and the early 1670s, includes an extended argument of the lawfulness of polygamy using examples of Abraham and other holy pillars of the Old Testament as justification.[86]

Certain advocates argued that polygamy was needed to increase population, and this line of reasoning stood to gain some currency in those regions most ravaged by the Thirty Years' War (1618–1648) where adult male populations had been drastically reduced.[87] It was alleged that in Nuremburg, in northern central Bavaria, a polygamy law was considered, although there is no evidence that it actually ever went into effect. Reportedly, to counteract the depopulation, the Regional Council of Catholic Franconia encouraged priests to marry in 1650 and authorized laymen to take two wives for the next ten years, a decree supposedly sanctioned by the archbishops of Bamberg and Würzburg.[88]

In the 1670s and 1680s, several publications exclusively devoted to advocating polygamy were printed and circulated throughout Europe. Two pro-polygamous publications in Latin and German—both written by German authors Johannes Leyser and Lorenz Beger—were published in liberal Amsterdam, evading certain censorship elsewhere.[89] Leyser's Latin text was translated into the Dutch-language equivalent as *Politisch discours tusschen monogamo en polygamo* (Political Discourse between Monogamy and Polygamy) and published anonymously in 1675.[90] These texts, like other writings, used Abraham's example, as well as those of other Old Testament patriarchs, such as David and Jacob, to bolster their argumentation.[91] Such heterodox views clearly remained in the minority, but were nevertheless considered "a threat to public morals" and taken seriously enough to warrant printed rebuttal.[92]

Of the two German pro-polygamous works, it was arguably Beger's 1679 book *Important Considerations on Christian Marriage* that stood to have the greatest impact. Published in German, the work was sponsored by his employer, Charles Louis, Prince Elector of the Rhenish Palatinate, son of the Winter King of Bohemia, Frederick of the Palatinate. The book treats marriage under natural, divine, and civil law, and considers polygamy; it was soon recognized to be a statement of Charles Louis's own position on his bigamous marriage.[93] Most interesting was the appendix, which comprised documents on the old case of Philip of Hesse, including the correspondence, legal statements, and signatures of Luther, Melanchthon, and Bucer. While news of Philip's bigamy was not unknown, this marked the first time the roles played by Luther and Melancthon were made public and the supporting documents became "common property in historical writings."[94] In short, these and other writings continued to challenge or reinforce marital traditions, and Abraham and his concubine were often included in the ongoing discussions.

Dutch Literature and the Question of Abraham's "Polygamy"

Now that we have summarized pan-European developments relating to the question of Abraham's apparent polygamy, we can turn to Dutch literary attitudes specifically. How did mainstream Dutch authors handle the matter? As we have seen, seventeenth-century Dutch Christian conduct literature sometimes used the story to reinforce monogamy. Diverse writers such as Cats, Dathenus, and Goeree used Hagar's story as a means of deterring adultery. How was it possible that the popular and esteemed Old Testament figure, the paragon of faith and obedience, strayed from the path of virtue at this juncture in the road? Was Abraham's behavior actually polygamous, as some critics claimed?

We return for a closer look at Cats's long poem cited earlier from the popular *Self-Strijt, dat is de krachtige beweginge van vleesch en geest* (Inner Conflict, That Is the Powerful Movements Between Flesh and Spirit). As we saw, the steadfast, chaste Joseph counters wily Potiphar's wife in a battle of rhetorical wits. Both draw on the story of Abraham's apparent polygamy to strengthen their opposing viewpoints.[95] For Potiphar's wife, Abraham's taking of multiple wives—she ascribes Abraham's behavior to natural (lustful) impulses—gives sanction to her own adulterous wishes. Fortunately, through the nimble Joseph, Cats manages to reclaim Abraham's impugned character, emphasizing that the patriarch's "error" was not driven by lust, but from a desire for progeny—and he shifts the principal blame onto Sarah for instigating it all. Here, to exonerate Abraham from sin, Cats justifies Abraham's conduct by taking up a tack that is reminiscent of Luther.

While Cats and others excused Abraham in various ways, Calvin, as we have seen, did not. Nor did several leading reformers in the half-century or more that followed. Calvinist theologian Theodor Bèze's *Van de Polygamie ofte Houwelick met veel Vrouwen* (Concerning Polygamy or Marriage with Plural Wives) was translated from Latin into Dutch and printed in 1595. Dedicated to the members of the executive committee of the states of Zeeland, it must have been one of the earliest official works in the northern Netherlands that used Abraham and Hagar to decry polygamy and to demonstrate how plural marriage brought about family conflict.[96] Bèze's firm views on the matter had been circulating in print since at least 1569: God may have "tolerated" polygamy in the Old Testament, Bèze said, but nevertheless, it was a sin today.[97]

However, the harshest condemnation of the polygamous Abraham appears in a collection of exegeses penned by the influential English Puritan theologian William Perkins, translated into Dutch, and published in Amsterdam in 1662.[98] While Abraham acted at Sarah's behest, Perkins does not let Abraham off the hook. For Perkins, Abraham not only broke the laws of marriage and of civic order (*burgelijk verbondt*) but, most egregiously, defied the laws God clearly set forth in Gen 1: "... and these two shall be joined of one flesh."[99] Here, Perkins makes his case by citing the same scriptural passage we have noted that Dathenus resorted to in 1624 to condemn extramarital sex. But Perkins makes no bones about the implications of Abraham's misconduct and he takes no prisoners: since all Old Testament patriarchs practiced polygamy outside of marital law, he writes, we must conclude that Abraham and the others are, in effect, adulterers (*overspelders*).[100]

In summary, the Dutch literary response to the question of Abraham's apparent polygamy was decidedly mixed. Mainstream authors and moralists like Cats took up traditional tacks to exonerate Abraham from the taint of polygamy. But others, most notably three of the most revered exponents of the orthodox Reformation, Bèze, Dathenus, and Perkins—the latter known as the father of English *and* Dutch Puritanism, no less—could not turn a blind eye to what they viewed as wrongdoing. While popular authors like Cats might blithely skirt around the issue, every Dutch churchman in the orthodox tradition would have had to at least acknowledge the problem, if not deal with it. Curiously, in Kattenburch's comprehensive sermon on Hagar's story, the minister leaves out precisely this issue, although his talk is crammed full of everything else, as we saw. Is this omission telling? The various literary and theological postures do make one thing clear: the consensus reflected that Abraham's conduct was, at the least, called into question. What implications this had for Dutch painting will be investigated in chapter 3.

Summary: The Polysemic Hagar in Dutch Literature

For the Dutch, then, the Pauline interpretation that presented Hagar and Ishmael as types did not always suffice: other explanations and contemporary analogies were needed to make sense of the complex ancient story in troubled times. The result is a curiously polysemic Hagar in Dutch literature: sometimes portrayed as a wrongdoer, other times as a sympathetic victim, often as both.

Certainly, as we have said, some Dutch Christian literature relied on the familiar Pauline typology or allegory; Hagar and Ishmael as the traditional foils for Sarah and Isaac can be found in many writings. But many other authors chose to talk about Hagar's story in remarkably sympathetic terms. Clearly, the story was used to appeal to the heart, as the minister Kattenburch, among others, shows us: the human emotions of jealousy, pride, loss, sorrow, and fear are all reflected in the twists and turns of the plot. But, fortunately, the story also illustrates, as Kattenburch and others showed, that sin and suffering may be followed by contrition and salvation. In fact, Hagar's story could be made to underscore a central tenet of Puritanism: in a Christian life, hardship or "affliction" is followed by humiliation, submission to God, repentance, and perseverance. Each step was seen as part of a continual spiritual process that led one to a gradual ascent from despair to peace, preparing one for "election" or salvation.[101] Simply put, Hagar's story could be adapted to serve as a spiritual "case study" for the conscientious Christian in his or her ongoing struggle with questions of affliction and assurance.

As we also saw, a surprising number of seventeenth-century Dutch writers used the story as a domestic homily, addressing practical concerns. The runaway Hagar and expulsion episodes in particular were employed to reinforce the virtues of humility, obedience, and diligence in the Dutch Christian household, and to promote family harmony.

Finally, we confirmed that aspects of Hagar's story raised concerns, particularly with regard to the question of Abraham's apparent polygamy. Certain Dutch authors addressed this issue, reflecting a range of attitudes. Some found ways to excuse Abraham; others condemned him. Criticism of Sarah's conduct was periodically voiced. Dutch attitudes toward Abraham's apparent polygamy dovetailed with a broader, Continental discussion that arose in the 1530s and resurfaced again in seventeenth-century literature, with particular impetus in the 1640s through the 1670s.

Now that we have completed our review of the subject in Dutch literature, we can begin a comprehensive analysis of Hagar's story in seventeenth-century Dutch art. Theological developments and literary attitudes serve as our best guide for assessing contemporary reactions to the pictorial record.

Notes

1. Grotius 1693, 133–34: ". . . niet der kinderen der vleesch . . . zy zeker zijn het niet. . . . [dit kan men er ook byvoegen dat Ismael van een woesten, en Izaak van een zagten aert was]" (". . . not the children of the flesh . . . they certainly are

not [the chosen]. . . . One can also add to this that Ishmael is from a savage nature, and Isaac from a gentle nature").

2. The three volumes are published under the aegis of Johannes Gravenhage; Jacobus Vosmaer and Jacobus Guillardus; and Matthias Oeveringius, respectively.

3. Mees 1673.

4. See Ainsworth 1621, N recto, verso; Pietersz 1629, 29; Twisk 1632, 577; Kattenburch 1737 (preached in Rotterdam on October 16, 1701, and in Amsterdam September 1717). Abraham's banishment of Hagar ("de Wet") prefigures how all hypocrites, mockers, and unbelievers will be driven from Christ's flock, in Pietersz 1632, 17–18. For gypsies, see van Kappen 1965, 27. Gypsies were called "Egyptenaren" (Egyptians), but were also known as "Heidens" (heathens, pagans), and "Saracenen" (Saracens).

5. Kattenburch 1737 (preached 1701), 247. "De zalighet der Joden moet het verlangen zyn der Christenen. . . . 't is onze pligt hierom te . . . bidden, en zoo Ismael onder de struiken sprakeloos of in swym legt, als Hagar, daar voor een geroep aan te heffen, ver van, als veelen doen, hun smerten te vergrooten, of door aanstotelyke handelingen . . ." ("The salvation of the Jews must be the desire of the Christians. . . . It is our duty to . . . pray . . . as Ishmael lies in a swoon under the reeds, unable to speak, [we must], as Hagar, raise a cry [for the Jew], and not do as others who add to their grief or increase their hardships. . . .")

6. Similarly, relatively sympathetic notions toward Jews can be detected in Dutch Millennialist/Pansophist thought; see Perlove 1996, 11:103–4.

7. De Koningh 1616, repr. in van Eemeren and Lenferink-van Daal 1990, 124–25, lines 775–90:

D'Egiptsche, vreemde, weijtsche Vrouw
Sijn d' misverstanden In onse landen.
Saraï is haer man getrouw,
Door d' reijne handen Van g'looves banden:

Maer Hagar waent door Hare Meesters minne,
En' s Heeren vrucht verbercht,
Waer doors' Haer vrouwe tercht,
Hier t' overwinnen.

Trotst Sara' V/vrij, soo lang gij wilt,
(Ô vreemde Christen!) M/met arme listen:
De Heer is haren loon en' schildt.

Of g' u vergisten In al uw' twisten
Door hoop' van dat g' als vrouwe, hier sult woonen;
Soo suldij, met Hagar,
Noch vluchten wijt en' varr;:
G'lijk wij vertoonen.

8. Image from the archives of the Warburg Institute, University of London.

9. The Latin reads: CEDAT SERVA DOMINAE, LEX GRATIA. The image itself, by the German engraver and etcher Matthaeus Merian (1593–1650), probably first appeared in the 1625–27 Merian *Icones Biblicae*, published in Frankfurt. Repr. in Claes Jans Visscher's Merian Bible, 1659. Collection: University of Amsterdam.

10. The accompanying poems are by Reyer Anslo (see folio 23). Another version also appears in Visscher's other post-1659 publication, *D'historien des ouden en Nieuwen Testaments, vermaekelyck afgebeeldt en g-etst door Pieter H. Schut, ende Nieulyckx uitgegeven door N. Visscher*, n.d., folio 24.

11. Visscher *Merian Bible*, ca. 1660, folio 23: "Hagar wordt met haer soon Ismael van Abraham uytgeleyt . . . [after Isaac was born and grew up], Ismaël als de outste gesproten uyt de dienstmaeght Hagar, bespottede Isaac, waer over Hagar met haer Sone Ismaël door Godts ordeninge van Abraham uytgeleydt ende wechgesonen wierdt, om een leeringh en af-beeldingh te geven des Oude en Nieuwe-Testaments, 't eene van de Dienstbaerheydt, 't ander van de Vryheydt, waer van het eene voor het andere wijcken moest. . . ." (Hagar and her son were sent away by Abraham . . . Ishmael, as the firstborn son from the maidservant, mocked Isaac, which resulted in Abraham sending away Hagar and her son Ishmael, as commanded by God, [in order to provide us with] a lesson and portrayal of the Old and New Testaments, the former [symbolizing] servitude, the latter freedom, of which the former must yield to the latter. . . .")

12. In the Royal Library, The Hague, trans. P. R. Sellin. The Latin title of the illustration is *Filii Lucis Adoptati*, p. 4, no. 28 (misprinted as no. 27).

13. Schabaelje 1654, 4, no. 28, *Filij lucis Adoptati. Gen. XXI. Vers. 9*: "Hier magh men beeldisch en figuerlick sien, hoe dat Abraham, den Vader des Geloofs, de Dienstmaeght van Egypten utystoot met haren Soone. Het welck ons tot een voorbeelt geschiet is, dat wy oock door de nieuwe geboorte des Geloofs in Jesu Christo den Levitschen bygevoeghden dienst des bedwanghs sullen uytstooten, ende sullen also Godt dienen in een nieuwe wesen des Heyligen Geestes; gelijck en Heylighen Paulus seydt. Het welck de vernieuwingh des levens in de menscheyt is, die uyt de geboorte des Heyligen wesens Christi haer af-komste ende kracht heeft. Daer mede stoot men, met den Abraham des Geloofs, de Dienstmaeght met haren Soon uyt; doch niet voor dat Izaak den Soon des Geloofs gebooren is. Dit neme een yder vry ter herten" ("Here one can see, pictorially and figuratively, how Abraham, the father of faith, throws out the Egyptian maidservant and her son. This takes place as an example to us that we too through the new birth of belief in Jesus Christ shall throw out the Levitical [priestly] added service of compulsion, through new birth of belief in Jesus Christ, and shall therefore serve God in a new being belonging to the Holy Ghost, as St. Paul says. This which is the renewal of life in humankind that is descended from and has its power from the birth of the

Holy Spirit of Christ. Therewith, one kicks out, with the Abraham of belief, the serving maid with her son. But not before Isaac, the son of belief, has been born. Everyone, take this freely to heart [without restraint].")

14. 240 x 185 mm. There is no date; this one was among seven of the twelve allegories first published by Philip Galle at Antwerp without Goltzius's monogram. In 1594, all twelve allegories with Goltzius's monogram were published by Hendrick Hondius in a new edition (Leiden: Prentenkabinet). (Hollstein VIIII, 73III; Bartsch 1978, 72). Other allegories include *Casting Out Evil*, *Relief of Sufferings*, and *Forgiveness of Transgressions*.

15. The printer has attributed this verse incorrectly to the book of Luke; the verse is actually from John.

16. Kunzle 2002, 191.

17. Ainsworth 1621: N recto, verso; Twisk 1632, 577; Kattenburch 1719 (preached in 1701).

18. Jacob Matam (after Abraham Bloemaert), 1603, *The Expulsion of Hagar and Ishmael*, engraving, 431 x 354 mm, signed at the bottom, Museum Boijmans Van Beuningen, Rotterdam.

19. Roethlisberger 1993, I:114–15, cat. no. 69.

20. Trans. Philip Levine. The Latin inscription reads: "Gen. XXI Dum petulans Dominae non insultare veretur, / Cum nato Iussa est vertere serva solum. / Christo, Christique gregi dum illudere certant, / Judaeos meritò par quoque poena premit."

21. Roethlisberger 1993, 115. Van der Coelen's translation from the French original is in Dutch: "Een ander groot Zinnebeeldig stuk over den waaren Godsdienst, de Joden ontnomen en tot de Heidenen overgebragt: een Landschap, waar in Hagar door Abraham verdreeven." Van der Coelen 1997, 281, citing the Dutch translation of the French original, *Fl. Le Comte, Het Konst-Cabinet der Bouw-Schilder-Beeldhouw-en Graveerkunde* . . . (Utrecht: A. Lobedanius, 1744–45).

22. Roethlisberger 1993, 115 and n. 18; McGrath 1984, 78 and n. 18.

23. "Now we, brethren, as Isaac was, are the children of promise. But as then he that was born after the flesh persecuted him that was born after the Spirit, even so it is now. Nevertheless, what saith the scripture? Cast out the bondwoman and her son: for the son of the bondwoman shall not be heir with the son of the freewoman . . ." (Gal 4:28–30, KJV).

24. Myers 1987, 913.

25. Huisman 1983, 54–55.

26. Kattenburch 1701, 1717, 1737, p. 244. "Dog wat daar van zy, de historie verzekert ons van een hooger hulp . . ."

27. For other biblical themes—such as the Flight into Egypt, the Massacre of the Innocents, and the Miracle of the Corn—that may express the pain and pathos of exile, see Kunzle 2002, 57.

28. Twisk 1632; Ainsworth 1621; Gen 16:1.

29. Thompson 2001, 36n90, mentions in this connection a preliminary study by Andrew Pettigree.

30. Pieter Jansz. Twisk 1632, 386.

31. Ainsworth 1621, N verso.

32. Kattenburch 1701, 1737, p. 241. "Ondertusschen moet men dit ook voor een merkwaarde eer rekenen, dat God niet alleen de Patriarchen met zyn aanspraak in de eerste eeuw verwaardigt, maar ook menschen van minder Godvrugtigheit als deze moeder en zoon . . ." ("Meanwhile, one must count this as a remarkable honor, that God not only found the patriarchs of the first age worthy, by speaking to them directly, but also those of lesser piety, such as this mother and son . . .")

33. Fruytiers 1573, folio 31r, v. "Op het rri. Capittel Genesis. Dare van Isaacs Besnydinghe ende Agars Uitdryven, ende troost des Enghels aen de Fonteyne ghehandelt wordt. Ghebede om Godes woordt tot eenenreghel te houden, voor onvruchtbare Elynden, om Godtsalige kinderen, ende vroedsamighe Huyshoudinghe."

34. Fruytiers 1573, folio 31r, v. "Wy dancken dy oock O Godt alles troostes van dyne groote ghenade die wy aen Agar ende heuren kinde speuren, soo dat ons dese Spreuke in haer leveichlyc wort afghebeeldet...soa neemt ghy Heere hem aen, ende troostet hem door dynen Enghelen. Doch Heere, als wy hier sien dat Hagar by de Waterfonteyne sittende . . . so bidden wy dyner grooter goetheit, dat ghy ons niet allenlick die dinghen gheeft die ons van noode zijn, maer oock wijsheyt om de self wel wete toe gebruyken . . ."

35. Dent 1640, chap. 9: "Wat wil ick veel verhalen, op hoe bysondere wijse Godt Hagar ende haer kindeken . . . in grooten anghst ende benautheydt gekomen waren, versorcht ende versien heeft: want sy souden alle beyde van honger ende dorst ghestoreven hebben: heeft Godt niet (ghelijck hy ghewoonlijck is te doen) gehopen, als alle hupe scheen verlooren te wesen? Genes. 21: vers. 17. Heeft den Engel Godts niet tot haer geroepen, uty den Hemel. Ende met eene spijs ende vertroostinge haer toegesonden! Wat will ick oock segge, hoe Godt buyten ghewoonte, ende op en sonderlinghe maniere zijne kercke in de woestijne voorsien heeft, ende alle nootwendighe dinghen versorcht . . ."

36. Getty Provenance Index, no. N-2040.

37. Groenhuis 1977, 116.

38. See also Kattenburch 1737 (preached 1701), 238, for this idea in connection with Hagar's story.

39. Verwijs and Verdam 1952, 9:2754.

40. Ainsworth 1621, Q3 recto.

41. See, for example, Luyken 1736, esp. 188–89, and illus. 6 and 8.

42. Vondel 1620, "Abraham, der gelovigen Vader," in *Den Helden Godes des Ouden Verbonds*. I thank Christian Tümpel for this reference (letter to author, May 17, 2005).

43. See, for example, among other studies, Franits 1993, *Paragons of Virtue: Women and Domesticity in Seventeenth-Century Dutch Art*.

44. Fruytiers 1573, folio 31r, v. "Op het rri. Capittel Genesis. Dare van Isaacs Besnydinghe ende Agars Uitdryven, ende troost des Enghels aen de Fonteyne ghehandelt wordt. Ghebede om Godes woordt tot eenen reghel te houden, voor onvruchtbare Elynden, om Godtsalige kinderen, ende vroedsamighe Huyshoud-inghe."

45. Cats 1658, "Proef-steen van den Trou-ringh," in *Al de Wercken van Jacob Cats*, 461, col. I.

46. Bor 1695.

47. Kattenburch 1717, 1737 (preached 1701), 232–33. "Ondertusschen moet ons dit tot een opmerking dienen, hoe in het allervolmaakste huwelyk mis-verstanden konnen ryzen; byzonder hoe tweederlei kinderen konnen aanleiding geven tot oneenigheden, zoo de ouders niet met groote voorzigtigheit en wysheit zyn voorzien. Laat die dan hier in 't voorbygaan leeren, by hun leven zorg te dra-gen, dat na hun overlyden onder kinderen van verscheidene bedden geen twisten ryzen over het erfdeel . . ."

48. Kattenburch 1701, 239. ". . . wat welsprekentheit kan die naar eisch ver-beelden? Moederlyke harten, die dus uw kinderen door uw eige schult van dorst moest zien versmagten, denk hoe gy zoud te moede zyn, en verbeel u daar door de ontroering van Hagars ingewanden!"

49. Kattenburch 1701, 240–41. ". . . willig zouw zig ook die moeder in de dood gegeven hebben, als mar Ismaël mogt leven."

50. Ridderus 1657.

51. Ibid., *5 verso.

52. Ibid., folio 24v.

53. Ibid., folio 23v., part 3.

54. de Saluste 1605, *The Vocation*, 2:516–17.

55. From "Vrouwe" in Cats's *Houwelijck. Al de Wercken van Jacob Cats*, 1658, chap. 4, p. 170.

56. The passage is cited in the recent study of prints by Van der Coelen 1997, 281.

57. Cats 1658, 56, lines 145–48.

58. Van der Coelen 1997, 281.

59. For more on servants, see Jongejan 1984; Carlson 1994, 1993; Dekker 1994.

60. Haks 1985, 167.

61. There is scholarly disagreement about female immigration figures; female records are difficult to trace, since they revolve around marriage, death, and birth events.

62. Haks 1985, 173–74.

63. Schama 1980, 11.

64. Authored by Jan Fruytiers, published in Emden by Goossen Goebens, 1573.

65. Fruytiers 1573, folio 31r: "Ghebedet. Op het rvi. Capittel Genesis. Dare van Agar, haer vlieden en troost door den Engel gehandelt wert. Ghebedt om een sterck geloofte nedergheslaghen herte, ende oprechte kenusse: dat oock alle Dienstboden en Meesters in heur behoorlicke beroepinge wandelen."

66. Ibid., ". . . wy dytte swacke schepsele vol van alle ghebreken die door onse sonden oock vluchtende zijn van dynen rechtuardigen oogen bidden dynre grontlooser varmherticheyt, dat ghy op ons als op Agar dyne genadig oogen wilt slaen, ene ons verootmoedigen met een nederghslagen herte, stercken met een vasaten gheloove, ende wederom tot u doet keeren, die verre van u door onse sonden geweken waren . . . niemandt voor dyne oogen verborgen can wesen: Ja dat ghyse beyde seit, den Hopen en den Dromen . . ."

67. Ibid., ". . . dat ghy hier mede onse Burgerlicke ordeninge bevestiget: So bidde wy dy dat ghy doch allen Dienstbode vast in heure herte wilt drucken, dat sy haer opgeleyde jock va uwer hant niet en verschuyve, maer in hare beroepinsge trouwelick volherde. Wilt doch ooc alley Huysheeren en Huys vrouwen also stercken day sy hun ymmers met onresdelicheyt tege hare Dienstbode niet en vergrype, denckende dat sy tot gelegener tyt daer van sulle moete rekenschap geven. En als het uwer Goetheyt oock eygentlick toecoet, de verdructe te troosten, en te recht een Godt alder vertrootstinge genaemt wort, gelijc ae dit exempel Agars . . ."

68. Ibid., ". . . dat ghy hier mede onse Burgerlicke ordeninge bevestiget: So bidde wy dy dat ghy doch allen Dienstbode vast in heure herte wilt drucken, dat sy haer opgeleyde jock va uwer hant niet en verschuyve, maer in hare beroepinsge trouwelick volherde. Wilt doch ooc alley Huysheeren en Huys vrouwen also stercken day sy hun ymmers met onresdelicheyt tege hare Dienstbode niet en vergrype, denckende dat sy tot gelegener tyt daer van sulle moete rekenschap geven. En als het uwer Goetheyt oock eygentlick toecoet, de verdructe te troosten, en te recht een Godt alder vertrootstinge genaemt wort, gelijc ae dit exempel Agars . . ."

69. Israel 1995, 677–78.

70. De Koningh 1616, 75–156.

71. De Koningh 1616, folio 30v, p. 150, lines 1221–26:

Dit's den ouwden gang der wereldt,
Wanneer ons t' geluk bepeerelt,
Wordt men fier en' over-trots;

Deugdes ootmoedt will men delven;

Naeeuw'lijks kentmen dan sich selven,

Noch de goede goedtheidt Gods.

72. Comment on de Koningh 1616, by his editor, G. van Eemeren, in the 1990 edition, p. 5.

73. Peter Paul Rubens gave Visscher an engraving of *Susanna and the Elders* as an "outstanding example of modesty" (an engraving by Lucas Vosterman, after a painting by Rubens). See McGrath 1997, 1:49. Cats dedicated his publication *Maagdeplicht* (The Duties of a Maiden) to Visscher (Schama 1988, 408–10). Visscher's collaboration seems especially meaningful here: does her participation suggest that the play, at least in part, was intended for a female audience?

74. Molhuysen 1912, 707.

75. Goeree, *Mengel-Poesy*, Amsterdam, 1734, 2:203, cited by van der Coelen 1997, 281 (my translation):

Toen Gerrit de eerste maal zijn Meyd hadt vuyl gebroed

Zo maakte hy dat staeg met de Bybel goed,

En zey, dat Abraham dat zelfde hadt bedreven,

Met Hgar zyne Maagd, gelyk'er staat geschreeven:

Hy hadt gelyk 't bewys is goed, het is geschied:

Marr eens is geens, gelyk het oude spreekwoord zeyt:

Doch nu heeft drooge Geurt ten tweedemaal zyn Meyd,

By ongeluk bestruyfd, en dat deed Abraham niet.

76. Schama 1980, 12.

77. Cats 1658. Cats first published *Self Strijt* in 1620 in Amsterdam. See *Al de Wercken van Jacob Cats*, 103–26.

78. Ibid., 106, col. 1; 107, col. 2; 109, cols. 1, 2.

79. Dathenus 1624.

80. Dathenus 1624, 83. "Als tot een exempel, zoudt gij, onvruchtbaar wezende, uwe dienstmaagd, zonder zonde, uwen man mogen tot een wijf geven, en zoude hij die met goede conscientie mogen aannemen?" There is disagreement in primary sources on this question of when the laws of monogamy were established. Some agree with Dathenus's interpretation of law and monogamy in the Old Testament; others do not consider the polygamy sinful, since it preceded the new law and God's covenant with Israel.

81. Dathenus 1624, 82–84. In the seventeenth-century Netherlands, when a marriage produced no children, spouses could not resort to divorce. The Reformed Church considered marriage indissoluble except in two instances: only in cases of adultery or desertion could a spouse receive a dispensation to remarry. Haks 1985, 22–23, 178–79.

82. Miller 1974, 52.

83. Ibid., 55.

84. P. R. Sellin 1984, 105–11. The Dutch edition was titled *Tractaet ofte Discours van de Echt-Scheydinge* (anonymous translator), Middelburgh: Iacob de Laet, 1655.

85. Miller 1974, 21–22. *Dialogue of Polygamy, Written Originally in Italian: Renderd into English by a Person of Quality; and Dedicated to the Author of that well-known Treatise call'd Advice to a Son* (London: John Garfield, 1657). Some attribute the book to Francis Osbourne.

86. Miller 1974, 7–12.

87. Ibid., 38, citing the eminent scholar Marinus Mersenne (1588–1648), *Quaestiones Celeberrimae in Genesim* (Outstanding Questions in Genesis), 1623, a book approved by the Faculty of Theology of Paris, among other sources.

88. Miller 1974, 40; Cairncross 1974, 74. The evidence of any Nuremburg decree, Miller points out, is lacking: "the depopulation is sometimes cited in [later] histories of marriage as the reason for the decree to have been enacted, but how long this [decree] went into effect . . . is unknown and [no evidence of it appears] in seventeenth century writings." Cairncross treats the development as a fact, but cites only secondary sources.

89. Lorenz Beger's *Important Considerations on Christian Marriage* (under the pseudonym Daphnaeus Arcuaris), 1679; and Johannes Leyser's *Polygamia Triumphatrix*, 1682 (under the pseudonym Theophilus Aletheus). Cairncross 1974, 75, 82–86. For more on Leyser and pro-polygamous publications in the 1670s, see Miller 1974, 60–95.

90. *Politisch Discours tusschen monogamo en polygamo, van de Polygamia ofte veelwyvery, opgestelde en met 300 argumenten verklaert uyt het Latijn en Hoogduyts vertaalt, en nu in 't Nederduyts overgeset, door Johannes Lyserus* Freiburg, 1675.

91. In *Polygamia Triumphatrix*, the example of Abraham (and Hagar) appears in various chapters: see theses 53, 60, 62, 63, 64, among others. In the Dutch *Politsch Discours*, see p. 2.

92. For a review of the literary refutations, see Cairncross 1974, 71, 88–90. Cairncross cites, among others, Bèze's *On Polygamy and Divorce*, published in Latin in Geneva in 1569, but not the official Dutch translation of Bèze's work, which appeared in 1595: *Van de Polygamie ofte Houwelick met veel Vrouwen* (Concerning Polygamy, or Marriage with Plural Wives). See also Miller 1974, 56–59, who notes three German works exclusively devoted to disproving the lawfulness of polygamy that appeared in the 1660s: William Zesch's *De Polygamia Successiva et Simultanea* (1662); Conrad Büttner's *Funus Polygamiae* (1667); and Michael Siricius's *Uxor Una, ex Jure Naturae et Divino, Moribus Antquis et Constitutionibus Imperatorum et Regum. Eruta contra Insultus Impugnantium Defensa* (1669).

93. Miller 1974, 96–104. In 1650, four months after he came to the Palatinate throne, Charles Louis married his dynastic wife Charlotte, daughter of

William V, Landgrave of Hesse-Cassel; in 1657, he arranged for a de facto separation to marry one of her ladies-in-waiting, Baroness Marie Suzanne Luise von Degenfeld.

94. Ibid., 100–104.

95. Cats 1658.

96. Bèze 1595.

97. In Bèze's *On Polygamy and Divorce* (Tractatio de Polygamia), first published in Geneva in 1569, cited by Cairncross 1974, 71, 225.

98. "Considered the father of the pietistic movement in Reformed Protestantism, Perkins' (1558–1602) orthodox views were marked by a 'practical' piety and morality strictly derived from scripture, which greatly influenced the Dutch." *Grote Winkler-Prins Encyclopedie* (1979), 17:570.

99. Perkins 1662, 149, cols. 1, 2; 150, col. 1.

100. Ibid., 149, col. 2.

101. Arshagouni 1988, 9–14, 44–47.

†

CHAPTER THREE

Paintings of Sarah Presenting Hagar to Abraham as Wife
(GEN 16:2–4)

We encounter Hagar for the first time in scripture in Gen 16:2–4, which tells us that a barren Sarah gave Hagar to Abraham as his wife in the hopes of procuring an heir and that the patriarch agreed to this plan. Only eleven surviving Netherlandish paintings show Sarah conducting the concubine to Abraham's bed, but if we include a handful or more of painted copies, the total comes closer to twenty. The subject was painted exclusively by northern Netherlandish artists, most appearing around mid-century or after, with one early Flemish exception executed in the late sixteenth century.[1]

These are erotically charged pictures in which an old, haggard Sarah directs a beautiful, young, partially clad or nude Hagar to an elderly Abraham waiting in bed. Psychologically, these works depict great variation: in some, Hagar is shown as a coy participant; elsewhere, she is an unwilling subordinate subject to her master's wishes. Abraham ranges from reluctant to aggressive, and is sometimes shown as a younger, virile man. Most remarkable of all, Sarah, celebrated as a female role model since the sixteenth century, has been reduced here to a leering procuress.

Certainly, the subject matter offered artists another opportunity to paint the nude. Just as they had exploited the Old Testament stories of Bathsheba, Susanna, and Lot with his daughters for their erotic potential, so they could turn to another nubile beauty of the Old Testament in a questionable situation. The depiction of nudes was obviously not new in the seventeenth century, and artistic tradition had lent it a certain status since ancient times.[2] Dutch artists began painting the female nude with greater frequency in the late 1630s and 1640s. Despite moral objections, for certain art lovers, "representations of nudes were held to be the pinnacle of a respectable painting tradition."[3]

In addition, the compositions using just three figures suited Dutch tastes, as we shall see, since the scene could be made to correspond to the common Dutch genre formula of "mercenary love" or "unequal lovers." The extreme contrast in ages could be played up, a ploy typical of Dutch followers of Caravaggio.[4] Furthermore, the characters could display a range of psychological nuance and varying emotions that added drama and dimension. All this must have made the topic attractive to artists after mid-century, under pressure to produce works for a competitive art market.

The presentation paintings mostly appeared during the mid- to late seventeenth century, though the expulsion and wilderness-rescue scenes were already popular before mid-century. Curiously, the appearance of the presentation images in the second half of the seventeenth century coincided with a renewed, Continent-wide discussion about marriage, monogamy, and polygamy, in which Old Testament examples of concubinage, including Abraham's story, were revisited. Following the end of the Thirty Years' War, the idea of polygamy may have made some inroads, however marginal, as we have seen, rendering the Hagar story even more topical.

Sixteenth-Century Imagery: Visual Precedents

Sixteenth-century visual precedents of the subject in northern Europe are few. An early portrayal of the scene appears in a sixteenth-century German bible illustrated by the engraver Hans Sebald Beham and published in Frankfurt in 1534.[5] This depicts the moment when the impatient, barren Sarah reinterprets God's promise—that she will one day bear Abraham's heir—on her own terms by persuading Abraham to take Hagar as his concubine. The caption beneath the image simply tells us "a barren Sarah permits Abraham to go to Hagar." In an interior, Sarah approaches Abraham, seated motionless next to a smiling Hagar on a bench. Face hidden under hood and cloak, Sarah's grief or anxiety at this moment is made clear: one hand covers her face; the other clutches a handkerchief in sorrow or distress. In short, the presentation is portrayed as an act of sacrifice on the part of a selfless Sarah, who only gives her husband another wife in a desperate effort to obtain the "promised seed." The presentation is depicted as Sarah's sincere attempt to respond to a patrilineal crisis, however misguided.

In one of five prints for a series on the life of Abraham engraved in 1543 by the Nuremburg artist Georg Pencz, the action takes place in front of Abraham's bed (fig. 4).[6] With one hand touching Abraham and the other Hagar, Sarah is shown instigating the event, as she does in the scriptural text. In placing her in this position, Pencz makes her the figural and literal link between the master and the maidservant. Abraham gestures with both arms as if offering an explanation to Hagar. Abraham's head-gear and boots are rendered in a contemporary style intended to make the biblical event more familiar and accessible to viewers.

In contrast to these two early presentation scenes is the remarkable engraving executed only a few years later, also by Pencz, and dated ca. 1548, issued as a separate plate (fig. 5).[7] The main action now takes place on the bed itself, upon which a nude Hagar and Abraham embrace. The bearded Abraham is surprisingly young. Both appear as eager participants, coupled like a pair of classical, mythological lovers. Sarah observes the proceedings from behind a curtain, reminding us that this event came about through her engineering; moreover, this action introduces a sense of transgression or clandestineness to the moment. A cup and a plate with

FIG. 4: **Georg Pencz.** *Sarah Presenting Hagar to Abraham,* **from the series** *The Story of Abraham,* **ca. 1543. Engraving, 50 x 82 mm, only state, signed with monogram at lower left. Rijksprentenkabinet, Rijksmuseum, Amsterdam.**

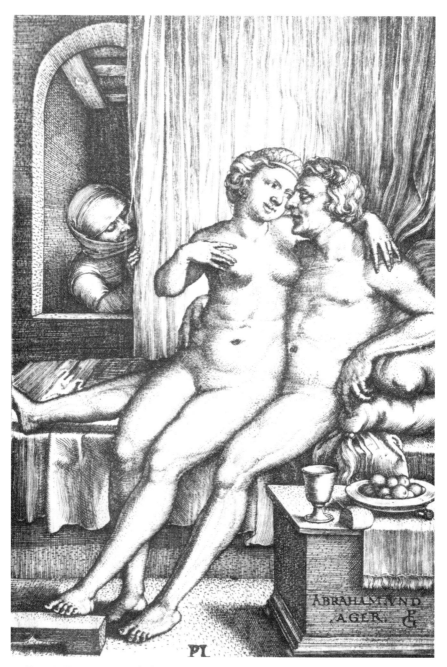

FIG. 5: Georg Pencz. *Abraham and Agar*, 1548. Engraving, 114 x 77 mm. Department of Prints and Drawings, British Museum, London.

fruit are placed on a low table, perhaps alluding to the "fruit" the sexual union will bring. On the side of the table, the artist inscribed the words ABRAHAM UND AGAR and signed his initials.

In this later version, Pencz tapped into the biblical story's erotic potential; his unique interpretation was obviously neither suited nor intended for a bible print, and may even have originally been designed to illustrate another subject. It caters to specific tastes in a secularized art market; for some viewers, the work may have resonated with other northern pictorial traditions in which sex, drink, and food are linked, such as the popular theme of the prodigal son.[8] One suspects that this work was made primarily as an erotic print.[9] If so, does Pencz depict a young, virile Abraham to better exploit the tale's erotic potential?

Most strikingly, the image appears at the same time when traditional Christian attitudes toward the episode were being reconsidered. Beginning in the 1530s, as we have seen, it became increasingly problematic for some, most notably for Protestant Reformers, to reconcile Abraham's behavior with contemporary Christian notions of morality, marriage, and civil law. Against this historical, social, and literary backdrop, we can view the images by Beham and Pencz with a fresh understanding. Did contemporary attitudes and misgivings lend some fire to the new, erotic tone in Pencz's interpretation? Pencz may be responding to the whims of the marketplace or catering to certain art lovers, but the timing is curious.

Seventeenth-Century Netherlandish Imagery

While the seventeenth-century Dutch paintings of the presentation scene do not appear until about the 1640s, prints are another matter. An illustration in the 1616 edition of *Liber Genesis* by the Dutch engraver Crispijn van der Passe I, titled *Longing for Posterity, Abraham's Concubine Agar* (fig. 6), provides us with an inscribed interpretation.[10] Originally published in Arnhem, *Liber Genesis* is thought to be the first authentic northern Netherlandish book of biblical prints.[11] Using compelling illustrations accompanied by moralizing text laid out in the manner of emblem books, the volume reinforced scriptural teachings and made the stories graphically accessible to those who had difficulty reading. It was also designed as a reference for other artists.[12]

Van der Passe the elder was very familiar with the latest developments in European bible prints, especially biblical imagery produced by Nurem-

FIG. 6: Crispijn van der Passe I. *Longing for Posterity, Abraham's Concubine Agar*, 1616. Engraving published in *Liber Genesis*, 1616, XXX. Universiteitsbibliotheek, Amsterdam.

berg artists.[13] His depiction of Gen 16 suggests he knew Pencz's 1548 print or descendants of it: as in the scenes by Pencz, van der Passe's action revolves around a bed upon which Abraham and Hagar embrace while Sarah holds the bed curtain aside to check on the lovers. However, van der Passe avoids nudity and the pair embrace fully clothed.

The accompanying captions and poetic text, written in Latin and German, clarify the action. The principal Latin caption immediately beneath the image says:

74

> Because of her love for offspring, Sara allows the old man
> the embraces of Hagar, since that was not yet grounds (cause)
>   for atonement.
> O, kindly mother of God [i.e., Sarah], do you behold the role
> [responsibilities] of love?
> Being a fostering mother, I [Sarah] both hold and behold the
>   responsibilities [roles or functions] of a spouse.[14]

This caption establishes that the event stemmed from Sarah's desire for an heir and reminds us that polygamy was permitted under Old Testament law. It good-naturedly chides Sarah for taking matters into her own hands and reinforces notions of Sarah as virtuous spouse. Below the caption, lengthier explanations follow. On the left, a register with Latin verse is balanced by rhyming German verse on the right:

In Latin

Destitute of offspring, Sara feels
  sorrow, badly wanting
The dear pledges of the nuptial tie,
But her womb withering away,
she promises her partner in wedlock
A bride who was in servitude,
Once upon a time born to parents
  far away on the Nile.
They approved the arrangements
  by a flattering marriage
And the joyful husband doubly has
  each in turn as mate:
Sara, needing to be called a mother
  by means
of another womb, holds her tongue.

Hope and desire for offspring gives up
  the joys
of the marriage bed to the bosom/lap
  of another woman;
their reputations remain spotless.
There are no crimes committed against
  this marriage, the greatest
Of all fathers is indebted to both sides
  that his lineage exists.

In German

Sarai was angry because
she could not bear a child
This is why she said to her husband
please go in, take my maidservant;
that I through her may obtain
Children/and multiply your seed
Abram followed her order:
and takes the Egyptian maid with him
And lays her at his side.
The wedding bed nevertheless remains
  spotless.
Abram is twice a husband
One man [for] Sarai and Agar.

Both the Latin and German reiterate that the concubinage came about solely out of desire for offspring and that the marriage remained virtuous and chaste. The Latin inscription goes so far as to claim that Hagar was given to Abraham as a second wife with her Egyptian parents' blessing![15] There can be no talk of misconduct here, since the Egyptian is seen to be Abraham's lawful wife at the time. A subscript at the bottom of the page, taken from Gal 4, confirms that the laws of monogamy were established later, in the New Testament;[16] this is probably placed here to remind us that, unlike Abraham, we are subject to these new laws.[17]

Like Pencz, van der Passe depicts the embrace of Abraham and Hagar on a bed, and he includes the motif of Sarah as observer or spy. Ostensibly, this shows that the event is conducted under Sarah's aegis, but it also lends a certain clandestineness or sense of transgression. Thus, although the text stresses marital virtues and relies on traditional teachings to justify the patriarch's actions, the scene is designed to heighten the viewer's delight.[18]

While van der Passe's image was circulated widely in Dutch artistic circles, paintings on the subject do not appear until the late 1630s or 1640s. In fact, the majority of paintings appear only in the last quarter of the century. Curiously, the Amersfoort-born artist Matthias Stomer painted the subject three times, during the late 1630s or 1640s, when he appears to have been active in Rome, Naples, and Sicily, although little is known about his patrons and circumstances there.[19] Most themes Stomer painted were inspired by the Amsterdam artist Gerrit van Honthorst and, according to inventories, the latter painted a presentation of Hagar in 1647 for the stadtholder Frederik Hendrik's palace, Honselaersdijk—curiously, painted in the same year that the stadtholder died—although the circumstances of the commission and the painting's whereabouts are unknown.[20]

In one of Stomer's paintings, the first of the three compositions, an old, wrinkled Sarah offers a young, bejeweled Hagar with one breast bared to the elderly Abraham in bed (fig. 7).[21] Nearby, a bright flame burns in a lamp, and beneath this, a chalice and part of a bowl are visible. Facial expressions and hand gestures help tell the story. Sarah guides an obedient Hagar with one hand; the upturned palm of her left hand seems to offer her up to Abraham. In contrast, Abraham's expression, reclining posture, and hand gesture suggest reluctance. The nature of Hagar's expression is unclear. In this context, the chalice reminds us of sensual pleasure, and the burning lamp may be more than ornamental, perhaps related to the flame and heat of amorous lust.[22]

Certainly, Stomer exploits the contrasting features of old and young here, a familiar Caravaggisti ploy. Moreover, it appears that Stomer realized

FIG. 7: Mathais Stomer. *Sarah Bringing Hagar to Abraham*, no date. Oil on canvas, 112.5 x 168 cm, inv. no. 2146. Photo: Joerg P. Anders. Gemäldegalerie, Staatliche Museen zu Berlin, Berlin, Germany. Photo credit: Bildarchiv Preussischer Kulturbesitz/Art Resource, NY.

that the three-figure composition of Abraham, Sarah, and Hagar had a natural affinity with the traditional, beloved Dutch theme of "unequal lovers" or "mercenary love." In scenes of "unequal lovers," a young woman accepts the embrace of an elderly man in exchange for money, sometimes stealing from his purse, often under the aegis of a leering crone. The depiction of an elderly Abraham and Sarah—with Sarah appearing particularly haggard next to a young and pretty Hagar—suited the conventional formula perfectly. The association with the "unequal lovers" theme is further made explicit by the simplified dark scene comprised of large figures illuminated by a single light source. This bears an unmistakable resemblance to Utrecht Caravaggisti genre paintings, such as Dirck van Baburen's *The Procuress* of 1622 (fig. 8), a variation on the "unequal lovers" theme.[23]

Like the figures in most "unequal lovers" imagery, Stomer's figures are depicted in half-length format.[24] Most striking among these three characterizations is Sarah, who has been transformed into the cunning procuress type. Her bearing and headgear are similar to stock types circulating in genre imagery at the time.[25] In this context, the upturned palm of her left hand would suggest she is expecting payment for her efforts. Her haggard, weathered face is placed close beside Hagar's plump visage and fair skin,

FIG. 8: Dirck van Baburen. *The Procuress*, signed and dated 1622. Oil on canvas, 101.6 x 107.6. M. Theresa B. Hopkins Fund, Museum of Fine Arts, Boston. Photo © 2006 Museum of Fine Arts, Boston.

recalling another beloved Dutch genre motif that pairs old and young females to moralize on vanity and the temporality of youth and beauty.[26] By incorporating this procuress type and formulaic elements from the "unequal lovers" theme, Stomer could make the intimate biblical scene all the more provocative, lively, and witty.

A second painting by Stomer painted during the same period shows a similar composition.[27] Here, Stomer has shifted the figures, placing Hagar between Sarah and Abraham. Abraham gestures with his right hand, as if to explain circumstances to the maidservant. A sanguine Hagar begins to disrobe, baring a breast. This aligns Hagar with other biblical females of questionable repute, such as Bathsheba and Mary Magdalene, who are often pictured with one bared breast. The hat Hagar wears is of a type that was thought to reflect ancient style accurately.[28] An attentive Sarah hovers behind Hagar, eager to promote the match. This time, Sarah is coercing the younger, smaller Hagar, with her hand clamped on the servant girl's wrist.[29] The same flame-burning lamp softly highlights the interaction between Hagar and Abraham, relegating Sarah to the shadows.

Most remarkable among Stomer's three versions is the work showing the principal figures in full length (fig. 9).[30] A small servant boy and dog have been added. The nude Hagar attempts to hide her nakedness by adopting the classic hand gestures of Venus pudica, an antique gesture of modesty. With one muscular arm, an eager Abraham appears to strip away what little remains of Hagar's clothing. From behind, Sarah also peels away the maidservant's dress. An obedient dog sits motionless near the foot of the bed. Luxurious draperies and garments enrich the scene. Hagar's somber expression hints at involuntary submission and her antique pose of modesty draws attention to her sexuality. The male servant, carrying a tray with drink, also surveys her nudity, increasing our sense of

FIG. 9: Mathais Stomer. *Sarah Brings Hagar to Abraham*, ca. 1640s. Canvas, 81.5 x 100 cm. Göteborgs konstmuseum, Göteborg, Sweden. Photograph © Göteborgs konstmuseum.

Hagar as a vulnerable sexual object and amplifying notions of indecency. All this raises the erotic stakes and lends titillation to the scene.

It was not until mid-century and after that several other artists— Salomon de Bray, Philip van Dyck, Caspar Netscher, Adraien van der Werff, and Willem van Mieris—portrayed a nude or partially clad Hagar. For the Haarlem painter Salomon de Bray, the subject appears to have

FIG. 10: Salomon de Bray. *Sarah Presenting Hagar to Abraham,* signed and dated 1650. Oil on panel, 12.5 x 9.75 in. Collection of Dr. Alfred Bader, Milwaukee. Photo: Rijksbureau voor Kunsthistorische Documentatie, Den Haag.

been an opportunity to paint a challenging nude, as his version of 1650 suggests (fig. 10).[31] We see the back of a nude Hagar, propelled by Sarah toward Abraham. All three figures are enclosed in a dense setting of elaborate, hanging draperies, by now a familiar motif, and of contemporary domestic furniture. De Bray gave Hagar a curvaceous, fleshy figure. This may be classed with the typical Dutch "topographical" nude: artists appear to have paid great attention to skin puckering, surface detail, unorthodox color modulations, and shading.[32]

As it turns out, de Bray's Hagar figure is similar to the central nude figure in the Flemish artist Jacob Jordaens' *Allegory of Fertility*, dated about 1623 (which, in turn, was a derivation of the antique sculpture of Aphrodite, goddess of fertility, by Praxiteles).[33] This suggests that de Bray depicted the erotic moment in terms of the patriarchal need for an heir, and to play up this aspect, he imported the allegorical figure of fertility as a stand-in for Hagar. He juxtaposes the fleshy, nubile Hagar with a fully cloaked and hooded Sarah, completely concealing the latter's figure to set off Hagar's sexual appeal. In this context, dress and undress serve as metaphors for barrenness and fecundity.

The artist maintains a relative physiognomic anonymity among the personages: only Abraham's facial expression is visible. Placed in three-quarter profile and turned away from the viewer, Sarah's emotions are obscured. Still, her gestures identify her as the choreographer here. Hagar holds a cloth before her in a familiar Venus pudica show of modesty, which increases her erotic value; although she may be attempting to conceal her nakedness from Abraham, her backside remains exposed to the viewer's scrutiny. Her body tapers up as she inclines away from the viewer; the result is that the back of her smallish, dark head is somewhat lost in the shadowy space between Abraham and Sarah. De Bray's Hagar is primarily cast as a body—specifically, as the surrogate body. Her body, figuratively and literally here, serves to concretize the physical union between sexual partners.

In the last quarter of the century, the presentation of Hagar paintings appear to emphasize the erotic and luxurious. Netscher's rendition (fig. 11) of 1673 is a good example.[34] Here, the setting has been transformed into a luxurious, bourgeois interior: the style is in keeping with an increasing elegance and formality that makes its way into Dutch interiors, particularly domestic scenes, after mid-century. This version was popular: six copies are known.[35]

FIG. 11: Caspar Netscher. *Sarah Leading Hagar to Abraham*, signed and dated 1673. Oil on Canvas, 58 x 49 cm. Collection of Sol Sardinksy, Philadelphia.

Pointing a finger at Hagar, Sarah presents a lavishly dressed maidservant to persuade Abraham to take her as a bedfellow. Dressed in a gold-brown robe, a red cloak, and a red cap, Abraham is seated on the left. Sarah wears a purplish robe, a gray-black cape, a pearl headdress, and a striped scarf. A statue-like Hagar is shown frontally, on display to the viewer, less anchored in the narrative. She wears a white robe and an undergarment with pearl embroidery on the sleeves and girdle; she acknowledges the viewer's gaze, looking out at us knowingly. At right, a gold ewer and plate stand on a carpet-covered table. Behind the figures is a bed. Barely visible among the folds of the bed curtain, a peeping figure, probably a maidservant, appears in the upper left-hand portion of the picture frame. This heightens the moral implications.

The refined texture and opulence of Hagar's dress resemble raiment worn by the highborn women in the so-called "polite" or "classical" domestic genre scenes that *fijnschilders* ("fine painters") produced in response to the tastes of growing second-generation wealth and international buyers. Here, the silky outer garment has fallen away to reveal the undergarment beneath. Hagar's one hand cradles her breast, the other, in a show of modesty, touches her thigh in an attempt to keep the outer garment from slipping off further, a variation on the Venus pudica motif.

Has the biblical episode become a parody of a brothel scene? With Sarah as stand-in for a procuress type and Hagar on display, it would not be difficult for Dutch viewers to read associations of prostitution into the scene, especially in so refined a setting.[36] Dutch viewers would have been conditioned by Dutch genre painting, where domestic interiors of all kinds sometimes doubled as brothels. What at first glance appeared to be an elegant scene of courtship could, upon more careful scrutiny, actually depict a crude transaction of coin between prostitute and solicitor. In such situations, Netherlanders knew, the devil was in the details.

Moreover, many of Netscher's details may have resonated with contemporary associations of prostitution. The business of prostitution was in the hands of women, specifically the madam. A pleasing environment, music, and private rooms were essential to the success of any bordello. As part of this sphere, prostitutes used makeup and fancy clothing to enhance their attractions. Such "production supplies" represented a sizeable investment, which most prostitutes could not afford. Their meager income barely covered the costs of basic necessities. Since a whore without finery would fail to attract good clientele, this is where the procuress stepped in. She supplied the makeup and finery, and the prostitutes rented these items with their paltry earnings. Predictably, little money would be left over. In effect, beautiful apparel indentured a prostitute.[37] Netscher may be punning on the nature of servitude in this context: Hagar is not only an indentured maidservant to her mistress, as the Bible prescribes, but also an indentured whore.

A refined elegance marks the interpretation by the Leiden artist Willem van Mieris from the last quarter of the century, where the action takes place in a lavish boudoir (fig. 12).[38] Abraham's nudity is covered by a rich fur bedspread as he anticipates the embrace of a graceful Hagar with an ornate hairstyle. Selective lighting focuses on Hagar's nude body. In the left foreground, a pile of discarded clothing serves as a repoussoir. Sarah holds her right hand out in a gesture of presentation. Can her gesture also be read as demanding payment for a business transaction?

FIG. 12: Willem van Mieris. *Sarah Bringing Hagar to Abraham*, ca. 1685–90, signed upper right: "W. van Mieris." Oil on panel, 44.2 x 36.3 cm. Private collection. Photograph © Jack Kilgore & Company, Inc., New York.

In Philip van Dijk's work, also from the last quarter of the century, a younger, muscular Abraham is poised as if he cannot wait to embrace a coy, nude Hagar.[39] Sarah presides over the pair and she is shown as younger and relatively comely, an exception to the rule. Her full cloak and hood are designed, as before, to contrast with and amplify Hagar's luminous nudity. Directly behind Sarah at the far right, a figure, probably a servant, is shown observing the proceedings. This, combined with lush draperies that envelop the action, once again lends a clandestine aura to the scene.

Did the ongoing discussions involving the apparent polygamy of Abraham and other Old Testament pillars prompt interest in the depiction of this episode or lend it a certain topicality? As we have seen, the appearance of these works parallels literary trends on the subject of polygamy and is, at the very least, a remarkable coincidence. Many of the presentation of Hagar paintings, as we have seen, include motifs that convey a sense of wrongdoing, paralleling those literary attitudes that challenged traditional views justifying Abraham's actions. These inclusions—peeping servants, states of dress and undress, drapery that conceals and reveals, cliched gestures of modesty—heighten the moral implications of a scene, thus increasing its sensual or erotic power overall, and perhaps even tapping into subconscious desires. By including these details to attract our prurient interest, is the artist placing Abraham's wrongdoing on the shoulders of all those looking at the painting? Here, the biblical narrative and its religious significance become secondary.

However, as we have seen, this does not hold true for all presentation scenes. Certain scenes tend to aggrandize or glorify the episode using allegorical or classicizing means, avoiding any hints of wrongdoing. For example, in Salomon de Bray's painting, the composition is designed to remind us of the patriarchal need for progeny, reflecting traditional readings of the episode. Likewise, an interpretation by the Rotterdam artist Adraien van der Werff, painted at the far end of the century, retains the religious significance of the narrative (fig. 13). Van der Werff's smooth, classicizing style followed the Leiden *fijnschilders* tradition, but was distinguished by greater elegance, grandeur, and richness of costume and interior. In his heyday, he was considered the most important Dutch painter of his time. In 1697, he was appointed court painter for Johan Wilhelm, Elector Palatine, and worked exclusively at the Düsseldorf court for six months of every year, painting primarily religious subjects.[40] At the Düsseldorf court in 1699, he painted *Sarah Presenting Hagar to Abraham* for the elector, and the

FIG. 13: Adriaen van der Werff, *Sarah Presents Hagar to Abraham*, signed and dated 1699. Oil on canvas, 76.3 x 61.2 cm. Bayerische Staatsgemäldesammlungen, Alte Pinakothek, Munich. Photo: Arthotek, Germany.

following year, its pendant, *The Expulsion of Hagar*.[41] Both are based on and closely resemble two pictures of the same themes he painted in Rotterdam in 1696, commissioned as pendants by Rotterdam pensionary Adraien Paets, Lord of Schoterbosch and a principal in the East India Company.

Unfortunately, we do not know the particulars of the commission, although the Maecenas traveled to Rotterdam and visited van der Werff's studio the same year that the artist completed the rendition for the Dutch pensionary. In the Düsseldorf version, van der Werff simplified the compositions and further refined his smooth style.[42]

We will concentrate on his presentation scene here, since the expulsion episode is discussed in chapter 4. Although Sarah retains the characteristics of the traditional procuress type, van der Werff avoids any genre formulas. Instead, he emphasizes classical motifs that must have suited his electoral patron. Abraham, partially nude, sits on the bed in the pose of a river god.[43] The monumental, classicizing draperies and ordered composition lends grandeur.[44] Hagar is bare-breasted here; her kneeling pose and bowed head suggest her submission and modesty.[45] The sensuality of the scene is muted by the classicizing imagery and grandeur. From above, an unseen light source falls down on the trio, lending a certain sacredness or preordained sanction to the event. Van der Werff's painting seems to offer the elegant mystique of a biblical event that is an important part of a divine genealogical design.[46]

Notes

1. These are ten original paintings by Dutch artists and one Flemish work (by Pourbus the younger) of the 1590s; I count six copies based on original compositions by Caspar Netscher and one copy based on Adraien van der Werff's scene for the elector (referenced as "unknown copyist after Rembrandt" by the Crocker Art Museum in Sacramento). I also count the sixteenth-century interpretation attributed to Lambert Sustris of Amsterdam, dated 1568, although it is not possible to review the image here.

2. De Jongh 2001, 30; Sluijter 2001, 37.

3. Sluijter 2001, 37.

4. Blankert 1986, 17–38.

5. Bible published by Christian Egenolph, Frankfurt, 1534. Schmidt 1962, 137, 175–77, fig. 127.

6. Georg Pencz, *Sarah Presenting Hagar to Abraham*, the first in a series of five engravings titled *The Story of Abraham*, ca. 1543. 50 x 82 mm, only state, signed with monogram at lower left. The four other scenes in the series include: *The Three Angels Visiting Abraham and Sarah*, *The Expulsion of Hagar*, and *Abraham and Isaac Ascending the Mountain* (image from Landau 1978, 78, fig. 1B. See also Hollstein 1996, 31:123, fig. 1; Bartsch 1978, no. 1).

7. 114 x 77 mm. Image from *The Illustrated Bartsch*, 8:322, no. 6.

8. For example, the popular "merry companies" featured a biblical or contemporary prodigal son feasting lustily alongside thieving whores and fools. Wining and dining with women led to adultery, corruption, etc.

9. Although there was a bustling market for such works, it is unlike anything else in Pencz's oeuvre, both in terms of subject matter and in the delicate handling of lighting and textures. Bartrum 1995, 122. See also Mellinkoff 1998.

10. *Longing for Posterity, Abraham's Concubine Agar*, engraving, published in *Liber Genesis*, 1616, XXX. Universiteitsbibliotheek, Amsterdam. See Veldman 2001, 71.

11. Van der Coelen refers to it as such (van der Coelen in Tümpel 1991, 168). Veldman refers to it as "the first book of biblical prints all by the same artist to appear in the Northern Netherlands," more or less, and published in two editions, 1612 and 1616 (Veldman 2001, 63). Van der Passe's interpretation of the episode differs from orthodox Calvinist teaching.

12. Veldman 2001, 62; van der Coelen in Christian Tümpel 1991, 168.

13. Veldman 2001, 62.

14. Translation by Philip Levine (Van der Passe 1616, XXX).

15. This line of argument can be traced to ancient rabbinical exegeses, which speculated that Hagar was the daughter of Pharoah (Gen 12) who gave the princess to Abraham as a second wife, and not as a servant. A Christian fascination with rabbinical exegeses, particularly those of Rashi (1040–96) and Nicholas of Lyra (fourteenth century), begins in the later Middles Ages. See Thompson 2001, 57, 64, 96–97. John L. Thompson, communication with author, February 7, 2001.

16. The citation is taken from the writings of the first Roman pope, Leo I (440–461), *Epistolae CLXVIII*: "Galat. IV. Abraham had two sons, one by the bondwoman and one by the freeborn. But the son of the bondwoman was born according to the flesh, whereas the son of the freewoman was born for remission of sins, which things are stated by way of allegory. But what does scripture say? Throw out the bondwoman and her son; for the son of the bondwoman will not be an heir along with the son of the freewoman." The writing has been adapted from a letter the pope sent advising a colleague who was marrying off his daughter. The inclusion of this is curious in a northern Netherlandish work, since it relies on a Catholic source. My thanks to John L. Thompson for identifying the citation and raising the question, April 16–17, 2002.

17. John L. Thompson concurs with this reading (April 16, 2002). He notes that "posteritus amor" resonates with Luther's reading of the incident: that Abraham and Sarah desired not just offspring, but were specifically intent on the procreation of the promised Messiah.

18. Veldman 2001, 64.

19. Slatke 1997, 697.

20. Albert Blankert, letter to author, August 10, 2003. The provenance of Honthorst's painting: "Inventory Honselaarsdijk, 1707, no. 31, as in the audience room: 'Abraham daer Sara hem met Hagar te bedt legt van Honthorst.'; Inventory Honselaarsdijk, 1755–58, no. 281, as in the anteroom of the west pavilion" (Judson and Ekkart 1999, 50, cat. no. 2).

21. Canvas, 112.5 x 168 cm, Staatliche Museen zu Berlin, Gemäldegalerie (image from Verdi 1999, fig. 15).

22. Stewart 1977, 65.

23. Weller 1998, 193; Slatke 1997, 696. *The Procuress*, Dirck van Baburen, signed and dated 1622, canvas, 101.6 x 107.6 cm, Museum of Fine Arts, Boston (image from Haak 1996, fig. 441). The Utrecht Caravaggisti: in the early seventeenth century, a group of painters from Utrecht traveled to Rome. There they were deeply influenced by the work of Caravaggio. Upon their return to northern Netherlands, they incorporated these new ideas into the style known as "Utrecht Caravaggism," which flourished there between 1620 and 1630. For more on the Utrecht Caravaggisti, see *Nieuw Licht op de gouden Eeuw: Hendrick ter Brugghe en tijdgenoten* (exh. cat. Ed. A Blankert and L. J. Slatkes). 1986–87, Utrecht: Centraal Museum.

24. Stewart 1977, 109.

25. See, for example, the "holy woman" procuress figure in the engraving from van der Passe the younger's *Le Miroir des Plus Belles Courtisannes de ce Temps*, 1635, C2 recto.

26. Van de Pol 1988, 124.

27. Sale, Sotheby's, London, December 11, 1991, illus. 51, 139 x 182 cm.

28. From Martha Hollander, communication with author, March 19, 2002.

29. In northern medieval visual tradition, this gesture signifies that one person has power over another (Wolfthal 1999, 41).

30. Mathais Stomer, *Sarah Brings Hagar to Abraham*, ca. 1640s, canvas, 81.5 x 100 cm, Göteborgs Konstmuseum, Göteborg, Sweden. Photo © Göteborgs Konstmuseum.

31. Salomon de Bray, *Sarah Presenting Hagar to Abraham*, signed and dated 1650, oil on panel, 12.5 x 9.75", collection of Dr. Alfred Bader, Milwaukee.

32. For more on the seventeenth-century Dutch nude, see Schott 2000, esp. 139, 174–78.

33. Jacob Jordaens, *Allegory of Fertility*, ca. 1623, signed, on canvas, 180 x 241 cm, Musée des Beaux-Arts, Brussels. Jordaens, in turn, appears inspired by a related figure found in several paintings by northern Netherlander Claes Moyaert, such as *Odysseus and Nausikaa*, ca. 1649, wood, 51 x 70 cm, Berlin, Kaiser-Friedrich-Museum. See Bader 1976, 22; von Moltke 1997, 4:701–2; A. Tümpel 1974, 77.

34. Caspar Netscher, *Sarah Leading Hagar to Abraham*, signed and dated 1673, canvas, 58 x 49 cm; collection of Sol Sardinksy, Philadelphia. Photo courtesy of

the Rijks Kunsthistorische Dokumentatie (see Wieseman 1991, 391, cat. no. 114; Slatter 1950, cat. no. 22).

35. Wieseman 1991, 391–92.

36. Wieseman 1991, 89, likewise notes: ". . . Netscher emphasizes the innate parallels with popular secular scenes of prostitute and procuress."

37. Van de Pol 1988, 135.

38. Willem van Mieris, *Sarah Bringing Hagar to Abraham*, ca. 1685–90, signed upper right, "W. van Mieris," oil on panel, 44.2 cm x 36.3 cm; private collection. Photo © Jack Kilgore & Company, Inc., New York.

39. Philip van Dijk, *Sarah Presents Hagar to Abraham*, ca. 1670s, on copper, 50 x 40 cm, Louvre, Paris.

40. Snoep 1973, 7; Gaehtgens 1987, 57–68, 138–42; Leistra 1997, 33:79–80.

41. Adraien van der Werff, Elector/Düsseldorf commission: *Sarah Presents Hagar to Abraham*, signed and dated 1699, oil on canvas, 76.3 x 61.2 cm, Bayerische Staatsgemäldesammlungen, Alte Pinakothek Munich. Photo: Arthotek, Germany. *The Expulsion of Hagar*, signed and dated 1701, panel, 77 x 61.5 cm, Rheinisches Landesmuseum, Bonn (see Gaehtgens 1987, cat. no. 52, 53). The Paets/Rotterdam commission: *Sarah Presents Hagar to Abraham*, signed and dated 1696, canvas, 86 x 68.5 cm, Hermitage, Leningrad; *The Expulsion of Hagar*, signed, canvas, 87.5 x 69.5 cm, Gemäldegalerie, Dresden (see Gaehtgens 1987, cat. no. 45, 46).

42. Gaehtgens 1987, 138, 142; Snoep 1973, 7.

43. Gaehtgens 1987, 138–39, 270–71, cat. no. 45, 45a.

44. Wieseman 1991, 89–90.

45. C. Tümpel 1991, 30.

46. Wieseman 1991, 89–90. Christian Tümpel, letter to author, May 17, 2005. What significance for elite patrons did this painted episode have, if any? In royal settings, Tümpel theorized recently, might a presentation scene reflect the special social structure of court life? Some elites kept both consort *and* mistress, exercising a certain latitude that non-elites could not.

CHAPTER FOUR

✝

The Runaway Hagar Encounters the Angel
(GEN 16:6–14)

Seventeenth-century Dutch artists also painted the two-figure compositions of the runaway Hagar and the angel at the well (Gen 16:10–12), but rarely. Ten extant works portray the earlier wilderness episode when the angel first appears to a pregnant Hagar beside the well at Beer-Sheba on the way to Shur, where the maidservant, fearful of the wrathful Sarah, has fled. In the scriptural text, the angel appears and instructs the maidservant to return to her mistress, foretelling the prophecy concerning Ishmael. The scene is graphically similar to and sometimes mistaken for the more popular wilderness-rescue paintings (Gen 21) that will be discussed in chapter 6.

Sixteenth-Century Visual Precedents

In sixteenth-century European art, the episode appears in a few bible prints and occasionally in tapestry cycles of the life of Abraham. In these, Sarah may appear angry or make a menacing gesture at a fearful Hagar, who is shown fleeing from the house to the wilderness—they belong to what has been called the "Hagar's flight" theme. Sixteenth-century precedents are epitomized by the 1576 woodcut by the Basle artist Tobias Stimmer (fig. 14): an angry Sarah, hands on hips, confronts a pregnant Hagar, who is already turning away.[1]

FIG. 14: **Tobias Stimmer.** *Neue Künstliche Figuren Biblischer Historien,* **gruntlich von** Tobias Stimmer gerissen / und zu gottsforchtiger—ergetzung andachtiger hertzen mit artigen Reimen begriffen durch J;F;S;W. Woodcut. Basle: Thomas Gwarin, 1576, no. 13.

Pieter Paul Rubens's Version
Shows Sixteenth-Century Influences

An early seventeenth-century version of the same moment, painted by Pieter Paul Rubens (ca. 1615), shows Stimmer's influence (fig. 15).[2] Rubens emphasized the rivalry between the mistress and the maidservant. He stresses Sarah's anger, with one hand placed on her hip and an arm raised up. The dog is also threatening. Hagar is not fearful, nor does she appear to be fleeing in haste, as she does in the biblical text. Between the two women, an old Abraham appears further back in the doorway. In this case, we are fortunate to know how the artist himself regarded it: Rubens used the term "galanteria" (pretty thing) to describe the small panel,[3] and in a letter to Sir Dudley Carleton in 1618, in which the painting is discussed, wrote to the English ambassador at The Hague: "The subject is . . . neither sacred or profane, so to speak, although drawn from Holy Scripture. It represents Sarah in the act of reproaching Hagar, who, pregnant, is leaving the house with an air of womanly dignity, at the intervention of the patriarch Abraham . . ."[4] The 1615 version has been identified as part of the consignment of paintings and tapestries delivered by Rubens to Carleton, in exchange for the ambassador's collection of antique marble sculptures.[5] Rubens's anecdotal treatment of the episode is more reminiscent of a domestic dispute than a biblical narrative; perhaps this is why Rubens refers to the work as "neither sacred nor profane."

Fig. 15: Pieter Paul Rubens. *Hagar Leaves the House of Abraham,* 1615. Oil on panel, 62.8 x 76 cm, inv. no. GE-475. The State Hermitage Museum, St. Petersburg.

Seventeenth-Century Dutch
Interpretations of Gen 16

However, it was not the confrontation between mistress and maid that interested the seventeenth-century Dutch. Netherlandish artists focused on the moment in the episode when the angel commands Hagar to return to her mistress, and the action takes place in a wilderness setting. This is the moment when the angel tells Hagar of Ishmael's birth and the prophecy about him, because, as the angel says, "the Lord has heard thy affliction" (Gen 16:11). This is also the moment—which so intrigued early modern commentators—when the rebellious maidservant shows submission and even "names" God (Gen 16:13). In addition to the paintings, several etchings and drawings on the theme also survive, once again signaling the peculiar significance Hagar's story had for Netherlanders. Surprisingly, the two-figure composition appears only in Dutch art and, to my knowledge, never in Italian painting.

Interest in this scene can be explained, at least in part, by the Dutch predilection for landscapes. Specialists in this genre, such as Bartholmeus Breenbergh, Cornelis Poelenburgh, and Jan Lievens, painted the subject. Breenbergh's version is especially vivid (fig. 16).[6] One of the initiators of the Italianizing landscape, Breenbergh places the two figures of Hagar and the angel in the right foreground as repoussoir for the expansive vista that opens to us on the left.[7] The angel's gesture of command further leads our eye to the distant castle and bluffs beyond. The majestic tree intercedes between foreground and background plane. The tree may also give expression to the angel's prophecy that Ishmael would become the wild, untamed patriarch of a great nation; the grapevine above the angel, clinging to the trunk, may symbolize fecundity or allude to God's people.[8] Here, the emphasis falls on the angel's command that Hagar return, fulfilling the divine prophecy. Reclining slightly backward, Hagar is seated and clothed in a manner that exposes her pregnancy to our view.

However, the majority of Dutch works concentrate on the angel and Hagar; landscape becomes secondary. Often the maidservant kneels in obedience, humility, or prayer, as a work by Ferdinand Bol from the 1650s shows.[9] Hagar has set her traveling hat and cloak aside and kneels obediently before an angel in white raiment standing in front of a stream. The stream presumably springs from the well, as the Bible prescribes; further back, a waterfall is visible. Cherubs hover above; this motif is traditionally found in annunciation scenes in the northern Netherlands.[10] Bol also pro-

FIG. 16: **Bartholomeus Breenbergh.** *The Angel Commands Hagar to Return to Sarah*, **signed and dated** 1632. Copper, 38 x 32 cm. Private collection. Photograph © Sotheby's, New York, January 30, 1997, lot no. 32.

duced a second copy after the original composition.[11] The inclusion of cherubs here suggests an awareness of the special status and heightened significance accorded to Hagar in scripture, a significance that, as we saw, first captured the attention of early modern commentators. Hagar is one of the few biblical figures to be visited by an angel of the Lord and, like the Virgin Mary, the prophecy Hagar hears concerns a child.[12]

FIG. 17: Attributed to Carel Fabritius. *Hagar and the Angel*, ca. 1643–45. Oil on canvas, 157.5 x 136 cm. Collection of Schönborn-Buchheim, Residenzgalerie, Salzburg. Photo: Fotostudio Ulrich Ghezzi, Oberalm.

In a flight scene attributed to Carel Fabritius (fig. 17), ca. 1643–45, Hagar sobs, crouching or kneeling against a tree trunk.[13] Hagar may not yet be aware of the angel who stands just behind her, almost touching her head with one hand. Presumably, this is the moment before the angel commands her to return to her mistress, foretelling Ishmael's prophecy.

In another flight scene, also attributed to Bol, Hagar kneels before the angel, her hands clasped in prayer. Storm clouds lace the sky.[14] In a landscape attributed to the little-known painter Jan Linsen, with figures attributed to history painter Salomon de Bray, Hagar listens carefully to the angel, her index finger touching her temple (fig. 18).[15] Pointing with his right hand, the angel appears to be delivering his message. Hagar leans against a well, fashioned after an antique Roman vessel. In another mid-century work in the manner of Govaert Flinck or Salomon de Bray, the angel speaks to an astonished Hagar, who has dropped her handkerchief, with one hand on her heart.[16]

As we have seen, most sixteenth-century Reformation literature interpreted Gen 16 as a lesson in obedience, humility, and faith, and some even dubbed Hagar a model of sincere confession; many of these same ideas would reappear in readings of the later wilderness-rescue scene. On the one end of the spectrum was Luther, who compared the runaway Hagar to those unbelievers who had "run away" from the church; he saw the "saintly Hagar" in Gen 16, however, as the model of a sinner who repents, one engaged in an act of true worship. On the opposite end, Calvin saw Hagar as a reprobate who repents only because she breaks down under extreme hardship. Both Luther and Calvin also adapted the episode to

FIG. 18: Attributed to Jan Linsen (with figures by Salomon de Bray?). *Hagar and the Angel*, ca. 1640s–50s? Oil on canvas, 106 x 132 cm. Collection of Dr. Alfred Bader, Milwaukee.

promote domestic harmony, advocating sensible household management and obedient, humble servitude.

Seventeenth-century Dutch Christian literature likewise adapted Gen 16 to foster obedience, humility, and repentance among Netherlanders, sometimes using it to address relations between masters and servants specifically, as we have seen. These pictures of the runaway maidservant, now recalcitrant and pious, would surely have reminded viewers (the household servants among them) of the virtues of obedience, penitence, or humility.

This notion of submission to authority is emphasized in the caption beneath a printed image of the episode added to the 1665 edition of *Joodse Oudheden* (*Jewish Antiquities*), written by the ancient Jewish exegete Flavius Josephus in Greek and translated into Dutch.[17] The image was engraved by Pieter Schut after Matthaeus Merian the elder in 1659 and reprinted here. Hagar and the angel stand close together. The angel speaks while Hagar listens, perhaps even protests. To the right, a contemporary well with rope and pulley has been included. Behind, a fringe of trees and a mountainous vista suggest a "wilderness" setting. In the margin to the left of the image, the caption reads, "the angel commands Hagar to humble herself before her mistress."[18]

The Dutch were fascinated by Josephus's style of storytelling, enriched as it was with psychological characterization.[19] In the biblical text, we are only told that a frightened Hagar flees to escape her mistress's wrath and she does not call out. But Josephus explains that it was Hagar's unwillingness to endure the humiliation of chastisement, for which she had only herself to blame. Josephus also tells us that an angel meets Hagar in the wilderness, commanding her to return home and advising her to secure well-being through self-control, because Hagar's plight was but "due to her arrogance and ingratitude" towards her mistress.[20]

Surely the Dutch recognized the didactic value of this biblical moment: the painted versions of the episode must have struck similar chords of obedience, penitence, or humility. In the paintings, Hagar never stands: the compositions by Bol, Fabritius,[21] and others imagine a kneeling, sitting, humbled Hagar, sometimes shown praying in the pose of the classic penitent, in the presence of the commanding angel.

This characterization is reminiscent of the repentant, rehabilitated Hagar presented by Abraham de Koningh in the theatrical play based on the same episode, discussed in chapter 2. In de Koningh's *Hagars Vlucht ende Wederkomst* (Hagar's Flight and Return), an angel of the Lord orders the domestic maidservant to return to her mistress. Aided by the allegorical personage of Obedience, an enlightened Hagar successfully battles Pride and Ambition to return to the contemporary Dutch household.

In short, in Dutch paintings of the runaway Hagar and the angel episode, the biblical maidservant is held up as a didactic exemplar of obedience, humility, and repentance for contemporary Netherlanders, just as she is in de Koningh 's play. In fact, the motif of Hagar's submission to authority may have been symbolic, on some level, of Dutch civic order and social control, as we have discussed. While de Koningh imagines a happy ending in his play, we know that in the biblical narrative, things only get worse after Ishmael is born. From the standpoint of the plot, the divine command that Hagar return to her mistress is what sets the maidservant up for the final fall.

Notes

1. Tobias Stimmer's woodcut from his book *Neue Künstliche Figuren Biblischer Historien*, Basle, 1576, no. 13; repr. 1923 by G. Hirsch as *Tobias Stimmer's Bibel* (D'Hulst and Vandenven 1989, 3:52, fig. 24). McGrath 1984, 89, mentions tapestries on the subject matter.

2. Pieter Paul Rubens, *Hagar Leaves the House of Abraham*, 1615, oil on panel, 62.8 x 76 cm., inv. no. GE-475, State Hermitage Museum, St. Petersburg.

3. McGrath 1984, 84n72, citing Rooses and Reulens 1899–1909, 2:150: "galanteria di mia mano."

4. Rubens, letter, May 26, 1618: ". . . I suggietto ne sacro ne profano per dir cosi benche cavato della sacra scrittura cioe Sara in atto di gridare ad Agar che gravidasi arte di casa in un atto donnesco assai galante con intervento anco del Patriarca Abraham . . . ," cited in D'Hulst and Vandenven 1989, 23; Rooses and Ruelens 1887, 2:170–74; Magurn 1955, 64–66.

5. D'Hulst and Vandenven 1989, 3:23; 1:55. In 1618, Rubens made an autograph replica of the same painting for Carleton, which the ambassador presented to Elizabeth, Queen of Bohemia, in honor of her twenty-third birthday in 1619. The replica is oil on canvas and slightly larger in size: 71 x 101 cm.; see Hoogsteder 2003, 202, fig. 11, for a reproduction.

6. Bartholomeus Breenbergh, *The Angel Commands Hagar to Return to Sarah*, signed and dated 1632, on copper, 38 x 32 cm., private collection. Photo © Sotheby's, New York, January 30, 1997, lot no. 32. For Jan Lievens's version, canvas, 69 x 87 cm, Museé des Beaux-Arts, Rouen, see Bialostocki et al. 1979, 136–37. The work by Poelenburgh is of oil on copper, 10 x 14″, Palazzo Pitti, Florence, cat. 1937, no. 1094.

7. Roethlisberger 1981, 1.

8. Ibid., 2:61, cat. no. 142.

9. *Hagar at the Well*, signed on lower right, oil on canvas, 115.6 x 97.8 cm, Muzeum Pomorskie, Gdansk. See Sumowski 1983, 1:328, fig. 89. Sumowski says the signature style is from the 1650s. See also van de Waal 1974, 148, and Blankert 1982, 89–90.

10. Van de Waal 1974, 151; Blankert 1982, 89.

11. This second painting, a good copy of the original composition, is in the Pushkin Museum, Moscow, with similar dimensions: 115 x 105 cm, also on canvas (Blankert 1982, 89–90).

12. Trible 1984, 28.

13. Attributed to Carel Fabritius, *Hagar and the Angel*, ca. 1643–45, oil on canvas, 157.5 x 136 cm, collection of Schönborn-Buchheim, Residenzgalerie, Salzburg. Photo: Fotostudio Ulrich Ghezzi, Oberalm. Sumowski attributes it to Fabritius. See Sumowski 1983, 5:3202, fig. 2071. Van de Waal attributes it to Govaert Flinck. See Van de Waal 1974, 151, fig. 8.

14. *The Angel Appearing to Hagar*, 78 x 59.5 cm, Berlin Art Market (van de Waal 1974, fig. 10); image via the Witt Library (as auctioned at Sotheby's, New York, June 6, 1976).

15. *Hagar and the Angel*, attributed to Jan Linsen (with figures by Salomon De Bray?), ca. 1640–50s?, oil on canvas, 106 x 132 cm, collection of Dr. Alfred J. Bader, Milwaukee.

16. Attributed to Ferdinand Bol or Salomon de Bray, *The Angel Commands Hagar to Return*, ca. 1650s, oil on panel, 35 x 25", private collection. See Moltke 1938–39, 224.

17. Pieter Schut (after an engraving by Matthaeus Merian the elder), 1659, reprinted in the 1665 Dutch edition of Flavius Josephus's *Boecken; te weten, twintigh van de oude Geschiedenissen der Joden* (Dutch), folio 10, trans. L. v. Boos and S. de Vries (Doordrecht: Jacob Savry), Royal Library, The Hague. For more on this bible print book and the complicated history of Netherlandish bible illustrations, see van der Coelen 1998, 172, and, 2:27–33.

18. Josephus (1665 Dutch edition), "De Engel vermaent Hagar haer onder harer vrouwe to verootmoedegen," folio 10.

19. C. Tümpel 1991, 26.

20. Flavius Josephus, *hoogh-beroemde Joodische Historien ende boecken* (Haarlem: Adriaen Roman, 1636), folio 7v, Royal Library, The Hague. For a modern English translation from Josephus's original Greek text, see the Loeb Classical Library edition of *The Jewish Antiquities* 4:188–89, trans. H. St. J. Thackeray et al. (Cambridge: Harvard University Press, 1930–1965), 4:93.

21. See, for example, Salomon de Bray's work, signed and dated 1649 (or 1659?), 64 x 47 cm, Hermitage, Leningrad, cat. 1958.

✝

CHAPTER FIVE

Paintings of the Expulsion of Hagar and Ishmael
(GEN 21:14)

Curiously, in the early modern period, a sympathetic Hagar figure first emerges in sixteenth-century imagery of Hagar's story, particularly in northern Netherlandish art.[1] Why?

Early Netherlandish Painting:
Lucas van Leyden's "Empathetic" Expulsions

Two engravings by the remarkable Dutch artist Lucas van Leyden, dated ca. 1506 and 1516, respectively, are perhaps the earliest examples of this change in tone.[2] In the earlier of the two images (fig. 19), van Leyden depicted a solemn Abraham handing a water vessel to a pretty, young Hagar. Her head is tilted down, presumably in sorrow. On the right, a small Ishmael holds the bread. To the left, a stony-faced, impassive Sarah observes the repudiation, holding Isaac's hand protectively. The rivalry between mothers and sons is implied. The composition is divided in half, contrasting the household manor and Sarah on the left with the wilderness and Hagar on the right, a sixteenth-century tradition; this has led some to question whether the setting functions as a *paysage moralisé*. The dry and verdant trees have been read as a symbol of choice, representing Abraham's alternatives.[3] Van Leyden emphasizes the tragic, human aspects of the story to secure the viewer's empathy, amplifying the emotions of its participants.

FIG. 19: Lucas van Leyden. *Abraham Dismissing Hagar*, ca. 1506. Engraving, 27.5 x 21.7 cm. Rijksprentenkabinet, Rijksmuseum, Amsterdam.

The later engraving of 1518 is also empathetic, envisioning a tender farewell. Here, van Leyden depicted the moment after Abraham has given Hagar the water. A grave Abraham gently touches Hagar's sleeve: she must go. This time, the pretty young Hagar appears to weep, holding a cloth to her face. A small, cherubic Ishmael appears to hang onto his mother's skirt as he looks up at his father. In one hand, he holds an apple. Mother and son are barefoot, suggesting their dispossession. Interestingly, Sarah and Isaac are not included in this genteel dismissal.

How can we account for the empathetic tone? In part, one attributes this to van Leyden's unusual gift for vivid storytelling and the skillful handling of emotional overtones. In a broader artistic context, he is part of a European trend in which imagery becomes increasingly naturalistic and humanistic during the baroque period. More specifically, van Leyden's images coincide with the heartfelt responses to the troubling story that were penned in the opening decades of the sixteenth century, attitudes that, thanks to the invention of the printing press, were circulated more widely than ever before. Just as Hagar and Ishmael attracted a certain attention and sympathy as the Pauline typology receded, so too a shift in artistic attitudes toward Hagar and Ishmael can be detected, particularly in Dutch art.

In the 1518 engraving, van Leyden imagines a weeping Hagar: does this resonate to some degree with the contrite, castigated maidservant that sympathizers such as Zwingli, Vermigli, Pellikan, Cajetan, and Luther lauded at roughly the same time? In the sixteenth century, the Pauline typology began to give way to literary expressions concerned with fundamentally human, heartfelt ("modern") values and emotion. Thus, Luther's portrait of the exiles anticipates particularly modern attitudes.[4]

Sixteenth-Century Northern Expulsions: A Tale of Two Half Brothers

Of course, we must remember that Lucas van Leyden's engravings were exceptional in their time. How was the expulsion scene treated elsewhere? A brief review of other sixteenth-century northern European treatments rounds out our understanding. In early northern European imagery, especially in bible prints, there is a tendency to depict the expulsion scene as the consequence of sibling rivalry.[5] Likewise, the handful of extant sixteenth-century northern Netherlandish expulsion paintings tend to portray the scene as the direct consequence of the fighting half brothers, with the older brother dominating the younger.[6] Perhaps the repeated focus on the physical antagonism between the siblings in the earliest expulsion paintings reflects the age-old European predilection for stories concerning fraternal rivalry, birthright, birth order, and inheritance, a recurrent theme in the Bible and in folk literature.[7] In the seventeenth century, the motif of the fighting half brothers disappears.

Cornelis Engelbrechtsz

An example of the sibling hostility appears in a painting ascribed to the Dutch painter Cornelis Engelbrechtsz, ca. 1500 (fig. 20).[8] Three different moments from the story are included in a continuous narrative. An expulsion scene with Abraham, Hagar, and Ishmael unfolds in the foreground. Further back at the right, Ishmael beats Isaac with a stick or spoon; at the left in the far background, a small scene of the angel appearing to Hagar (presumably to show her the source of water) has been inserted. Both literally and figuratively, then, Ishmael's abuse of Isaac is shown as the direct cause of and justification for the expulsion. The outcasts are depicted as barefoot, emphasizing their disgrace and vulnerability. As in other sixteenth-century expulsion scenes, the artist depicts the half brothers as closer in age than the fourteen-year difference indicated in the Bible.[9]

FIG. 20: Cornelis Engelbrechtsz. *The Expulsion of Hagar*, ca. 1500. Oil on panel, 34.5 x 47 cm, inv. no. GG 6820. Kunsthistorisches Museum, Vienna.

FIG. 21: Jan Mostaert. *The Expulsion of Hagar and Ishmael*, ca. 1525 (1527?). Oil on oak, 94 x 131 cm. Collection of Thyssen-Bornemisza. Copyright © Museo Thyssen-Bornemisza, Madrid.

Jan Mostaert

In an exemplary work painted by the Dutch artist Jan Mostaert about 1525, different moments from the biblical episode are woven into the scene in a continuous narrative (fig. 21).[10] In the foreground, Abraham expels Hagar and Ishmael. In the background at left, Sarah observes Ishmael striking Isaac from the doorway of the house. In the landscape in the right background, we see an open doorway leading our eye to the wilderness beyond. An angel appears to Hagar to show her the water source, while further back, Ishmael weeps under a tree. Beyond this, we now see Hagar at a small lake, presumably the source of water the angel showed her. Behind this, even smaller figures of Hagar and Ishmael proceed further into the wilderness. Above them on a rock, Abraham's sacrifice of Isaac is portrayed. This is probably included to reinforce our notion of Abraham's faith and obedience: at God's command, he was willing to sacrifice not *one*, but *both* sons.

Here, the sibling hostility is interpreted in contemporary terms: Ishmael is in the act of striking Isaac with a golf club. The two golf balls nearby indicate the boys were in the midst of a game. The artist links the expulsion directly to the assault: Ishmael carries a golf club into the wilderness, instead of his typical attributes of quiver and bow. Golf is one of the oldest games in the Netherlands, a popular outdoor sport. In this manner, the artist uses the biblical episode as a pretext to comment on contemporary domestic life. Mostaert's interpretation was apparently popular, since at least two copies were made.[11]

Certain iconographic elements suggest that Mostaert's expulsion painting lends itself to a "symbolic" or allegorical reading.[12] In the left background, Sarah is associated with the manor, placed on a higher plane (a symbol of heavenly Jerusalem); in the right background, the banished Hagar appears in front of Mount Sinai (earthly Jerusalem). Meanwhile, the banished Ishmael lies under a tree that has withered branches but is crowned with green leaves. Bleyerveld suggests that this is probably the symbol of the tree of knowledge, brought back to life through Christ; the tree symbolism suggests that the Old Testament (or old covenant) must make way for the New (Hagar must go, ceding to Sarah).[13] If this is so, Mostaert's painting relies, to some degree, on the traditional Pauline allegory for meaning.

Seventeenth-Century Dutch Paintings of the Expulsion Scene

As we saw in seventeenth-century Dutch literature, the Pauline typology was increasingly set aside to reconcile the complex, ancient story with contemporary values. Something analogous is also at work in seventeenth-century Dutch-painted expulsion scenes, under pressure to satisfy the needs and serve the interests of a mercantile audience in a competitive art market. Certainly, the Pauline allegory would continue to resonate in any depiction of the expulsion scene for those viewers familiar with traditional Christian teachings on the subject, as we have said. But, as we shall see in this chapter, other interpretations, influences, and concerns quintessentially Dutch are brought to bear in seventeenth-century paintings of the episode.

We begin with the painting by Pieter Lastman dated 1612, (fig. 22)[14] and the famous etching that his former pupil Rembrandt produced in 1637 (fig. 23).[15] Much of the expulsion imagery from this time up through the 1670s draws on these two compositions, suggesting Lastman's and Rembrandt's lasting influence. This helps to account, to some

FIG. 22: Pieter Lastman. *The Expulsion of Hagar and Ishmael,* 1612, signed and dated "Anno 1612 Lastman fecit." Oil on canvas, 49 x 71 cm, inv. 91. Photo: Elke Walford. Hamburger Kunsthalle. Photo Credit: Bildarchi Preussischer Kulturbesitz/ Art Resource, NY.

degree, for the increasing popularity of the expulsion theme in the opening decades of the century.[16]

Pieter Lastman's Expulsion Painting of 1612

Lastman belonged to a group of artists known as the "pre-Rembrandtists" who forged a new naturalistic style in Dutch painting after the turn of the century, influenced by Caravaggio, Adam Elsheimer, and the Caracci.[17] Here, the foregrounded Abraham, Ishmael, and Hagar are well modeled against a heroic, Italianate landscape. The turban and oriental clothing evoke ancient times. Abraham wears sandals; the outcasts are barefoot. The landscape is capped by Roman buildings and a picturesque bridge stretches its arches over the river winding beneath it. Rising in the distance, more edifices top craggy cliffs. In the left mid-ground, appearing in an archway in front of a house, a mother holds a child; presumably they are Sarah and Isaac. Nearby, a maidservant milks a cow.

Lastman emphasizes the moment before the departure, not the expulsion itself,[18] and he uses several devices to deepen the meaning and tenderness of the moment. Abraham places his hand on Ishmael's head; the

FIG. 23: Rembrandt van Rijn. *Abraham Casting Out Hagar and Ishmael*, 1637. Etching and drypoint, only state, 125 x 95 mm. Collection of Rembrandt House Museum, Amsterdam. Photograph © Rembrandt House Museum.

inclusion of a blessing gesture in the expulsion episode appears to be a sixteenth-century Dutch innovation.[19] The young Ishmael weeps. Hagar's right hand is on Ishmael's shoulder. With the palm of her left hand upright, she appears to plead with Abraham. Ishmael functions as the physical link between both parents, figuratively and literally.[20]

PICTURING ABRAHAM

In seventeenth-century theological and literary writings, Abraham was generally held up as an exemplar of faith, obedience, and hope, admired for his hospitality, and considered a role model for fathers in the Dutch household. This helps account for his great popularity in Dutch painting.[21] But when it came to the expulsion episode, Abraham's harsh role required explanation. Sarah was sometimes criticized for her jealousy, and this too had implications for Dutch painting: she is treated in highly unsympathetic terms in many works, as we shall see.

The rejection of mother and son is tempered by Lastman in a number of touching ways. Most remarkably, Abraham is shown as a tender, caring patriarch: he has accompanied the outcasts some distance away from the house. The blessing gesture not only reminds us of the biological bond between father and son, but it also alludes to the divine promise that, through Abraham, Ishmael will be divinely blessed with "a nation" (Gen 21:12–13). Thus, when expelling mother and son, Abraham is shown trusting in God; Lastman reinforces notions of an obedient, faithful, admirable patriarch.

Rembrandt van Rijn's Expulsion Etching of 1637

Although many artists in Rembrandt's circle painted the subject, remarkably, we have no surviving painting by Rembrandt himself on the episode. However, his masterful etching in 1637 inspired and influenced numerous paintings of the expulsion in the decades that followed. Rembrandt's composition, in which the expulsion unfolds from left (Sarah and Isaac) to right (Hagar and Ishmael), recalls the configuration in the 1543 etching by sixteenth-century Nuremberg artist Georg Pencz (fig. 24).[22] Rembrandt divides the scene, contrasting civilized, domestic life on the left (house), with the wilderness on the right, recalling sixteenth-century iconography.[23] Abraham straddles both spheres: he appears as the central figure here, as he does in the scriptural passage.

Rembrandt uses various means to bring the expulsion to life. With one foot on the stoop, Abraham appears to balance his loyalties to Sarah and Isaac with his concern for Hagar and Ishmael.[24] His stately robes and broad stance convey heroism and majesty. Sarah is shown smiling, while Hagar turns away, handkerchief to her face, overcome with grief: this underscores the contest between the mothers, the victor in laughter, the loser in tears.[25] Is Sarah's glee at this moment malicious? Perhaps, but

FIG. 24. Georg Pencz. *The Expulsion of Hagar and Ishmael,* **from the series** *The Story of Abraham,* **ca. 1543, signed with monogram at lower left. Engraving, 50 x 82 mm, only state. Rijksprentenkabinet, Rijksmuseum, Amsterdam.**

Rembrandt may be alluding to Sarah's laughter in Gen 21:6, in the moment after Isaac is born and just a few short verses before the expulsion itself (Gen 21:14):[26] "And Abraham was an hundred years old, when his son Isaac was born unto him. And Sarah said, God hath made me to laugh, so that all that hear will laugh with me" (Gen 21:5–6, KJV).

Still, this contrast between the smiling Sarah and a sorrowful Hagar appears in other works by artists from Rembrandt's circle, as we shall see.

Like Lastman, Rembrandt adds special touches designed to reinforce a sense of the patriarch's faith and humanity in this awful moment. Abraham's left hand appears to reach out as if attempting to bless Ishmael, recalling Lastman's gesture, but too late. Abraham has already given the outcasts bread and water, as the Bible indicates, but, more than this, he has provided Hagar with a knife and purse, affixed to the bottom of her dress. Moreover, Ishmael's costly garment and boots suggest he hasn't been entirely neglected.[27] Hagar wears sandals.

If Lastman and Rembrandt evoke sympathy for Hagar and Ishmael in the expulsion scenes, it is partly because of the way Abraham, the traditional Dutch paragon of virtue, is rendered. Lastman and Rembrandt show a heroic, resolute father envisioned as compassionate. This compassionate Abraham distinguishes the Dutch expulsions from other European interpretations, most notably, Italian versions. For example, the classicizing, Michelangelesque Abrahams in the expulsion paintings by Naples artist Luca Giordano (early 1630s) and Roman painter Francesco Ruschi (fig. 25, ca. 1644–45) tyrannically banish mother and son. Hagar looks like a courtesan, while Abraham is portrayed as a "Herculean graybeard": as a result, the Italian expulsion becomes a "pompous [scene] of judgment" or a "Herculean labor."[28] By contrast, Lastman and Rembrandt picture their Abraham, the "father of many nations" (*vader van veeler volcken*),[29] as a benevolent authority, and Hagar as pitiful. The Dutch expulsions convey a remarkable tenderness and sense of tragedy.

Salomon de Bray's Expulsion of 1662

The blessing motif is intensified in Salomon de Bray's version of the expulsion painted in 1662 (fig. 26).[30] Abraham presses both hands down on the head of a kneeling Ishmael. The patriarch looks up to the heavens, presumably toward the divine force driving the painful decision he must make. Ishmael's back is turned toward us. In the foreground, weeping Hagar descends the steps leading away from the house, her descent underscoring the doom of banishment. The Rembrandtesque beam of light

FIG. 25: Francesco Ruschi. *The Expulsion of Hagar*, ca. 1644–45. Oil on canvas, 55 x 75 in. Collection of Bob Jones University.

FIG. 26: Salomon de Bray. *The Expulsion of Hagar,* 1662. Oil on panel, 21¹/₄ x 18⁵/₈ in. (54.0 x 47.3 cm). Norton Simon Art Foundation, Gift of Mr. Norton Simon.

that falls across patriarch and son lends the aura of divine sanction: the expulsion is depicted as a test of Abraham's faith.

A Mid-Seventeenth-Century Expulsion Scene Attributed to Jan Victors

In scripture, Abraham is reluctant to part with Hagar and Ishmael; it is only after God tells Abraham to hearken to Sarah's words that he acts. In certain Dutch scenes, Abraham's powerlessness or reluctance in the matter is emphasized.[31] In one example, a mid-century expulsion scene attributed to Jan Victors, the patriarch's left hand makes the familiar commanding gesture, but he stands close to Hagar, perhaps touching her protectively, suggesting sympathy.[32] In fact, the placement of the figure almost appears to impede Hagar's departure. From the half-door, Sarah is shown smiling as she watches the event unfold, while another figure, presumably Isaac, leans out a window. Hagar, depicted here as a sympathetic blond peasant girl or maidservant, holds her hand to her face in shock or despair.[33] Ishmael looks up at his mother, perhaps in distress. In this depiction, the emphasis falls on the plight of the outcasts. In expulsion scenes with a passive or nonheroic Abraham and a smiling Sarah, our focus and sympathies necessarily shift to Hagar and Ishmael.

Gabriel Metsu's Expulsion Scene of the Early 1650s

One expulsion scene, painted by Gabriel Metsu in the early 1650s, has a unique Abraham (fig. 27).[34] He forcefully propels a sad, protesting Hagar out the door, pointing in the distance. Ishmael looks up at his mother in alarm. A figure, perhaps Sarah or Isaac, waves them away from the window above. In this precipitant expulsion, Hagar and Ishmael don't even get the provisions of bread and water mentioned in the Bible. Metsu's expulsion reminds us that not everyone viewed Abraham as compassionate or heroic in this moment. The comely Hagar, wearing a scarlet red dress with a low neckline, is central in the composition. Our sympathies go to the beleaguered mother, not to the resolute-looking Abraham.

The Dutch Expulsion Paintings: Plumbing the Narrative for Emotional Riches

However, Metsu's "ejection" is a great exception to the rule. The Dutch expulsion scene is almost always shown as a sorrowful, unavoidable "farewell" rather than as an act of repudiation.[35] These Dutch "farewells" are a far cry from the harsh Pauline edict that called upon the righteous to throw out the carnal bondwoman and her son. It appears that the Pauline strictures were simply obsolete in the seventeenth-century Netherlands: a conflicted or compassionate Abraham, a jealous Sarah, an attractive, pitiful Hagar, or a cherubic, weeping Ishmael charged the pictures with rich emotions. In short, the biblical domestic tragedy was plumbed to explore fundamental human values, emotions, and experiences—jealousy, familial

FIG. 27: Gabriel Metsu. *The Expulsion of Hagar*, ca. 1650–55, signed "Gmetsu." Oil on canvas, 115 x 89 cm, inv. no. S 2209. Collection of Stedelijk Museum De Lakenhal, Leiden, the Netherlands. Photograph © Stedelijk Museum De Laken-hal, Leiden.

strife, love and loss, among others—to satisfy the popular appetite.[36] Like their literary counterparts, artists realized that the expulsion episode could be made to appeal to the heart.

As a result, there is a strange dichotomy at work in these scenes: on the one hand, the expulsion paintings reenact the repudiation of mother and son, faithful to the scriptural narrative. At the same time, the paintings attribute to the outsiders sympathetic human values and emotions. The paintings comply with scriptural fact, but they increasingly appeal to the heart, dissolving the traditional theological blame on Hagar. The human, tragic aspects of the story are exploited at the expense of the original religious meaning. Over and over again, this idea of a painful familial split comes to the fore.

The Curiously Sympathetic Hagar in Dutch Expulsion Scenes

While the "good Hagar" made some headway in Dutch literature, as we have seen, nowhere does she receive greater sympathy or attract more attention than she does in Dutch art, especially when it comes to the painted expulsion and wilderness-rescue scenes.

Barent Fabritius: Hagar Breaks Down

Hagar becomes even more sympathetic in expulsion compositions in the mid-seventeenth century. Among the most sympathetic portrayals is one painted by Barent Fabritius around 1650.[37] Here, at the center of the composition, a sobbing Hagar has fallen into Abraham's arms. Her hands are clasped together in a begging gesture, presumably asking for forgiveness. Abraham supports the distraught maidservant. A winsome Ishmael holds up the bottle of water in his left hand (in the Bible it is carried by Hagar). Sarah and Isaac, unusually, are not included in this picture. The intimacy between the master and maidservant is unique.

Jan Steen: Inviting Hagar Back In?

Jan Steen also painted a highly sympathetic Hagar and Ishmael in an expulsion scene of about 1660 (fig. 28).[38] The figural arrangement, setting, and, to a degree, the figure types used are drawn from Rembrandt's famous etching of 1637 (fig. 23).[39] As in the Rembrandt etching, Steen shows the moment just after the outcasts have been dismissed. Hagar carries the pro-

FIG. 28: Jan Steen. *The Expulsion of Hagar*, ca. 1660, signed in full on the corner-stone of the archway. Oil on canvas, 54 x 43.5 in. Gemäldegalerie Alte Meister, Staatliche Kunstsammlungen, Dresden.

visions of bread and water and weeps into her apron. In the foreground, a coy or knowing Ishmael looks out at the viewer as he prepares his bow, like a cupid. Inside the house, Sarah picks lice from Isaac's head, a common maternal activity in Dutch domestic genre paintings. The background is enlivened by the inclusion of a herder and livestock. Two dogs have been added. Here, Abraham stands on the stoop, as he does in Rembrandt's etching, balanced between two sets of mothers and sons. But in Steen's version, Abraham seems, unusually, to point back to the house with his right hand. His other hand touches Hagar on the shoulder. Does Steen show a conflicted Abraham who can't decide whether to throw poor Hagar out or invite her back inside?[40] If so, Steen has found a humorous way to reflect the patriarch's quandary.

Nicolaes Maes: The Dignified Hagar

Typically, the Dutch expulsion scenes show a weeping Hagar as we have seen, wiping her tears or covering her face with a handkerchief. However, Hagar does not always resort to tears to gain our sympathy, as a unique work by Nicolaes Maes demonstrates (fig. 29).[41] Maes's version reflects the essentials of Rembrandt's 1637 composition, but he has added a number of innovations. Maes's Hagar is dry-eyed, subdued, richly dressed, and remarkably dignified in the manner in which she, like Ishmael, turns away from Abraham.[42] With one hand, Abraham reaches out toward Ishmael. Is this an aborted blessing, or are we seeing the moment just after the blessing has been given? The steep descent of the staircase adds a sense of finality to the banishment.[43] Maes's Ishmael must be one of the most striking depictions of childhood misery anywhere in Dutch art; a child prematurely bearing the emotions of an adult, beleaguered, yet moving forward into the unknown. In these ways, Maes intensifies our sense of the tragedy and pulls on our heartstrings. Here, too, we sympathize with Hagar and Ishmael far more than we do with Abraham. Sarah and Isaac have been left out altogether.

Picturing Sarah

However, in most expulsion scenes, as we have seen, Sarah and Isaac are a constant presence. Sarah appearing as old and decrepit is to be expected, since the Bible tells us she is eighty-nine years old. Particularly in the presentation of Hagar scenes (chapter 3), we noticed how artists stressed her haggard appearance to contrast with the beauty of a youthful Hagar. The juxtaposition of contrasting ages and figure types were a typical ploy of the Caravaggisti, but in this context, the contrast also heightens notions of rivalry and sensuality. In some scenes, such as Victors's expulsion painting, Sarah appears at the half-door wearing a smile as she observes the dismissal. In other instances, she shows a stony-faced indifference. In either case, Sarah's attitude is designed to contrast with Abraham's compassion-

FIG. 29: Nicolaes Maes. *Abraham Dismissing Hagar and Ishmael*, 1653, signed and dated. Oil on canvas, 34.5 x 27.5 in. Metropolitan Museum of Art, New York.

ate bearing. This serves to further ennoble the patriarch's conduct and to endear Hagar to us.

Probably the most unflattering portrayal of Sarah in Dutch painting, or literature, for that matter, appears in *Sarah Demanding Hagar's Banishment* of 1680 by Rembrandt's former pupil, Aert de Gelder.[44] The subject matter is rare in European prints, rarer still in painting, Netherlandish or otherwise: it depicts the event that leads to the expulsion, when Sarah entreats a reluctant Abraham to expel Hagar and Ishmael (Gen 21:9–10). A sneering Sarah addresses a calm Abraham, sitting in a majestic chair. A pudgy Isaac leans against her knee, his turban nearly obscuring his impish face. Beside the pudgy boy, Sarah appears "all the more vehement in her protestations."[45] To modern aesthetic sensibilities, the characterizations of Sarah and Isaac are strikingly unappealing, even repugnant. What inspired de Gelder here? Is this simply an instance of the "expressive naturalism" that characterizes de Gelder's style and that of certain other seventeenth-century Dutch painters?[46]

As we have seen sprinkled throughout the literature, Sarah was sometimes censured for her conduct in connection with the expulsion. She was not only criticized for her jealous, typically "womanish" behavior; commentators traditionally found Sarah's behavior—specifically, her bossing Abraham around—problematic, since this was considered unacceptable conduct for wives.[47] Perhaps traditional criticisms such as these allowed de Gelder to take greater creative license and to apply an extreme form of naturalism in the moment when Sarah takes charge, portraying the matriarch and heir in an unsympathetic fashion.

For the Sake of the Family: The Expulsion as Domestic Homily in Dutch Painting

As we saw in chapter 1, Hagar's story, and the expulsion episode in particular, appears to have been commonly used to foster good household management, encourage domestic harmony and order, and advocate humility and obedience to readers. The expulsion story was often employed to enforce the primacy of the Christian family and order in domestic life. As in literature, so in art: certain iconography suggests that the expulsion episode could function as a domestic homily in Dutch art.

One expulsion scene by an unknown artist, probably painted in the first quarter of the century, makes this association explicit (fig. 30).[48] The expulsion takes place in front of a house, maintaining the traditional division between household and landscape. Abraham is poised between two sets of mothers and sons. On the left, Sarah and Isaac are affiliated with the household, while Hagar and Ishmael are placed outside. The figures wear contemporary dress; Ishmael wears the long, seemingly girlish dress that young boys usually wear in portraits, but not customarily boys in his-

FIG. 30: Artist unknown. *The Expulsion of Hagar and Ishmael*, early 1600s?. Dimensions, present location unknown. Photo: Rijksbureau voor Kunsthistorische Documentatie, Den Haag. RKD note below image: "Collection of C. E. Schlyter, Stockholm; photograph Karl Schultz, Stockholm; collection of Sonja Ahlklo, Lidmg 1974" [*sic*].

tory paintings.[49] In the distance, a river, a bridge, and a hamlet round out the scene.

Sarah is reading from a book to Isaac, presumably a pious teaching. It appears that Sarah has interrupted the boy at play, because six small figural carvings lie on the ground beneath him. Perhaps these are "bikkels," figures made of wood or stone for children's play.[50] One is tempted to question whether these pieces represent idolatrous figures, the result of Ishmael's bad (as it were, Catholic?) influence?[51] We remember that old sources accused Ishmael of the sin of idolatry, endangering Isaac. If so, this suggests that Sarah's teaching causes Isaac to leave the idols of Ishmael behind.

On the right, the concubine weeps, carrying the jug of water in one hand and bread in her apron. Ishmael carries a hoop, a contemporary children's toy. In Dutch domestic genre painting, the hoop can function as a symbol of folly or the trials of fortune. It may also simply signify childhood.[52]

Other details, also common to domestic genre painting, enliven the expulsion: on the left half of the picture, a spinning wheel and spindle, a dog, and an owl are aligned with the domestic realm, Sarah and Isaac. Placed on the right half of the scene, the cat and rooster are associated with the rejected maidservant, her son, and the "wilderness."

What do these elements mean? The spinning wheel and spindle, placed close beside Sarah, are traditional symbols of female virtue and diligence. Dogs often function as allusions to marital fidelity in Dutch domestic genre painting. In contrast, cats were associated with cunning or mischief.[53] The owl and rooster may mirror virtue and vice respectively; much has been written about birds as erotic metaphors in Netherlandish art.[54] The rooster may be symbolic of lasciviousness or lewdness,[55] while the owl may allude to watchfulness and sharp-sightedness.[56] In short, the animal symbolism may be included to warn against dangers that threaten family harmony.

Thus artists, as this painting suggests, were interested in the domestic aspects of the story: the expulsion scene could be adapted to reinforce the ideals of the Christian family and the sanctity of the household. Moreover, if our reading of the tiny figures as idolatrous carvings is correct, the painting also takes a swipe at Catholicism. Is Abraham's rejection of the rebel mother and son shown here necessary for the sake of the well-being of the Christian (Protestant?) family?

Jan Pynas: Hagar's Expulsion as a Warning against Pride

Didactic symbolism may crop up elsewhere. In an expulsion scene with a picturesque farmyard by Jan Pynas, signed and dated 1614, Ishmael once again carries a hoop as he departs, probably a symbol of folly (fig. 31).[57] On the left, a peacock is perched in front of the doorway, observing the action.[58] In Dutch art and literature, the peacock sometimes functioned as a traditional symbol of pride or arrogance. In medieval Christian thought, the vice of pride was one of the "seven deadly sins," which included covetousness, lust, envy, gluttony, anger, and sloth. Here, the peacock may allude to Hagar's pride or arrogance. If so, this resonates with a phrase from Cats's poem *Lamentation of Hagar*, when the maidservant tells us it was her pride that brought about the fall, "so komt den hoogmoed voor den val" (so pride comes before the fall).[59]

FIG. 31: Jan Pynas. *The Departure of Hagar*, signed and dated 1614. Oil on panel, 78 x 106 cm. Private collection, the Netherlands. Photo courtesy of Rijksbureau voor Kunsthistorische Documentatie, Den Haag.

Reinforcing Humility, Obedience, and Diligence: Abraham Bloemaert's "Bad" Hagar versus the "Good Dutch Maidservant"

In Abraham Bloemaert's *Expulsion of Hagar and Ishmael*, signed and dated 1638 (fig. 32), the scene takes place in a contemporary farmyard.[60] It is characteristic of the artist's later, picturesque style. A certain classicism attenuates the realism of the setting. The space leads from left to right; the foreground consists of figures and a framing by trees.[61] In the background, a diminutive expulsion with Abraham, Hagar, and Ishmael is taking place.

In the center foreground, a kneeling female worker, with stout arms and sleeves rolled up, works on a basket. Directly behind her, a group of domestic workers observes the expulsion, taking place just across the hedge. Some gossip. A peacock sits in the tree above the small, raised hut.

The foregrounded worker here is a model of domestic virtue, shown as diligent and obedient. She wears contemporary garb similar to maidservants in domestic genre interiors. Roethlisberger suggested that in this context, the image of Hagar's banishment functions as a punishment incurred for the disregard of authority; the dog probably alludes to fidelity.[62] Or, given the literary parallels, we could infer that the painting reinforces notions of domestic harmony. Domestic order, the painting insists, is sustained through humility and discipline, epitomized by the image of a graceful maidservant hard at work. The layout of the scene, composed of dominant orthogonal lines, graphically reinforces our sense of stability and calm, overriding the calamity in the background.

At about the same time, Bloemaert also produced another expulsion scene, neither dated nor signed, and somewhat smaller in size.[63] It shows a similar setting and includes the peacock. The dog lies in the same passive position. This time the model maidservant is on her knees milking a

FIG. 32: Abraham Bloemaert. *The Expulsion of Hagar and Ishmael*, signed and dated 1638. Oil on canvas, 57.75 x 71 in. The J. Paul Getty Museum, Los Angeles. Photo © The J. Paul Getty Museum.

goat. The position of the dog and vessel create an axis angling upward, leading the eye to the female figure first, then to the expulsion unfolding behind her. Thus, we see the maidservant in the act of observing the expulsion. Despite the distraction, she does not stop working, a Dutch paragon of humility, diligence, and obedience. Other laborers in the scene also keep busy.

In these paintings, the expulsion of Hagar, the "bad servant" in the background, serves as foil to the "good servant" in the foreground to reinforce notions of humility, diligence, and domestic order. This parallel construction of opposing scenes is a tradition of the previous century, reminiscent of the inverted sixteenth-century kitchen scenes by Pieter Aertsen.[64] Bloemaert inverts the repudiation of disobedience (Abraham's expulsion of Hagar) against the dominant setting of domestic order (the ideal maidservant, hard at work). Thus, Bloemaert's expulsion scenes present the viewer with a choice of foreground or background: the rebel biblical maidservant and her wretched fate or the hardworking maidservant and the virtuous ideal.

Bloemaert's ideal maid mirrors the positive servant stereotypes praised in contemporary domestic conduct books and celebrated in innumerable domestic genre paintings.[65] If the model maid functions as a symbol of domestic order, what then of Bloemaert's Hagar, the rebel maidservant, as symbol of disorder? In contrast to countless genre paintings of orderly interiors inhabited by capable mistresses and docile maidservants, the expulsion scenes, as Bloemaert's painting suggests, may have offered an alternative picture of household management, of domestic order threatened or fractured.

In the seventeenth century, the innumerable domestic genre scenes centered on the threshold of the house reveal a peculiarly Dutch obsession with the household, the doorway as a site of social "transition," and the proper actions of males, females, and children in these settings.[66] The expulsion of Hagar and Ishmael—which always takes place in front of and never inside the home, close to the doorway but in sight of the wilderness—may represent a statement about the maintenance of the family or the defense of domestic territory. Abraham typically stands between Hagar and the house, while Sarah watches from inside a doorway or window, often appearing in the upper half of the doorway. In this sense, the expulsion narratives reflect values that belong to the same cultural continuum as the "ideal" domestic scenes and may help to account, in part, for their popularity: both pictorial genres are concerned with preserving the domicile as a sanctified space for familial transactions.

Exploiting Hagar's Visual Appeal: Styling the Maidservant

In scripture, Abraham is central to the expulsion episode. Likewise, he plays the principal role in a few expulsion scenes, such as Rembrandt's magnificent etching of 1637 (fig. 23). However, as we cannot fail to notice, Hagar claims a special presence in many works: artists imbue her with personal emotions not described in the Bible. She comes to share center stage with Abraham, sometimes upstaging the patriarch altogether. By mid-century, Hagar is portrayed in ways that are calculated to boost her visual appeal.

In the biblical text, Hagar is obviously much younger than the ancient Sarah. Her age is not specified, but it only made sense to assume her to be nubile, since she was evidently fertile. Accordingly, Hagar is portrayed as pretty, young, and often, plump. Sometimes, Hagar wears a fitted bodice with a low neckline and, underneath, a plain white undergarment (shift) with voluminous sleeves, a traditional costume used in antique, biblical, or domestic genre scenes. The white shift, characterized by billowing sleeves, had been a basic undergarment for centuries.[67] In certain mid-century works, such as scenes by Jan Victors and Gabriel Metsu (fig. 27), the neckline of Hagar's shift has been lowered to partially reveal a breast, emphasizing her sexual appeal; on the other hand, her sleeves are rolled up, presumably alluding to her household status as servant. Often, she is shown with bare feet, increasing our sense of her vulnerability or penury.

In many mid-century scenes, Hagar wears a hat, reflecting a variety of styles and signaling eminent departure; Dutch women generally wore hats as a special kind of travel or riding dress.[68] In Maes's expulsion scene (fig. 29), Hagar's striking hat has been identified as a gypsy "bern," one of several headdresses familiar in depictions of gypsies since the sixteenth century. The belief that gypsies were descendants of Egyptians and therefore descendants of Hagar and Ishmael persisted in seventeenth-century culture, as we have seen. Thus, Maes's Hagar wears a bern, as she does in another expulsion painting by an artist from Rembrandt's "circle."[69] Hagar's hat is used as a convincing tool to connect the maidservant with her ancient, historical associations. Moreover, the headgear lends the maid-servant "exotic" appeal.

In several works, including Metsu's expulsion scene reviewed earlier (fig. 27), Hagar wears a straw hat, reflecting contemporary fashion. Worn by women of all classes, straw hats were the conventional, proper head-gear used for the outdoors. They were associated with country life and "became a stock attribute of country girls in painting and theater."[70] In a mid-seventeenth-century painting attributed to Adriaen van den Tempel, a comely Hagar is equipped with a wide-brimmed straw hat, a basket, and a dress with a deep décolletage and billowing sleeves.[71] The artist attempts to boost Hagar's appeal by modeling the outcast after the seduc-tive, rustic shepherdesses inhabiting Arcadian landscapes, so popular in Dutch genre painting at this time.[72]

After mid-century, Hagar is more likely to don an elegant gown than the common bodice-and-shift dress. Elegant attire is especially prevalent in the wilderness-rescue scene in Gen 21 (chapter 6), surely appealing to the luxurious tastes of an aspiring Dutch merchant class. Artists and their patrons could have found some theological justification for the lavish trappings: rabbinical exegeses known to the Dutch speculated that Hagar was the daughter of Pharoah from Gen 12, who gave the princess to Abra-ham as a second wife and not as a servant.[73]

By the last quarter of the century and into the early 1700s, Hagar takes on greater sensuality and a schematic primacy. In Philip van Dijk's expulsion of the 1680s, Hagar appears as antique goddess (fig. 33).[74] The composition maintains the conventional division between the residence (tent, in this case) and the outdoors. Here too, Hagar wears classical garb that exposes a shoulder, breast, and legs. With the dog at her side, Hagar is more reminiscent of the mythical huntress Diana than the banished biblical maidservant.

In a painting signed and dated by Willem van Mieris in 1724, Hagar again appears as a kind of antique femme fatale, in classical drapery bar-ing one breast and exposing her thighs.[75] The composition draws on the traditional formula, with Abraham standing on the stoop and Sarah lean-ing out a window; the conventional division between house and "wilder-ness" persists.

In short, by the last quarter of the century and beyond, not only has the theological or didactic significance of the expulsion episode vanished altogether, but what Hamann called the "domestic, intimate" tone of the

FIG. 33: Philip van Dijk. *Abraham Expels Hagar and Ishmael,* late seventeenth century. Oil on copper, 40 x 50 cm. Louvre, Paris, France. Photo Credit: Réunion des Musées Nationaux/Art Resource, NY.

Dutch interpretations is also gone. Instead, Hagar has become an antique concubine-goddess at the center of an erotic, classical tragedy, a trend we also noticed in the presentation of Hagar scenes (chapter 3). This pattern also holds true for the last painted episode from Hagar's story, the wilderness-rescue scene.

Notes

1. Van der Coelen 1997, 281; Mellinkoff 1998, 49.

2. *Abraham Dismissing Hagar*, ca. 1506, engraving, 27.5 x 21.7 cm; same subject, 1516, engraving, 14.8 x 12.5 cm (images from Hollstein 1996, plates 17 and 18).

3. Jacobowitz and Stepanek 1983, 50–51.

4. Thompson 1997, 228.

5. See, for example, German artist Johan Teufel's woodcut *Feast for the Circumcision of Isaac and the Expulsion of Hagar*, 1572 Wittenberg Bible (Schmidt 1962, 274–81, fig. 202); Flemish artist Marten de Vos's expulsion scene in the print bible *Thesaurus veteris et novi testamenti* (Antwerp: Gerard de Jode, 1585); or Dutch artist Willem Willemsz Thibaut's *The Story of Hagar and Ishmael*, ca. 20.5 x 23.8 cm, nos. 1–4, dated 1563 (date altered to 1580, added in the second state at lower right), Rijksprentenkabinet, Rijksmuseum, Amsterdam.

6. See, for example, *A River Landscape with the Expulsion of Hagar and Ishmael*, circle of Paul Bril, oil on copper, 23 x 30.5 cm, auction, Sotheby's, London, October 28, 1987. Photo: Witt Library, London. Anonymous, *Abraham's Dismissal of Hagar and Ishmael*, glass panel, The Hague: C. J. Berserik, inv. no. 2000-07, probably late sixteenth century. Photo: RKD. Another variation of the rival half brothers theme (see Bleyerveld 1991, 122–23, fig. 103, 104): two drawings show the moment before the expulsion. Sarah appeals to Abraham, presumably for the repudiation of Hagar and Ishmael, while the half brothers play (or fight?) nearby: one drawing is for a windowpane, Pierpont Morgan Library, attributed to Pieter Coecke van Alest, after 1534; the other is *Sara Advises Abraham to Send Hagar Away*, ascribed to either Aertgen van Leyden, the Master van Ruth and Naomi, or David Joriszoon, drawing, collection of Dr. A. Welcker, Amsterdam.

7. Boswell 1988, 257.

8. Cornelis Engelbrechtsz, *The Expulsion of Hagar*, ca. 1500, oil on panel, 34.5 x 47 cm, inv. no. GG 6820, Kunsthistorisches Museum, Vienna.

9. In some seventeenth-century paintings, communication between the two brothers is suggested, but the interaction is never depicted as physical strife. See, for example, A. van der Werff's *The Expulsion of Hagar*, 1701, Rheinisches Landesmuseum, Bonn (Gaechtgens 1987, cat. no. 53).

10. Jan Mostaert, *The Expulsion of Hagar and Ishmael*, ca. 1525 (1527?), oil on oak, 94 x 131 cm, collection of Thyssen-Bornemisza; copyright © Museo Thyssen-Bornemisza, Madrid. The work was originally signed and dated 1525 (1527?) and signed "IM," but after a cleaning, the data disappeared; top edge and sides have been cut.

11. Bleyerveld 1991 (scriptie), 117–18: Jan Mostaert, *The Expulsion of Hagar*, oil on panel, 94 x 129 cm, auction of the collection of Sir. G. L. Campbel of Succoth e.a., Christie's, London, 1947–46, no. 128, as Bruegel; Jan Mostaert, *The*

Expulsion of Hagar, oil on panel, ca. 150 cm wide, collection of C. Benedict, Paris, 1937. Photo: RKD.

12. Bleyerveld 1991, 120; Busch 1982, 108. Both point out that similar symbolism appears in Lucas van Leyden's engraving *The Expulsion of Hagar*, ca. 1506, British Museum, Department of Drawings, London (Bleyerveld 1991, 118–19, fig. 99).

13. Busch 1982, 108. Bleyerveld 1991, 120. The motif of the withered tree that simultaneously sprouts new growth is also reflected in the fence and yard of the house.

14. Pieter Lastman, *The Expulsion of Hagar and Ishmael*, 1612, signed and dated "Anno 1612 Lastman fecit," oil on canvas, 49 x 71 cm, inv. 91. Photo: Elke Walford, Hamburger Kunsthalle. Photo Credit: Bildarchiv Preussischer Kulturbesitz/Art Resource, New York.

15. Rembrandt van Rijn, *Abraham Casting Out Hagar and Ishmael*, 1637, etching and drypoint, only state, 125 x 99 mm; collection of Rembrandt House Museum, Amsterdam. Photo © Rembrandt House Museum.

16. See A. Tümpel 1974; Hamann 1936, 471–580.

17. Haak 1996, 190–92.

18. C. Tümpel 1991, 30.

19. Hamann 1936, 574.

20. Ibid., 481.

21. C. Tümpel 1991, 27.

22. Georg Pencz, *The Expulsion of Hagar*, ca. 1543, etching, 5.2 x 8.5 cm. C. Tümpel 1970, cat. no. 6; van der Coelen 1997, fig. 3; Bartsch 1978, no. 3.

23. Van der Coelen 1977, 276–77. For more examples, see the symmetric division between the "lived-in world" and the wilderness in expulsion scenes by Pencz of 1543; Matham's engraving after Bloemaert, 1612; Lucas van Leyden, 1506; Antonio Tempesta (ca. 1600).

24. Van der Coelen 1997, 278.

25. For more on the theme of rivalry between Sarah and Hagar in medieval depictions, see Mellinkoff 1998.

26. In medieval depictions of Abraham being visited by the three angels (Gen 18:2–13), Sarah sometimes appears laughing or smiling in accordance with scriptural text (Mellinkoff 1998, 40–42). Sarah first laughs when she overhears the divine promise that God will bless the couple with a child, despite their old age: "Therefore Sarah laughed within herself, saying, After I am waxed old shall I have pleasure, my lord being old also?" (Gen 18:12, KJV).

27. Van der Coelen 1997, 278.

28. Hamann 1936, 567–69, figs. 133, 134: Luca Giordano (1632–1705), *The Expulsion of Hagar*, ca. 1650–53, Dresden, Gemälde-Galerie; and Francesco Ruschi (Rusca), *The Expulsion of Hagar*, early 1630s, Rome, Treviso (until 1656),

Bob Jones University Art Collection, Greenville, SC (Pepper 1985, 265). A Ruschi copy of the same image is at the Museo Civico, Treviso.

29. Twisk 1632, 21.

30. Salomon de Bray, *The Expulsion of Hagar*, 1662, oil on panel, 21-1/4 x 18-5/8″ (54.0 x 47.3 cm), Norton Simon Foundation, gift of Mr. Norton Simon.

31. C. Tümpel 1991, 216.

32. Jan Victors, *The Expulsion of Hagar*, Budapest Museum of Fine Arts, Hungary (see Hamann 1936, 530, fig. 84).

33. Hamann says her face and the shape of her head recall an antique Venus type (Hamann 1936, 530).

34. Gabriel Metsu, *The Expulsion of Hagar*, ca. 1650–55, signed "GMetsu," oil on canvas, 115 x 89 cm, inv. no. S 2209; collection of Stedelijk Museum De Lakenhal, Leiden. Photo © Stedelijk Museum De Lakenhal, Leiden. See also C. Tümpel 1991, 216, plate 7.

35. Hamann characterizes the Dutch expulsions as "peaceful farewells" (Hamann 1936, 481, 568–69).

36. C. Tümpel 1991, 30.

37. *The Expulsion of Hagar*, ca. 1650, panel, 50 x 36 cm; Metropolitan Museum of Art, New York.

38. Jan Steen, *The Expulsion of Hagar*, ca. 1660, signed in full on the cornerstone of the archway, oil on canvas, 54 x 43.5″, Gemäldegalerie Alte Meister, Staatliche Kunstsammlungen, Dresden. See also Kirschenbaum 1977, 182, fig. 41.

39. Hamann 1936, 558–59.

40. Ibid., 558.

41. *Abraham Dismissing Hagar and Ishmael*, 1653, oil on canvas; 34.5 x 27.5″, Metropolitan Museum of Art, New York.

42. Walsh 1972, 110.

43. Ibid., 10.

44. *Sarah Demanding Hagar's Banishment*, early 1680s (suggested), signed "A. de Gelder," canvas, 116 x 138 cm; private collection, Germany (image from Moltke 1994, 24, cat. no. 5, plate 5).

45. Moltke 1994, 24.

46. Blankert et al. 1997, 32–42.

47. Thompson 1997, 219.

48. Image from RKD, The Hague. Identified as "'Onbekende Praerembrandtisten'; collection of C. E. Schlyter, Stockholm. Photo: Karl Schultz, Stockholm; Collection Sonja Ahlklo, Lidmg [*sic*] 1974." Dimensions and location unknown.

49. Albert Blankert, correspondence with author, August 19, 2003.

50. Yvonne Bleyerveld, correspondence with author, June 2, 2003.

51. Nicolas of Lyra, among other medieval exegetes, accused Ishmael of idolatry, as we saw in chap. 1.

52. Durantini 1983, 215.

53. Ibid., 268.

54. For example, the word "vogelen" or "birding" meant copulation, and "vogel" (bird) served as the synonym for penis. See the principal article on bird symbolism by De Jongh 1968–69, 27.

55. Among the many examples, the word "haenken" (cock) was used to refer to philanderers in sixteenth-century theater. Depictions of men slyly offering roosters to women are common in genre imagery.

56. For more on the symbolism of owls in Dutch art, see Bax 1979, 208–12; and De Jongh and Luijten 1997, 87.

57. Jan Pynas, *The Departure of Hagar*, signed and dated 1614, oil on panel, 78 x 106 cm, private collection, the Netherlands.

58. In fact, the peacock appears in several Dutch expulsion paintings in the decades that follow. See, for example, Gerard van den Eeckhout's *The Expulsion of Hagar*, 1666, North Carolina Museum of Art, Raleigh; a 1642 painting signed and dated by van den Eeckhout, 64 x 51 cm, RKD no. L14315; a mid-century painting attributed to van den Eeckhout, or Barent Fabritius (Hamann 1936, fig. 90), or alternatively, to Carel van den Pluym (Bader 1976, 28–29, plate 9); and a mid-century pen-and-ink drawing by an unidentified artist from the Rembrandt school (Hamann 1936, fig. 88).

59. C. Tümpel 1991, 30.

60. Abraham Bloemaert, *The Expulsion of Hagar and Ishmael*, signed and dated 1638, oil on canvas, 57.75 x 71″, J. Paul Getty Museum, Los Angeles. Photo © The J. Paul Getty Museum.

61. Roethlisberger 1993, 1:341.

62. Ibid., 1:115. Roethlisberger is referring to Jacob Matham's 1603 etching of the expulsion from a print by Abraham Bloemaert.

63. Roethlisberger dates this 1635. *The Expulsion of Hagar*, ca. 1635, oil on canvas, 99.7 x 148.5 cm, private collection (image from RKD, The Hague).

64. Roethlisberger 1993, 1:29. For more on the development of this format in seventeenth-century scenes, see Hollander 2002, 145–46; for sixteenth-century scenes, see Falkenburg 1988, 114–26.

65. Franits 1993, 110.

66. De Mare and Vos 1993, 108–31. Hollander 2002, esp. 184–200.

67. De Winkel 2001, 62.

68. Ibid., 56.

69. Walsh 1972, 112. Christian Tümpel notes that this style was called an "Egyptian hat," letter to the author, May 17, 2005.

70. De Winkel 2001, 56–57.

71. Attributed to A. van den Tempel, *The Expulsion of Hagar*, ca. 1650, oil on canvas, 111 x 134 cm, private collection. Photo © Sotheby's, London (Lokeren de Vuyst, January 22, 1986, lot. no. 391).

72. For more on this genre, see Kettering 1983.

73. John L. Thompson communication to author, February 7, 2001. The Christian fascination with rabbinical exegeses, particularly those of Rashi (1040–96) and Nicholas of Lyra (fourteenth century) begins in the later Middle Ages (Thompson 2001, 57, 64, 96–97).

74. Ca. 1680s, signed on the lower right "Pv Dijk," oil on copper, 40 x 50 cm, Louvre, Paris (image from RKD, The Hague).

75. Willem van Mieris, *The Expulsion of Hagar*, signed and dated 1724, canvas, 44 x 35.5 cm, collection of The Hermitage, St. Petersburg (see Hamann 1936, fig. 152).

CHAPTER SIX

✝

Saving Hagar and Ishmael

THE WILDERNESS RESCUE
(GEN 21:15–19)

The majority of Dutch wilderness-rescue paintings depict the moment when the angel appears, pointing out the water well to the distraught mother and her child dying of thirst. What was the significance of this for Netherlanders? Seventeenth-century Dutch literature tended to interpret the rescue of mother and son as evidence of God's benevolence, mercy, and grace: despite their bad behavior, God offers the errant, outcast maidservant and her son consolation (*troost*), redemption, and salvation. Sermons, Christian conduct books, and prayer books encouraged Netherlanders to turn to God in bad times, just as Hagar did. When it came to Gen 21, Hagar and Ishmael were even seen as exemplars of penitence. Calvin's harsh view—that the ungrateful reprobates were saved despite their unworthiness—was not adopted.

In Dutch paintings of the wilderness-rescue scene, similar chords of mercy, contrition, and salvation are struck. Like their literary counterparts, the pictorial Hagar and Ishmael are depicted as highly sympathetic types; Hagar is shown seated or often kneeling in the classic pose of the penitent, sometimes with hands folded in prayer.

Previously, scholars thought that the wilderness-rescue theme was favored by the Italians and was of less significance to the Dutch; one survey counted thirty extant Italian works from various regions.[1] However, it appears that Netherlanders were just as touched by the angelic rescue as the Italians, arguably, more so. Nearly forty paintings by Dutch artists survive.

The Dutch wilderness-rescue episode pivoted on four brief biblical verses (Gen 21:15–19, KJV):

And the water was spent in the bottle, and [Hagar] cast the child under one of the shrubs. And she went, and sat her down over against him a good way off, as it were a bowshot for she said, Let me not see the death of the child. And she sat over against him, and lift up her voice, and wept. And God heard the voice of the lad; and the angel of God called to Hagar out of heaven and said to her, What aileth thee, Hagar? fear not; for God hath heard the voice of the lad where he is. Arise, lift up the lad, and hold him in thine hand; for I will make him a great nation. And God opened her eyes, and she saw a well of water; and she went, and filled the bottle with water, and gave the lad drink.

Following this, two short verses conclude the story of Hagar and Ishmael, telling us that God is with Ishmael as he grows up in the wilderness; Ishmael becomes an expert bowman; and Hagar finds a wife for him from her native Egypt (Gen 21:20–21).

It may be that the Dutch predilection for landscapes accounts for the appeal of this episode in Dutch painting, as is already evident in early bible illustrations.[2] Van de Waal posited that the episode naturally lent itself to pastoral scenes, which might account for its popularity, since there "certainly did not seem to be any theological basis" for Dutch interest in the pictorial theme.[3] However, as this chapter clarifies, the wilderness-rescue paintings were popular for several reasons—primarily for theological notions of contrition and redemption—paralleling literary attitudes.

Seventeenth-Century Images

The painted angelic rescue of Hagar and Ishmael first becomes popular in the early seventeenth century in the Netherlands. Painters began to place the rescue in an Italian landscape, influenced by Adam Elsheimer, Maarten van Heemskerck, and Italian art. To mirror the world of ancient Israel, Dutch artists typically chose exotic Italian plants or mountains, incorporating antique or baroque architecture to add drama and a touch of fantasy.[4] Biblical figures often wear antique or oriental costumes, lending historicity. Sometimes artists created landscape "hybrids" comprised of both Italianate features and bosky elements from the Dutch national landscape,[5] as the "pre-Rembrandtist" Jacob Pynas did in an early work dated 1620 or 1626.[6] This is the moment when the angel points out the water

well to Hagar; her hands are clasped, as if in obeisance, prayer, or gratitude. The angel has arrived just in the nick of time: the tiny figure of a
dying Ishmael is placed at some distance, as the Bible tells us, beneath a
tree in the left mid-ground.

However, only a handful of seventeenth-century paintings emphasize
landscape. The majority of scenes concentrate on Hagar and the angel, as
we shall see, most notably in Pieter Lastman's *Hagar and the Angel*, dated
1614 (fig. 34).[7] Lastman's work sets the standard for most compositions
that follow.

The exchange between Hagar and the angel is the focus here. Lastman styled a plaintive, exhausted Hagar, her arms outstretched; her position echoes that of the unconscious Ishmael lying farther back in the
lower left picture plane. Depicted in motion, the angel counterbalances
Hagar's pose, surging toward the viewer. The foreshortening of his ener-
getic body contrasts with Hagar's beleaguered form.[8] In the right foreground, a single flower blooms near the overturned, empty water vessel

FIG. 34: Pieter Lastman. *Hagar and the Angel*, 1614. Oil on panel, 20 x 26⁷/₈ in.
(50.8 x 68.3 cm), M.85.117. Los Angeles County Museum of Art, purchased
with funds provided by the Ahmanson Foundation, Mr. and Mrs. Stewart Resnick,
Anna Bing Arnold, Dr. Armand Hammer, and Edward Carter in honor of Kenneth Donahue. Photo © 2005 by Museum Associates/LACMA.

and, above it, a burgeoning vine with fruit glistens with dewdrops, miraculous elements in this otherwise arid landscape. These may be a sign of the water well nearby.[9]

The angel points in two directions simultaneously. With one muscular arm, he reaches out to indicate the water well. However, his right hand points to the heavens, to indicate the celestial source behind this miracle. The image thus becomes a visual reminder of God's saving grace,[10] a reminder of the divine source of sustenance or mercy.[11] In fact, a number of angels in the Dutch wilderness-rescue paintings use one hand—the index finger is often specified—to point heavenward. The gesture appears to be distinctively Dutch: Italian wilderness-rescue scenes do not incorporate it.[12] Most Italian angels usually gesture with one hand directed downward at Ishmael and the other off to the side, as illustrated by a lovely mid-century painting by the Italian artist Francesco Cozza, to indicate the water well nearby.[13] Thus, a number of Dutch wilderness-rescue scenes portray the angel in a manner that simultaneously pays tribute to the glory of God. This has its parallels in Dutch Christian literature, as we have seen: Reformers and moralists chiefly drew on the episode to speak of God's benevolence and mercy or recognized the moment as a divine act of charity.

Mortals Encountering Angels

Clearly, the Dutch had a penchant for paintings of angelic visitations, so characteristic of baroque art. The wilderness-rescue scene belongs to this trend, which helps to account for its appeal at least in part.[14] Angels appear in countless extant depictions of Tobias, Abraham, Lot, or Elijah, among others.[15]

In Gen 21, there is no mention of an angelic visitation and no dialog between the angel and Hagar: the Bible says only that the angel calls to Hagar from a remote distance, presumably from the heavens. And Hagar does not speak in return.[16] The Bible tells us that Hagar "lift[ed] up her voice, and wept" (Gen 21:16). And it is not necessarily Hagar's cry that God responds to, but Ishmael's: the text says only "God heard the voice of the lad" (Gen 21:16–17). This scriptural wrinkle raised questions among early commentators, as it does today; perhaps this was the result of careless editing of the original text or may reflect, as feminist interpreters suggest, the embedded patriarchy of the narrator. Nevertheless, traditional Christian depictions of this scene, both Italian and Dutch, depart from scripture to graphically realize an instance of physical exchange between the angel and Hagar. In both Christian literature and art, then, scripture is glossed so that the episode can serve as a reassurance of divine mercy and reinforce notions of penitence and salvation.

A bible print of the wilderness-rescue scene from a 1670s Dutch publication *Icones Biblicae praecipuas sacrae Scripturae historias eleganter et graphice repraesentantes* (Biblical Images Showing the Principal Stories of Holy Scripture, Handsomely and Perfectly Wrought) confirms this reading (fig. 35).[17] In the foreground, Hagar sits under a tree, while the angel gestures toward a source of water. Ishmael languishes nearby, the empty water vessel beside him. Hagar's hands are piously clasped together. The same image appeared in several publications of bible prints during the seventeenth century, offering the same or similar inscriptions that emphasize the comfort the angel brings. In one instance, an inscription beneath the image reads: HAGAR, IN THE UTMOST DIFFICULTY, IS SUCCORED BY THE ANGEL.[18] In another instance, a verse from I Tim 4:10 was added: GOD IS THE SAVIOR OF ALL MEN.[19]

FIG. 35: **Matthaeus Merian.** *Hagar's Rescue*, **in** *Icones biblicae praecipuas Sacrae Scripturae historias eleganter et graphice repraesentantes. Biblische Figuren etc. mit Versen und Reymen in dreyen Sprachen.* **Strassburg: Zetzner, 1625, vol. I; 1627, vol. 2; 1630, vol. 3; 1629, vol. 4.**

In the 1654 *De Grooten Emblem Sacrae* (The Great Sacred Emblems), a collection of bible illustrations accompanied by didactic text, the author explains the significance of the wilderness-rescue scene, including a reprint of the 1588 etching by Peter van der Borcht.[20] The image, titled *Relief That Comforts*, shows the servant girl (*dienstmaeght*) weeping beneath a tree. Ishmael lies nearby. Her hands clasped piously, she turns to discover the angel behind her. She weeps, the text explains, because she has been thrown out of God's "house" for her worldly behavior. She becomes a symbol of penitence and redemption: Hagar reminds us, the author says, to set aside worldly interests and concentrate on the spiritual, through proper "service" (*doende onse dienst*) to God for the sake of honor and "reward" (salvation).[21]

Thus, Dutch artists, like Dutch authors, used the wilderness-rescue scene to give shape to a merciful force that encouraged penitence and offered comfort, protection, and salvation in times of crisis.

Hagar as a Model Penitent

A few paintings appear to emphasize Hagar as a model penitent, and exclude the angel altogether. These surface in the last quarter of the century, probably reflecting the growing influence of critical biblical commentary and the development of Enlightenment thought, when popular belief in angels diminished.[22] Willem van Mieris shows a sympathetic Hagar kneeling with hands folded in prayer in a painting dated 1686.[23] The composition now centers on Hagar's votive act.

A unique composition by the little-known Amsterdam painter Johannes Voorhout of 1700 also forgoes the traditional angel (fig. 36).[24] The figures of Hagar and a boyish Ishmael dominate here, shown in classical garb and kneeling, and placed on a stone ledge. Ishmael reaches for Hagar; Hagar's arms reach up toward a tumultuous sky, palms upturned. Together, their intertwined forms create a spiral that leads the eye up into the sky. Just as Ishmael seems to seek the comfort of his mother, so Hagar appears to reach toward the heavens above. To the left, a small, broken vase depends on a large, erect monument for support, loosely echoing the positions of mother and child. In the distance, a shepherd herds a flock of sheep up the hilltop. In the sky, swirling clouds and feathered treetops lend a mystical quality. The sun appears to be setting on the horizon.[25]

What moment is depicted here? Is Hagar appealing to the heavens for help?[26] In the biblical text, she cries out after she has placed the dying Ish-

FIG. 36: Johannes Voorhout. *Hagar and Ishmael in the Wilderness*, ca. 1700, signed by the artist. Canvas, 112 x 84 cm. Collectie Centraal Museum, Utrecht. Photo © Centraal Museum, Utrecht.

mael away at the distance of a bow's shot. But Hagar does not look grief-stricken: does this painting imagine the moment she is brought to repentance? Or is it the moment after the pair have been saved, Ishmael has been revived, and an enlightened Hagar kneels in thankful obeisance for their salvation? The surreal sky and setting sun suggest that the divine force has just receded.

Regardless of the moment, Hagar takes on a monumentality here, underscored by the stone slab that supports the outcast mother and son; here too, the subject matter focuses on Hagar's votive act rather than on the moment of rescue. The formerly rebellious Hagar is now shown as reliant on the divine. Without the angel, Voorhout presents Hagar as a classical model of penitence.

Hagar and Dutch Notions of Divine Charity (Mercy) and Maternity

The suffering that this mother of a dying son undergoes lent Hagar some pathos and a certain heroism in this moment, as Reformation exegeses and Dutch Christian literature shows. As Kattenburch said in his sermon, this mother would have willingly given her own life, if only Ishmael could live.[27] He even compares Hagar's love for Ishmael to God's love for man. Here too, Hagar is admired for her restraint and perseverance, as she was in sixteenth-century Protestant literature: even in dire straits, she does not blame or curse Abraham and Sarah.[28] In art, as in literature, certain works suggest that Hagar's maternal devotion in the face of adversity came to be admired.

The picture of a desperate Hagar and her dying child was the epitome of hardship. Thus, on one level, these images belong to the vast iconography featuring mothers and children as symbols of charity and mercy, or alternatively, as symbolic victims of cruel fates. One of the many examples is Cesare Ripa's allegorical figure of "Misery" in *Iconologia*, represented by a woman of "dismal and gloomy countenance" with a child "languishing for want of food."[29] In pictures, then, Hagar and Ishmael become the classic social victims.

Traditionally, artists preferred to paint Ishmael as a small child or toddler in the wilderness scenes, despite his age in the Bible: Ishmael is thirteen years old or more when he is banished, by seventeenth-century standards verging on adulthood, the age of a first apprenticeship. One contemporary raised his age to eighteen at the time of the expulsion, but he is very rarely shown as a full-grown boy.[30] By depicting Hagar with a small child, artists enhanced the drama of the rescue, emphasizing the pair's vulnerability and securing greater compassion from the viewer.

In seventeenth-century Italy and France, the rescue of Hagar and a young Ishmael in the wilderness was directly associated with the concept of charity in at least two pictorial instances. In Treviso, in the Monte di Pieta, a painted frieze in the Capella dei Rettori dated 1598 and attributed to the Flemish artist Lodewijck Toeput (also known as Pozzoserrato) pairs scenes from the Bible of man's acts of charity for his fellowman with God's acts of mercy for mankind: the good Samaritan is depicted opposite a portrayal of Hagar in the wilderness.[31] A mid-seventeenth-century print by the French artist J. Valdor II, *Hagar in the Wilderness*, was dedicated, according to the French caption underneath, to Magdalena Fabry, the wife of the French chancellor Pierre Séguier, in recognition for her great charity on behalf of the poor and needy. Here, the theme of Hagar in the wilderness was chosen to convey the motif of mercifulness or charity.[32]

Netherlanders developed a special regard for women and children, traditionally the most vulnerable sector of society, if Dutch painting is any indication. Wilderness-rescue paintings were among the many images of acts of charity, divine or otherwise, on behalf of suffering mothers and children in the Dutch Republic: an abundant number of Regent portraits and genre paintings show needy mothers with children receiving charity, emblematic of the social impetus to help the poor.[33] Indeed, performing charitable acts and good works, particularly on behalf of those most disadvantaged, reflected Calvinist beliefs and was part of the national consciousness.[34] Republican ideals promoted the protection and safeguard of widows, orphans, and *arme vreemdelingen* (poor foreigners), and this was not just rhetoric. In Amsterdam, for example, a remarkable number of Dutch charitable civic institutions were already in place and justly famous by the early seventeenth century. Charities included orphanages, homes for the aged, and poor houses. One institution provided relief specifically for women and children (*Huyssitene-armen* or "housebound poor") who could not support themselves because of "bad times and other miseries," according to a Dutch historian writing in 1614.[35] Estimated at six thousand cases in 1611, many of those admitted were foreigners, supposedly "without distinction of religion." There were several hospitals (*gasthuizen*): the main hospital comprised two hundred beds, divided equally into one section for men and the other for women; there was a veteran's hospital for sick, wounded, or dying soldiers; the leper house; and an insane asylum.

During the winter, hospitals offered "a free walk-in clinic (*Den Beyert*), where eligible poor people and travelers could receive shelter for up to three days."[36] Most remarkable among these civic institutions was the famous "Rasphuis," a reformatory prison for male offenders, and a similar, smaller correctional prison for women known as the "Spinhuis." The Spinhuis reportedly included a rehabilitation program aimed at teaching female inmates—thieves, drunks, runaways, beggars, the homeless, prostitutes—domestic skills such as spinning, sewing, or knitting. Innovative policies such as these reflected the Dutch realization that economic and social turmoil was linked, to some degree, with crime, remarkable at a time when standard European law prescribed brutal punishments.[37]

KAREL DU JARDIN'S PAINTING OF 1662

With this in mind, we may better consider Karel du Jardin's unusual wilderness-rescue scene, painted about 1662 (fig. 37).[38] Although no direct influence has been identified, it was painted within the context of the classicizing trends in Amsterdam. It shows Italian influences and is characteristic of du Jardin's mature history works. For reasons of style and scale (187.1 by 142 cm), it is closely connected with another of du Jardin's monumental paintings, *Conversion of Saul*, dated 1662.[39]

Most rescue paintings depict the moment in the narrative when the angel first appears to Hagar and points out the water well. Du Jardin's painting represents the moment after Hagar and Ishmael have been rescued and Hagar has filled a vessel of water for Ishmael (Gen 21:19). From the upper left, a raking light bathes the figures in a sacred glow. Hagar is kneeling, chastened and humbled, in the classic posture of prayer or repentance.[40] She proffers drink to her son and looks gratefully in the direction of the light source. The angel points with one hand to the fountain and, with the other, toward the heavenly light. The narrative moment appears to be unique in Dutch painting, as Kilian notes, but not in Dutch prints. A sixteenth-century visual precedent is suggested in the last scene from Willem Willemsz Thibaut's 1563 series of four etchings.[41] Hagar and Ishmael are shown at the well, the moment after the angelic rescue. Hagar offers Ishmael a drink from a vessel. The Latin inscription beneath Thibaut's etching reads, THENCE THE AFFECTIONATE, KIND MOTHER, WHO IS DUTIFUL [religious], REVIVES HER NURSLING, FAINT FROM THIRST WITH WATER, DIVINELY REVEALED, FROM THE RUNNING SPRING.[42]

FIG. 37: Karel du Jardin. *Hagar and Ishmael in the Wilderness*, ca. 1662. Oil on canvas, 73³/4 x 56¹/4 in, SN 270. Bequest of John Ringling, Collection of the John and Mable Ringling Museum of Art, State Art Museum of Florida, Florida State University.

Du Jardin's wilderness-rescue work and the *Conversion of Saul*, too large to have been painted for the open market, point to thematic concerns—mercy, repentance, and conversion, respectively—suited to public institutions.[43] Moreover, Hagar is wearing on her shoulder the colors of reddish orange, white, and blue, the same colors and descending order as the national flag of the United Provinces. Did Hagar and Ishmael symbolize an aspect of statehood in some capacity in a picture large enough for public space? Ishmael drinking from the vessel with a small cherub at his elbow can be read as an act of mercy, the administering of drink to the thirsty. The beautiful mother and child are idealized types. The nearly life-sized Hagar is shown here as a nurturing, maternal ideal, not unlike those dutiful mothers so beloved in Dutch genre painting.[44]

Could du Jardin's nourishing image have been used to reinforce the idea of divine mercy (or charity) and penitence? Perhaps this painting was done for one of Amsterdam's charitable institutions like those that cared for the *Huyssitene-armen* (the housebound poor) or for a women's reformatory such as the Spinhuis. Du Jardin had previously secured institutional commissions, the Spinhuis among them.[45] Furthermore, the depiction of mother and child—rendered with distinctive dark hair and complexions perhaps not typically Netherlandish, and sharply contrasted with the light-haired celestials—is noteworthy. In addition to touching on concepts of divine mercy (or charity), penitence, and salvation, might this image also connote conversion?

Hagar as an Erotic Concubine in Peril

An interest in an erotic Hagar increases in Dutch paintings during the last quarter of the century, as we have seen in other episodes from Hagar's story. Not surprisingly, the wilderness rescue mirrors these developments. Several Dutch compositions foreground young, alluring Hagars in central, suggestive poses, sometimes wearing luxurious gowns. Bared arms and legs or low-cut necklines make her sensuality explicit. Awkward works by Jan Andreas Lievens[46] and an artist from the circle of Barent Graat the elder[47] show an elegantly attired Hagar laid out in the manner of a reclining Italian erotic female. Clearly, there was some demand for a penitent, erotic Hagar in distress.[48]

The painter Gérard de Lairesse's interpretation, dated ca. 1675, is characteristic of the refined, classical elegance he became admired for among Amsterdam's wealthy in the last quarter of the century (fig. 38).[49] The fig-

FIG. 38: Gerard de Lairesse. *Hagar in the Wilderness*, ca. 1675–80, signed at the right "G. Lairesse f." Oil on canvas, 74 x 60 cm, inv. no. GE-622. The State Hermitage Museum, St. Petersburg.

ures of Hagar and the angel are framed by the large tree trunk and mountain range in the background. A dying Ishmael lies further back in the picture plane. The angel and Hagar are posed in a highly refined, classical manner, accentuated by their elegant garb. Hagar's theatrical gesture of weeping suggests that this must be the moment before Hagar first sees the angel. Hagar's profile and hair is Greco-Roman. The angel's delicate, fluttering raiment enhances her graceful pose. Does Hagar's bared right breast indicate she has the capacity to suckle Ishmael and nourish a future race? Nevertheless, the bared breast aligns Hagar with other biblical females shown in this manner, such as Bathsheba, Mary Magdalena, or the Virgin Mary.

In Herman van der Myn's painting, dated 1718, Hagar has been transformed into an antique goddess, with one breast bared (fig. 39).[50] She is dressed in velvet and silk, sitting on a stone bench, looking up at an angel who calls to her from some distance above. The overturned water vessel

FIG. 39: Herman van der Myn. *Hagar in the Desert*, signed and dated "H. Van Der Myn 1718." Oak panel, 47.5 x 38.5 cm, inv. no. 212. Collection of the Budapest Museum of Fine Arts. Photo © The Budapest Museum of Fine Arts.

identifies this as Gen 21; Hagar's tears express her fear and grief. Van der Myn is painting in a refined "French academic" style, while incorporating the realistic rendering of cloth and details of plant life.[51] Hagar occupies most of the canvas. The once heroic angel has been reduced here to a small wood nymph, only a small light source glows behind him to indicate the divine, and the dying child has been omitted altogether. What we are left with is an abandoned woman in the wilderness and all the connotations implied: notions of female sexuality, powerlessness, and victimhood are linked. The bared breast, elongated neck, and loosened sandal ensure her erotic appeal.

Nevertheless, van der Myn incorporates traditional symbols to convey meaning. The blooming poppy, symbol of death, stands for the life-threatening ordeal that tests Hagar. Above her head, the fig leaf is an old symbol of suffering (in the Middle Ages, this was often an attribute associated with the Virgin Mary) and, on the right, the oak leaf and tree trunk are, in traditional emblems, symbols of strength, stamina, or constancy.[52] Despite the erotic tone of the painting, these motifs remain compatible with notions we encountered in seventeenth-century Dutch Christian literature.

Notes

1. Offerhaus 1962, 7n9.
2. C. Tümpel 1991, 180.
3. Van de Waal 1974, 91.
4. C. Tümpel 1991, 52.
5. A. Tümpel 1991, 17.
6. Jacob Pynas, *Hagar in the Wilderness*, ca. 1620 or 1626, copper, 34.5 x 49 cm; private collection, Paris (see ibid., 24, fig. 8).
7. Signed and dated on rock: 1614, 51 x 68 cm, Los Angeles County Museum of Art (image from Consibee, Levkoff, and Rand 1991, 37). See also C. Tümpel 1980, 48.
8. Conisbee, Levkoff, and Rand 1991, 37.
9. Ibid.
10. Ibid., 146.
11. In this sense, the Dutch gesture may reflect Protestant thought and values: painting should express, as Luther demanded, "the interconnection between mankind's poverty, insignificance, and unworthiness, and God's magnanimity, goodness, and mercy" (C. Tümpel 1980, 48). Luther's theological approach, at

the core of Reformation thought, is rooted in the belief that a great distance separates God from his subjects. As a consequence of the fall, sinful mankind could never bridge this gap. Only through divine mercy could a connection between God and man be achieved, and only through this connection could man be saved (Mijnhardt and Kloek 2001, 68).

12. There may be one exception: Bernardo Strozzi's *Hagar and the Angel* (Seattle Art Museum, Kress Collection). The vertical composition may be unique: the two figures and a vessel are placed in extreme close-up, perhaps why the artist includes the upward gesture. Ishmael has been left off. Strozzi's works show influences of northern artists.

13. Signed and dated "Francus Cozza Pint 1665," canvas, 72 x 97 cm, Rijksmuseum, Amsterdam (image from the archives of the Warburg Institute, London).

14. C. Tümpel 1991, 236.

15. Blankert notes that many artists in Rembrandt's circle depicted themes where angels and humans interact. He posited that such scenes are about the "brief moment of reversal from one extreme of emotion to the other," serenity turning into fear, despair and grief into hope. This idea surfaced in seventeenth-century Dutch literary theory, based on the Aristotelian concept known as *peripeteia* in ancient Greek tragedy. It is thought that history paintings were highly appreciated "because [they] offered the painter an opportunity . . ." as the Dutch playwright Joost van den Vondel put it, to portray ". . . the affects, passions, desires and suffering of mankind" (Blankert 1982, 34–35).

16. Trible 1984, 24–25. However, in contrast, Gen 16 tells us that the angel does appear to Hagar beside the well at Beersheeba, where she has fled.

17. Matthaeus Merian, *Hagar's Rescue*, in *Icones biblicae praecipuas Sacrae Scripturae historias eleganter et graphice repraesentantes. Biblische Figuren etc. mit Versen und Reymen in dreyen Sprachen* (Strassburg: Zetzner, 1625 [vol. 1], 1627 [vol. 2], 1630 [vol. 3], 1629 [vol. 4]).

18. P. Hendricksz Schut, engraving, after Merian's design, for *Toneel ofte Vertooch der bybelsche historien* (Amsterdam: N. Visser, 1659), fig. 15. "Ager sÿnde in de uyterste ongelegenheyt wert van den Engel getroost. Genesis. 21.17."

19. See, for example, p. 41 in *Icones biblicae praecipuas Sacrae Scripturae historias eleganter & graphice representantes* (Amsterdam: D. Danckertsz, Reyer Anslo, M. Merian): "Hagar wort van den Engel getroost." In Johannes Vollenhove's *Afbeeldingen van de heilige historien des Ouden- en Nieuwen Testament* (Amsterdam: N. Visscher, post-1659), p. 15, the same Merian image appears with an additional caption: "Godt is een behouder van alle menschen" (1 Tim 4:10).

20. Included in J. P. Schabaelje's *De Grooten Emblem Sacrae*, 1654 (Royal Library, The Hague), 4, no. 29. The title in Latin is "Solatium refocillans," GEN. XXI. VERSE 15.

21. "Het welck ons tot een voorbeelt geschiet is, dat wy oock in ons selven gewaer sullen worden, hoe dat wy om onse eygenschaps wille uyt den vryen Wesen Gods gestooten worden, . . . daerom blijft den selven dienst in 't Huys Godts . . ." (Schabaelje 1654, 4, no. 29).

22. Christian Tümpel, communication with author, May 17, 2005. See also A. Tümpel and C. Tümpel 1974, 36–37, 143, 147.

23. *Hagar in the Wilderness* canvas, 28 x 36 cm, private collection, Stockholm (image from RKD, The Hague).

24. Signed by the artist, ca. 1700, canvas, 112 x 84 cm, Centraal Museum, Utrecht (image from RKD, The Hague). See also A. D. de Vries and Bredius 1885, 92–93; Centraal Museum, Utrecht, cat. 1952, 460.

25. Centraal Museum, Utrecht, cat. 1952, 460.

26. Ibid.

27. Kattenburch 1701, 1717, 1737, 240. ". . . zo zyn ook de tranen en het geroep van Hagar, in God's ooren en oogen, als die Ismaël zelf gestort hadde: willig zouw zig ook die moeder in de dood gegeven hebben, als maar Ismaël mogt leven" ("So are also the tears and the crying of Hagar, in God's ears and eyes, as disturbing as those Ishmael himself had made: willingly would the mother have given her own life, if only Ishmael might live.")

28. Kattenburch 1737, 239. "[Hagar] word met geen beklag tegens Abraham of Sara ingevoert . . ." ("Hagar is not presented as railing against Abraham or Sarah . . .")

29. From Ripa's *Iconologia*, 1593, 1779, 1979, 2:154.

30. Ainsworth 1621, Q3 recto. Published in Amsterdam, where Ainsworth, a refugee from England, lived.

31. Dated 1598. Offerhaus 1962, 12–13. Image from the archives of the Warburg Institute, University of London. Next to Hagar, a scene of the poor man and the rich Lazarus appears, followed by a scene of Elijah being fed by the ravens.

32. Offerhaus 1962, 12–13. Séguier, who became chancellor in 1635, was one of the founders of the Académie Française. Offerhaus identifies the print as follows: "een vroegere staat van deze prent is voorzien van het jaartal 1644. De prent is gemaakt door J. Valdor II (zie L. Lebeer, Bibliographie Nationale . . . de Belgique, t. 26, col. 64)."

33. Muller 1985, 97.

34. For more on the Dutch mentality and civic institutions, see J. T. Sellin 1944.

35. P. R. Sellin 1988, 208–9n63: Sellin is quoting from Johannis Pontanus's contemporary description of the city: *Historische beschrijvinghe der seer wijt beroemde Coopstadt Amsterdam*, trans. P. Montanus (Amsterdam: Jodocum Hondium, 1614).

36. P. R. Sellin 1988, 208–9n63.

37. Ibid., 209n63.

38. *Hagar and Ishmael in the Wilderness*, ca. 1662, signed on a fragment of the cornice, lower left: "K Du Jardin fe," canvas, 187.1 x 141.9 cm, John and Mable Ringling Museum, Sarasota, Florida (image from Blankert 1980, plate 64).

39. 186.5 by 134.5 cm, National Gallery, London (image reproduced in Kilian 2005, vol. 2, plate 82).

40. From Ripa's *Iconologia*, 1593, 1779, 1979, 2:154.

41. Willem Willemsz Thibaut, *The Story of Hagar and Ishmael*, dated 1563 (date altered to 1580, added in the second state at lower right), ca. 20.5 x 23.8 cm, nos. 1–4, Rijksprentenkabinet, Rijksmuseum, Amsterdam (image from Hollstein 1949, 30:215–17).

42. P. R. Sellin translation. The Latin text reads "Languentem inde ʃiti recreat pia mater alumnia Irrigui ʃontis monstrata calitus Unda. 4."

43. Kilian 1993, 1:52, 108. *Conversion of Saul* may have been commissioned by the Orveille family, since it was included in the sale of their possessions in 1705.

44. See, for example, the painting attributed to the Haarlem classicist painter Reyer Jacobsz van Blommendael, active in the guild there between 1662 and 1675. Bloch 1940, 57:17–18, fig. 6. A mother offers her son milk using a remarkably similar pose and vessel.

45. Du Jardin also painted a portrait of the regents of the Spinhuis in the 1660s (Kilian 1996, 9:380).

46. Jan Andreas Lievens, *The Angel Shows Hagar the Well*, canvas, 83 x 163 cm, private collection, Amsterdam (Iconoclass/D.I.A.L. inv. no. 71C26.7; or Sumowski 1983, 3, 1770, 1773).

47. *The Angel Shows Hagar the Well*, canvas, 105 x 137 cm (image from RKD, The Hague).

48. See also the central Hagar figure in Nicolas Verkolje's painting signed and dated on lower left, 1695, 55 x 45 cm, private collection? (image in RKD, The Hague).

49. Gerard de Lairesse, *Hagar in the Wilderness*, ca. 1675–80, signed at the right "G. Lairesse f," oil on canvas, 74 x 60 cm, inv. no. GE-622, State Hermitage Museum, St. Petersburg.

50. Herman van der Myn, *Hagar in the Wilderness*, signed and dated "H. Van Der Myn 1718," oak panel, 47.5 x 38.5 cm, inv. no. 212, collection of the Budapest Museum of Fine Arts. Photo © The Budapest Museum of Fine Arts.

51. Although the Amsterdam-born artist spent most of his career in France and England painting commissions, there is evidence that he was in the Netherlands around the time that this work was painted (Ember 1987, 100–101).

52. Ibid.

✝

Summary and Conclusion

Literature

Developing a literary framework of the story of Hagar and Ishmael in Dutch literature clarifies its peculiar significance in Dutch thought, provides a sound cultural context for the paintings, and enables us to detect literary and visual parallels.

The theological implications of Hagar's story evolved until, in the sixteenth century, a change of heart toward the rebel mother and son took place, as traditional Pauline attitudes began to give way to more sympathetic, heartfelt responses toward the outcasts and their plight. In addition, some commentators tapped into the story for didactic purposes, specifically to reinforce good household management and proper conduct among its members.

In seventeenth-century Dutch literature, Hagar's story was used, more or less, in three different ways: theologically, allegorically, and also as a practical homily on domestic life. Certainly, the Pauline allegory persists in seventeenth-century Dutch thought. On a traditional theological level, the story, the expulsion episode in particular, reenacted this biblical-historical moment of division, and for many Netherlanders could mark the emergence of a purified faith, a redemptive covenant, or a reformed "church." The Dutch explicitly relied on the familiar Pauline allegory as a polemical tool, as some literature and inscriptions on bible prints showed. The expulsion episode could simply be used to promulgate greater adherence to the faith, but it could also be appropriated to assert religious or political superiority, or epitomize the Republic's struggle for independence. On a fundamental level, then, many Dutch viewers would have been familiar with the traditional Pauline associations and teachings when viewing illustrations of Hagar's story, the expulsion episode in particular.

For the Dutch, the Pauline allegory did not always suffice in troubled times: other explanations and contemporary analogies were needed to make sense of the complex ancient story. When push came to shove, the Dutch could simply not abandon Hagar and Ishmael to fend for themselves but sympathized with the biblical exiles' plight and despair. Thus, Dutch literature developed a curiously ambivalent attitude toward Hagar and her story: at times, she is portrayed as the archetypal reprobate, at other times, as sympathetic victim, occasionally as both. Certainly, some Dutch Christian literature relied on the familiar Pauline allegory, but many other authors talked about Hagar's story in remarkably sympathetic terms, particularly when it came to the wilderness-rescue episode, portraying the repentant maidservant as an exemplar of contrition and Christian "perseverance," or a model of maternity in the face of hardship.

Clearly, the story was used to appeal to the heart, as the minister Kattenburch showed us: the human emotions of jealousy, pride, loss, sorrow, and fear are all reflected in the twists and turns of the plot. But, fortunately, the story also illustrated, as Kattenburch and others explained, that sin and suffering may be followed by contrition, solace, and the wellspring of salvation divinely revealed. For the Dutch, the miraculous rescue of the undeserving Hagar and Ishmael was as much a question of grace and mercy as it was of faith.

A surprising number of Dutch writers used the story, the runaway Hagar and expulsion episodes in particular, as a domestic homily to reinforce the virtues of humility, obedience, diligence, and contrition in the Dutch Christian household and family life. From the biblical tragedy, valuable teachings were culled—specifically intended for masters and servants, husbands and wives, parents and children, siblings and stepsiblings, and young, marriageable women—to warn against disturbing family harmony. This particular usage of the story may reveal what mattered to the Dutch most and, perhaps, lay at the heart of the fledgling Republic's survival and success: the maintenance of order and harmony in domestic life meant, in turn, the well-being of the "family" of the beleaguered seven United Provinces as a whole. In fact, as we have suggested, the biblical story of the formerly rebellious maidservant who becomes a model of humility, obedience, and contrition appears to have been symbolic, on some level, of ideal Dutch civic order.

Aspects of Hagar's story were complex, troubling, and raised concerns, especially concerning the matter of Abraham's apparent polygamy. Many Dutch authors felt compelled to address this issue, reflecting a range of literary attitudes: some excused the patriarch; others condemned him. Criticism of Sarah's conduct was periodically voiced; in particular, she sometimes shouldered the blame for Abraham's apparent "polygamy."

Dutch Painting

These literary developments had implications for the iconography. This is especially true of the runaway Hagar (Gen 16) and wilderness-rescue scenes (Gen 21). In Gen 16, a sympathetic Hagar is often shown seated or kneeling before the angel, sometimes in the classic pose of the penitent with hands folded in prayer. As in the literature, the subject of the runaway maidservant, who begins recalcitrant then submits to the angel, was designed to remind Netherlanders of the Christian virtues of obedience, penitence, or humility.

Similarly, depictions of Gen 21, when the banished Hagar and Ishmael encounter the angel in the wilderness, were also devised to touch on themes of sin and redemption. These images visualized a divine, merciful force that relieved human sorrow and suffering, which must have brought viewers some comfort and assurances of salvation in uncertain times. Furthermore, the angelic rescue of the sinners encouraged contrition, obedience, and repentance: the formerly rebel maidservant was now humbled. In addition, the desperate mother with a small, dying child appealed to the compassion of the viewer as symbolic victims of misfortune. The moment depicted a divine act of charity. In some paintings, the grieving mother, distraught over her dying son, was an object of admiration as well as pity.

Thus, the Dutch paintings of the runaway Hagar and the wilderness-rescue scenes touched on the familiar patterns of sin and grace, faith and repentance. These themes lay at the core of the Protestant Reformation, but were equally cherished by Catholics.[1] As the painted and literary renditions of Gen 16 and 21 suggest, it appears that what the Dutch needed was a lowly, biblical model of human sin, suffering, and contrition, a non-apocryphal figure whose story of salvation defied the odds but was supported by scripture: the maidservant fit the bill.

As far as the runaway Hagar and wilderness-rescue scenes are concerned, the parallels between art and literature are relatively straightforward. With the expulsion episode, the matter is more complex. On the one hand, the expulsion imagery could readily have been associated with traditional Pauline teachings for many Christian viewers, as we have seen: the villainous Hagar and Ishmael must go. Theologically, the Dutch identified with the line leading from Abraham, Sarah, and Isaac. But, at the same time, they developed a curiously ambivalent attitude toward Hagar's story. This literary ambivalence meant that artists were freer to imagine the expulsion scene as a tender "farewell" rather than as a repudiation, and to construct a sympathetic, endearing Hagar. In fact, the shift in theological attitudes left the door wide open for Dutch artists to plumb the narrative for emotional riches and intensified drama. Maes, Fabritius, and Steen, among other artists, amplified the tragedy by envisioning a recalcitrant, comely, nubile Hagar, a compassionate, conflicted Abraham, a jealous, haggard Sarah, or a cupid-like Ishmael, to better pull on Dutch heartstrings.

In the literature, Hagar is an ambivalent figure—depicted in either positive or negative (traditional) terms, or both, depending on context. In early to mid-century Dutch painting, she is, in contrast, almost always portrayed as a sympathetic type. In fact, by mid-century a strange dichotomy was at work in the expulsion scenes: on the one hand, they reenact the repudiation of mother and son, faithful to the scriptural narrative. At the same time, they breathe human values and emotions into their protagonists to heighten the painfulness of the moment. The paintings, based on a specific scriptural passage, increasingly work against it by appealing to fundamental human emotions protesting this cruelty. The theological significance of the expulsion scene begins to dissolve.

Only a few expulsion scenes did not favor Hagar. In these instances, the banishment was adapted to reinforce the ideals of the Dutch Christian family and the sanctity of the household, made explicit by the inclusion of didactic symbolism. In both literature and painting, those episodes disapproving of Hagar speak to the maintenance of Christian virtues and the proper conduct of members of the family household. Hagar serves as a foil to others, as in Bloemaert's ideal: the beautiful, diligent, "good maidservant" is placed in the foreground, while a reprobate Hagar appears in the unfolding expulsion in the background. The remarkable expulsion painting by the unidentified pre-Rembrandtist artist also foregrounds Sarah and Isaac as models of the Christian family ideal; Hagar and Ishmael, seen negatively, are placed further back in the picture plane. Thus, in expulsion scenes with overt didactic functions, Hagar necessarily takes a backseat.

Hagar-themed paintings after mid-century, however, are governed by a different set of principles. In later expulsion scenes, Hagar assumes a centrality and a visual presence that simply isn't warranted by scripture. Religious meanings recede as Hagar's erotic appeal takes over. This held true for the majority of later renditions of Hagar's story. An increasing elegance and eroticism creeps into the portrayals of Hagar, particularly in the last quarter of the century. A nude or partially dressed Hagar brings erotic pathos to the fore, boosting the subject's appeal. In later wilderness-rescue scenes, for example, we are no longer looking at a biblical maternal crisis, but a sexualized female expressing an erotic form of suffering. Religious connotations seem to have vanished. In the last decades of the century, the religious subject degenerates into an erotic pabulum.

But even these later works remind us that Hagar simply cannot escape her traditional theological baggage—her vilification by Paul—and her unfortunate historical role as Abraham's rejected concubine. Ultimately, Hagar's "baggage" meant she could be transformed into an erotic figure,[2] which artists begin to realize in the second half of the century. In fact, Hagar's appeal in Dutch seventeenth-century art pivots around this notion of dual identity: villainess or victim? Is she wrong or wronged? Notions of female sexuality, villainy, and victimization could be intertwined and, in Hagar's case, made explicit.

Obviously, the presentation of Hagar scenes follow this pattern more or less. Appearing mostly after mid-century, these erotically charged pictures offered Dutch artists another opportunity to paint the nude. The works adopted compositional conventions taken from domestic genre painting to maximize appeal. Sarah's physical decrepitude and her "procuress" role became essential to the pictorial formula. The essentially elderly Abraham was sometimes shown as reluctant or passive, but he could also appear as eager, young, or aggressive. Hagar's persona ranged from coy and knowing to coerced or powerless. The appearance of these paintings coincided with a continental theological debate concerning Abraham's apparent polygamy. Did the ongoing discussions in print help fuel interest in the depiction of this episode or lend it a certain topicality? Some of the paintings found ways to incorporate a sense of wrongdoing. Netscher's version even turned the biblical episode into a parody of a brothel scene. Clearly, many of the presentation of Hagar paintings reflected—and exploited—recent theological and literary developments that challenged the traditional view of the episode and called Abraham's conduct into question.

The ambivalence found in both literature and painting suggests that, up through the mid-seventeenth century, the Dutch struggled to make historical sense of the outwardly cruel biblical story of a fractured family, so at odds with their own ideals. While Pauline allegory and Calvin renounced the outcasts in harsh terms, the Dutch had trouble doing so. In fact, in spirit and tone, certain authors took cues from the sympathetic Luther, among other forbears. Why? To do so was human. Moreover, authors realized that there was greater emotive potential in portraying a vilified but mistreated handmaiden than a stereotypical villainess.

Something analogous is also at work in Dutch painting, the expulsion scene in particular, which formed the core of this study. What does Hagar the victim and Abraham the reluctant tell us about Dutch society? These emotional pictures treat the fraught experiences of expulsion, exile, and family division with a remarkable tenderness and mournfulness. Moreover, the Dutch identified with the favored patriarch and the tarnished, powerless outcast simultaneously. This biblical moment was of particular significance to the war-torn northern Netherlanders: these "children of Israel" had sacrificed and suffered so much from the split of the Dutch national "family," the north from the south.

Up through the mid-seventeenth century, by which time most of the works appeared, what we are seeing in these paintings and in the expulsion scenes in particular is the intersection of literature, art, and human experience and the manner in which these forces work upon each other in the Dutch cultural sphere. Shaped by these special conditions and raised up by sympathetic literature, the pictorial maidservant becomes extremely attractive, enhanced with a new, peculiarly Dutch, sense of humanity. Hagar is thus rescued from her traditional "exile" of ignominy and neglect, at least as far as the Dutch Golden Age was concerned. Nowhere does Hagar claim greater interest or sympathy than she does in seventeenth-century Netherlandish painting.

Notes

1. Thompson 2001, 238.
2. I am grateful to Ruth Mellinkoff for sharing her findings in 2003 on Old Testament female figures in medieval art.

Hagar and Ishmael in Scripture
THE BIBLE TEXT FROM
GENESIS AND GALATIANS

The interpretation of Hagar's story in exegeses, literature, and art is based on two chapters of scripture from the Old Testament and on the Apostle Paul's allegorical reading of the story in his Epistle to the Galatians in the New Testament.

The passages cited below are from the King James Version of the Bible.

Genesis 16:1–16

Now Sarai Abram's wife bare him no children: and she had an handmaid, an Egyptian, whose name was Hagar. And Sarai said unto Abram, Behold now, the LORD hath restrained me from bearing: I pray thee, go in unto my maid: it may be that I may obtain children by her. And Abram hearkened to the voice of Sarai. And Sarai Abram's wife took Hagar her maid the Egyptian, after Abram had dwelt ten years in the land of Canaan, and gave her to her husband Abraham to be his wife. And he went in unto Hagar, and she conceived; and when she saw that she had conceived, her mistress was despised in her eyes. And Sarai said unto Abram, My wrong be upon thee: I have given my maid into thy bosom; and when she saw that she conceived, I was despised in her eyes: the LORD judge between me and thee. But Abram said unto Sarai, Behold, thy maid is in thy hand; do to her as it pleaseth thee. And when Sarai dealt hardly with her, she [Hagar] fled from her face. And the angel of the LORD found her by a fountain of water in the wilderness, by the fountain on the way to Shur. And he said, Hagar,

Sarai's maid, whence camest thou? and whither wilt thou go? And she said, I flee from the face of my mistress Sarai. And the angel of the LORD said unto her, Return to thy mistress, and submit thyself under her hands. And the angel of the LORD said unto her, I will multiply thy seed exceedingly, that it shall not be numbered for the multitude. And the angel of the LORD said unto her, Behold, thou art with child, and shall bear a son, and shalt call his name Ishmael; because the LORD hath heard thy affliction. And he will be a wild man; his hand will be against every man, and every man's hand against him; and he shall dwell in the presence of all his brethren. And she called the name of the LORD that spake unto her, Thou God seest me: for she said, Have I also here looked after him that seeth me? Wherefore the well was called Beerlahairoi; behold, it is between Kadesh and Bered. And Hagar bare Abram a son: and Abram called his son's name, which Hagar bare, Ishmael. And Abram was fourscore and six years old, when Hagar bare Ishmael to Abram.

Genesis 21:8–21

And the child [Isaac] grew, and was weaned: and Abraham made a great feast the same day that Isaac was weaned. And Sarah saw the son of Hagar the Egyptian, which she had born unto Abraham, mocking. Wherefore she said unto Abraham, Cast out this bondwoman and her son: for the son of the bondwoman shall not be heir with my son, even with Isaac. And the thing was very grievous in Abraham's sight because of his son. And God said unto Abraham, Let it not be grievous in thy sight because of the lad, and because of thy bondwoman; in all that Sarah hath said unto thee, hearken unto her voice; for in Isaac shall thy seed be called. And also of the son of the bondwoman will I make a nation, because he is thy seed. And Abraham rose up early in the morning, and took bread, and a bottle of water, and gave it unto Hagar, putting it on her shoulder, and the child, and sent her away: and she departed, and wandered in the wilderness of Beersheba. And the water was spent in the bottle, and she cast the child under one of the shrubs. And she went, and sat her down over against him a good way off, as it were a bow shot: for she said, Let me not see the death of the child. And she sat over against him, and lift up her voice, and wept. And God heard the voice of the lad; and the angel of God called to Hagar out of heaven, and said unto her, What aileth thee, Hagar? fear not; for God hath heard the voice of the lad where he is. Arise, lift up the lad, and hold him in thine hand; for I will make him a great nation. And God opened her eyes, and she saw a well of water; and she went, and filled the bottle with water, and gave the lad drink. And God was with the lad; and he grew, and dwelt in the wilderness, and became an archer. And he dwelt in the wilderness of Paran: and his mother took him a wife out of the land of Egypt.

Galatians 4:21–31

Tell me, ye that desire to be under the law, do ye not hear the law? For it is written, that Abraham had two sons, the one by a bondmaid, the other by a freewoman. But he who was of the bondwoman was born after the flesh; but he of the freewoman was by promise. Which things are an allegory; for these are the two covenants; the one from the mount Sinai, which gendereth to bondage, which is Agar. For this Agar is mount Sinai in Arabia, and answereth to Jerusalem which now is, and is in bondage with her children. But Jerusalem which is above is free, which is the mother of us all. For it is written, Rejoice, thou barren that bearest not; break froth and cry, thou that travailest not: for the desolate hath many more children than she which hath an husband. Now we, brethren, as Isaac was, are the children of promise. But as then he that was born after the flesh persecuted him that was born after the Spirit, even so it is now. Nevertheless, what saith the scripture? Cast out the bondwoman and her son: for the son of the bondwoman shall not be heir with the son of the freewoman. So then, brethren, we are not children of the bondwoman, but of the free.

Bibliography

Agrippa, Henricus Cornelius. 1529. *Declamation on the nobility and preeminence of the female sex.* Ed. and trans. A. Rabil Jr. Chicago: University of Chicago Press, 1996.

Ainsworth, Henry. 1621. *Annotations upon the first book of Moses called Genesis wherein the Hebrew words and sentences are compared with and explained with the ancient Greek and Chaldee versions, but chiefly, by conference with Holy Scriptures.* Amsterdam.

Aletheus, Theophilus (alias Johannes Lyser). 1682. *Polygamia Triumphatrix, id est Discursus politicus de Polygamia.* Amsterdam.

Arshagouni, Mary Ellen. 1988. *John Donne's "Devotions upon emergent occasions": A Puritan Reading.* Diss., University of California, Los Angeles: University of California.

Bader, Alfred. 1976. *The Bible through Dutch Eyes: From Genesis through the Apocrypha.* Milwaukee: Milwaukee Art Center.

Bange, Petty, et al. 1985. *Tussen heks en heilige: Het vrouwbeeld op de drempel van de moderne tijd, 15de/16de eeuw.* Uitgeverij Sun, Nijmegen: Nijmeegs Museum.

Bailey, Wilma Ann. 1994. Hagar: A model for an Anabaptist feminist? *The Mennonite Quarterly Review* 68, 5:219–28.

Bartrum, Giulia. 1995. *German Renaissance prints 1490–1550.* London: British Museum Press.

Bartsch, Adam von. (1757–1821). *The illustrated Bartsch.* Ed. Walter L. Strauss. New York: Abaris Books, 1978.

Bax, D. 1979. *Hieronymus Bosch: His picture-writing deciphered.* Rotterdam: A. A. Balkema.

Bellis, Alice Ogden. 1994. *Helpmates, harlots, and heroes: Women's stories in the Hebrew Bible.* Louisville, KY: Westminster/John Knox.

Bernt, Walther. 1970. *The Netherlandish painters of the seventeenth century.* 3 vols. Munich: Verlag F. Bruckmann/Phaidon Press.

Bèze, Theodor. 1595. *Van de Polygamie ofte Houwelick met veel Vrouwen.* Trans. Henrico Heiningo. Middelburgh: Richard Schildres Drucker der Heeren, Staten van Zeeland.

Bialostocki, Jan, et al. 1979. *Jan Lievens: ein Maler im Schatten Rembrandts.* Braunschweig: Herzog Anton Ulrich-Museum Braunschweig.

Bildarchiv Foto Marburg. 1976–. *Marburger Index: Bilddokumentation zur Kunst in Deutschland.* Bildarchiv Foto Marburg im Forschungsinstitut für Kunstgeschichte der Phillipps-Universität, Rheinisches Bildarchiv Köln.

Blankert, Albert, et al. 1997. *Rembrandt: A genius and his impact.* Exhibition catalog, National Gallery of Victoria, Melbourne. Zwolle: Waanders.

Blankert, Albert, with Leonard Slatkes. 1986. *Holländische Malerei in neuem Licht: Hendrick ter Brugghen und seine Zeitgenossen.* Exhibition catalog, Centraal Museum, Utrecht. Braunschweig: Limbach.

Blankert, Albert. 1982. *Ferdinand Bol (1616–1680), Rembrandt's pupil.* Doornspijk: Davaco.

———, et al. 1980. *Gods, saints and heroes: Dutch painting in the age of Rembrandt.* Washington, D.C.: National Gallery of Art.

Bleyerveld, Yvonne. 2000–2001. Chaste, obedient and devout: Biblical women as patterns of female virtue in Netherlandish and German graphic art, ca. 1500–1750. *Simiolus: Netherlands Quarterly for the History of Art* 28, 4:219–50.

———. 2000. *Hoe bedriechlijck dat die vrouwen zijn: Vrouwenlisten in de beeldende kunst in de Nederlanden circa 1350–1650.* Amsterdam: Primavera Press.

———. 1991. *Het Oude Testament in de Nederlandse schilderkunst, tekenkunst en grafiek (1430–1533), in het bijzonder de uitbeelding van oudtestamentische vrouwen* (scriptie). Amsterdam: Vrije Universiteit.

Bloch, Vitale. 1940. Haarlem classicists. *Oud Holland* 57:14–20.

Bor, Salomon. 1695. *De verkore Godsdienst Binnens Huys geoeffent: en d'Opvoeding der Kinderen in de Selve.* Utrecht: Willem Broedelet.

Boschma, C., J. M. de Groot, G. Jansen, J. W. M. de Jong, and F. Grijzenhout, eds. 1998. *Mesterlijk Vee: Nederlandse Veeschilders 1600–1900.* Zwolle: Waanders.

Boswell, John. 1988. *The kindness of strangers: The abandonment of children in Western Europe from late Antiquity to the Renaissance.* New York: Random Books.

Brenner, Athalya. 1986. Female social behaviour: Two descriptive patterns within the "Birth of the Hero" paradigm. *Vetus Testamentum* 36, 3:257–73.

Burnett, Mark Thornton. 1992. The "trusty servant": A sixteenth-century English emblem. *Emblematica* 6, 2:237–53.

Busch, Werner. 1982. Lucas van Leydens "Große Hagar" und die Augustinishce Typologieauffasung der Vorreformation. *Zeitschrift für Kunstgeschichte* 45:97–129.

Cahn, Walter. 2001. The expulsion of the Jews as history and allegory in painting and sculpture of the twelfth and thirteenth centuries. In *Jews and Christians in twelfth-century Europe*. Ed. M. A. Signer and J. van Engen. Notre-Dame, IN: University of Notre Dame Press.

Cairncross, John. 1974. *After polygamy was made a sin: The social history of Christian polygamy*. London: Routledge & Kegan Paul.

Calvin, Jean. (1509–64). *Commentaires Bibliques: Commentaires sur l'Ancient Testament. La Livre de la Genese*. Ed. André Malet. Aix-en-Provence: Editions Kerygma, 1978.

Carlson, Marybeth. 1994. A Trojan horse of worldliness? Maidservants in the burgher household in Rotterdam at the end of the seventeenth century. In *Women of the Golden Age: An international debate on women in seventeenth-century Holland, England, and Italy*. Ed. Els Kloek, Nicole Teeuwen, and Marijke Huisman. Hilversum: Verloren.

———. 1993. Domestic service in a changing city economy: Rotterdam, 1680–1780. Diss., University of Wisconsin-Madison.

Caron, Marlies, et al. 1988. *Helse en hemelse vrouwen: Schrikbeelden en voorbeelden van de vrouw in de christelijke cultuur*. Utrecht: Rijksmuseum Het Catharijneconvent.

Carrasso-Kok, M., and J. Levy-van Halm. 1988. *Schutters in Holland: kracht en zenuwen van de stad*. Zwolle: Uitgeverij Waanders.

Cats, Jacob. 1658. *Al de Wercken van Jacob Cats*. Repr. in the modern edition. Schiedam, the Netherlands: H.A.M. Roelants, n.d.

Van der Coelen, Pieter. 1998. *De Schrift verbeeld. Oudtestamentische prenten uit renaissance en barok*. Diss., Nijmegen: Kunsthistorisch Instituut, Katholieke Universiteit Nijmegen.

———. 1997. Het Oude Testament in Print: Voorstellingen van de Verstoting van Hagar en Ismael. *Antiek*, 6:274–82.

———. 1996. *Patriarchs, angels & prophets: The Old Testament in Netherlandish printmaking from Lucas van Leyden to Rembrandt*. Amsterdam: Museum Het Rembrandthuis/Rembrandt Information Centre.

Conisbee, Philip, Mary L. Levkoff, and Richard Rand. 1991. *The Ahmanson gifts: European masterpieces in the collection of the Los Angeles County Museum of Art.* Los Angeles: Los Angeles County Museum of Art.

Cossa, Frank. 1980. John Evelyn as penitent Magdalen: "Saints" and "malcontents" in seventeenth-century English portraiture. *Rutgers Art Review* 1:37–48.

Dathenus, Petrus. 1624. *Eene Christelijke Samenspreking uit Gods Woord.* 'S Graven-hage: Anthony Jansz.

Dekker, Rudolf. 2000. *Childhood, memory and autobiography in Holland: From the Golden Age to Romanticism.* Basingstoke: Macmillan.

———. 1995. *Uit de Schaduw in 't grote licht: Kinderen in egodocumenten van de Gouden Eeuw tot de Romantiek.* Amsterdam: Wereldbibliotheek.

———. 1994. Maid servants in the Dutch Republic: Sources and comparative perspectives, a response to Marybeth Carlson. In *Women of the Golden Age: An international debate on women in seventeenth-century Holland, England, and Italy.* Ed. Els Kloek, Nicole Teeuwen, and Marijke Huisman. Hilversum: Verloren.

Dent, Arthur. 1640. *Voetpat der eenvoudiger menschen.* Dedicated to and approved by Dominee Otto Badius. Amsterdam.

De Witt, David Albert. 2000. *Jan van Noordt (1624–1676), '. . . famous history- and portrait-painter in Amsterdam,' the Netherlands.* Diss., Queen's University at Kingston: UMI Research Press.

D'Hulst, R.-A., and M. Vandenven, eds. 1989. *Rubens, The Old Testament.* Corpus Rubenianum Ludwig Burchard, pt. I, 3. Trans. P. S. Falla. New York: Oxford University Press.

Durantini, M. F. 1983. *The child in seventeenth-century Dutch painting.* Diss., University of California, Berkeley. Ann Arbor: UMI Research Press.

Van Eeghen, P., and J. Ph. van der Kellen. 1905. *Het Werk van Jan en Casper Luyken.* Amsterdam: Frederik Muller & Co.

Eisler, Colin, ed. *Early Netherlandish painting: The Thyssen Bornemisza Collection.* London: Sotheby's Publications, 1989.

Ember, Ildikó, et al. 1987. *Niederländische Malerei des 17. Jahrhunderts aus Budapest.* Köln: Wallraf-Richartz-Museum der Stadt Köln mit dem Museum der Bildenden Künste, Budapest, und dem Centraal Museum, Utrecht.

Emmerson, Grace I. 1989. Women in ancient Israel. In *The world of ancient Israel: Sociological, anthropological and political perspectives.* Ed. R. E. Clements. Cambridge: Cambridge University Press.

Evenhuis, R. B. 1967. *Ook dat was Amsterdam: der Kerk der Hervorming in de Gouden Eeuw.* 3 vols. Amsterdam: ten Have.

Evett, David. 1990. "Surprising confrontations": Ideologies of service in Shakespeare's England. In *Renaissance Papers.* Ed. Dale B. J. Randall and Joseph A. Porter. Southeastern Renaissance Conference.

Falkenburg, R. L. 1988. Iconographical connections between Antwerp landscapes, market scenes and kitchen pieces, 1500–1580. *Oud Holland* 102, 2:114–26.

Ferrari, Oreste, and G. Scavizzi. 1992. *Luca Giordano: L'Opera Completa.* Naples: Electa Napoli.

Franits, Wayne. 1993. *Paragons of virtue: Women and domesticity in seventeenth-century Dutch art.* New York: Cambridge University Press.

———. 1992. Housewives and their maids in Dutch seventeenth-century art. In *Politics, gender, and the arts: Women, the arts, and society.* Ed. R. Dotterer and S. Bowers. Selinsgrove, PA: Susquehanna University Press.

———. 1989. The depiction of servants in some paintings by Pieter de Hooch. *Zeitschrift fürKunstgeschichte* 52, 1:559–66.

———. 1986. The family saying grace: A theme in Dutch art of the seventeenth century. *Netherlands Quarterly for the History of Art* 16, 1:36–49.

Fruytiers, Jan. 1573. *Schriftmetige Gebeden op deerste Boeck Moysi Genesis. Insgehelijcs op all de Psalmen des Konincklicken Propheets Davids.* Emden: Goossen Goebens.

Gaehtgens, Barbara. 1987. *Adriaen van der Werff 1659–1722.* Munich: Deutscher Kunstverlag.

Gaskell, Ivan. 1990. *Seventeenth-century Dutch and Flemish painting.* London: Philip Wilson Publishers for Sotheby's Publications.

Getty Information Institute. 1996. *Getty Provenance Index cumulative edition* (GPI). CD-ROM. Comp. J. Montias and M. J. Bok. Pasadena, CA: Getty Information Institute.

Goddard, Stephen H., ed. 1988. *The world in miniature: Engravings by the German little masters 1500–1550.* Laurence, Kansas: Spencer Museum of Art, University of Kansas.

Grimm, Claus. 1990. *Frans Hals: The complete works.* New York: Harry N. Abrams.

Groenhuis, G. 1977. *De Predikanten.* Groningen: Wolters-Nordhoff.

Grotius, Hugo. 1693. *Aentekeningen over de Brieven van den Apostel Paulus aen die van Rome, Korinten, Galatie, Ephesen, Philippe en Colossen, uit het Latijn vertaelt door David van Hoogstraten.* Amsterdam.

Haak, Bob. 1996. *The Golden Age: Dutch painters of the seventeenth century.* New York: Stewart, Tabori & Chang.

Haks, Donald, and Marie Christine van der Sman, eds. 1996. *Dutch society in the age of Vermeer.* Zwolle: Waanders.

Haks, Donald. 1985. *Huwelijk en Gezin in Holland in de 17de en 18de Eeuw.* Utrecht: Hes Uitgevers.

Hamann, Richard. 1936. Hagars Abschied bei Rembrandt und im Rembrandt-Kreise. *Marburger Jahrbuch fur Kunstwissenschaft* 8–9:471–580.

Havlice, Patricia Pate, ed. 1977. *World painting index.* Metuchen, NJ: Scarecrow Press.

Van der Heijden, Manon. 1998. *Huwelijk in Holland: stedelijk rechtspraak en kerkelijk tucht, 1550–1700.* Amsterdam: B. Bakker.

Held, Julius S. 1964. *Rembrandt and the book of Tobit.* Northampton, MA: Gehenna Press.

Hollander, Martha. 2002. *An entrance for the eyes: Space and meaning in seventeenth-century Dutch art.* Berkeley: University of California Press.

———. 1994. The divided household of Nicolaes Maes. *Word and Image* 10:138–55.

Hollstein, F. W. H. 1996. *The new Hollstein Dutch & Flemish etchings, engravings and woodcuts, 1450–1700: Lucas van Leyden.* Compiled by J. P. Filedt Kok. Ed. G. Luijten. Rotterdam: Sound & Vision Interactive.

———. 1996–. *The new Hollstein: German engravings, etchings and woodcuts 1400–1700.* Rotterdam: Sound & Vision Interactive.

———. 1949. *Dutch and Flemish etchings, engravings and woodcuts, ca. 1450–1700.* 53 vols. Amsterdam: M. Hertzberger.

Hoogsteder, Willem Jan. 2003. Die Gemäldesammlung von Friedrich V und Elizabeth in Königshaus in Rhenen/Niederlande. In *Der Winterkönig, Friedrich von der Pfalz: Bayern und Europa im Zeitalter des Drießigjährigen Krieges.* Ed. Peter Wolf et al. Stuttgart: Konrad Theiss Verlag.

Huisman, C. 1983. *Neerlands Israël: Het Natiebesef der Traditioneel-Gereformeerden in de Achttiende Eeuw.* Dordrecht: J. P. van den Tol.

Hummelen, W. M. H. 1968. *Repertorium van het Rederijkersdrama 1500–ca.1620.* Assen: van Gorcum & Comp.

Irmscher, Gunter. 1986. Ministrae voluptatum: Stoicizing ethics in the market and kitchen scenes of Pieter Aertsen and Joachim Beuckelaer. *Simiolus: Netherlands Quarterly for the History of Art* 16, 4:219–32.

Israel, Jonathan. 1995. *The Dutch Republic: Its rise, greatness, and fall 1477–1806.* Oxford: Clarendon Press.

Jacobowitz, Ellen S., and Stephanie L. Stepanek. 1983. *The prints of Lucas van Leyden and his contemporaries.* Washington, D.C.: National Gallery of Art.

Jongejan, Marlies. 1984. Dienstboden in de Zeeuwse steden, 1650–1800. *Spiegel Historiael* 5:214–21.

De Jongh, Eddy. 2001. The model woman and the women of flesh and blood. In *Rembrant's Women.* Ed. J. Wiliams et al. Edinburgh: Trustees of the National Galleries of Scotland.

De Jongh, Eddy, and Ger Luijten. 1997. *Mirror of everyday life: Genreprints in the Netherlands, 1550–1700.* Rijksmuseum Amsterdam: Snoeck-Ducaju & Zoon, Ghent.

De Jongh, Eddy. 1986. *Portretten van Echt en Trouw: Huwelijk en Gezin in de Nederlandse Kunst van de Zeventiende Eeuw.* Zwolle: Waanders.

———. 1968–69. Erotica in vogelperspectief. *Simiolus: Netherlands Quarterly for the History of Art* 3, 1:22–74.

Josephus, Flavius. (37–100 AD). *hoogh-beroemde Joodische Historien ende boecken.* Haarlem: Adriaen Roman. 1636.

Josephus, Flavius. (37–100 AD). *Boecken; te weten, twintigh van de oude Geschiedenissen van der Joden.* Trans. L. v. Boos and S. de Vries. Doordrecht: J. Savery, 1665.

Josephus, Flavius. (37–100 AD). Trans. H. St. J. Thackeray et al. 10 vols. Loeb Classical Library. Cambridge: Harvard University Press, 1926–1965.

Judson, J. Richard, and Rudolf E. O. Ekkart. 1999. *Gerrit van Honthorst 1592–1656.* Doornspijk: Davaco.

Kaplan, Paul H. I. 1982. Titian's "Laura Dianti" and the origins of the motif of the black page in portraiture. *Antichita Viva* 21, 1:11–18.

Van Kappen, O. 1965. *Geschiedenis de Zigeuners in Nederland. De Ontwikkeling van de Rechtspositie der Heidens of Egyptenaren in de Noordelijke Nederland, 1420–1750.* Assen: van Gorcum and Comp.

Kattenburch, Adrianus van. 1737. *Een-en-twintig predikatien over verscheide mest historische stoffen des ouden testaments.* Leiden.

Kettering, Alison McNeil. 1983. *The Dutch Arcadia: Pastoral art and its audience in the Golden Age.* Montclair, NJ: Abner Schram Ltd.

Kiers, Judikje, and Fieke Tissink. 2000. *De Glorie van de Gouden Eeuw: Schilderijen, beeldhouwkunst en kunstnijverheid.* Zwolle: Waanders/Rijksmuseum te Amsterdam.

Kilian, Jennifer M. 2005. *The paintings of Karel du Jardin, 1626–1678: catalog raisonné.* Philadelphia, PA: John Benjamins Publishers.

————. 1996. Karel Du Jardin. *Dictionary of Art*, vol. 9. Ed. J. Turner. New York: Grove Dictionaries.

Kirsch, Jonathan. 1997. *The Harlot by the Side of the Road: Forbidden Tales of the Bible.* New York: Ballentine Books.

Kirschenbaum, B. *The Religious and Historical Paintings of Jan Steen.* New York: Allanheld & Schram, 1977.

De Koningh, Abraham. 1616. *Hagars vluchte ende weder-komste.* Ed. G. van Eemeren and A. Lenferink-van Daal. N.p.: Centrum Renaissance-drama, 1990.

Korwin, Yala H., ed. 1981. *Index to two-dimensional art works.* Metuchen, NJ: Scarecrow Press.

Kunzle, David R. 2002. *From criminal to courtier: The soldier in Netherlandish art 1550–1672.* Leiden/Boston: Brill.

————. 1978. The World Upside Down. . . . In *The reversible world: Symbolic inversion in art and society.* Ed. Barbara Babcock. Ithaca, NY: Cornell University Press.

————. 1973. *The early comic strip: narrative strips and picture stories in the European broadsheet from c. 1450 to 1825.* Berkeley: University of California Press.

Kussmaul, Anne. 1981. *Servants in husbandry in early modern England.* Cambridge: Cambridge University Press.

Landau, David. 1978. *Catalogo completo dell' opera grafica di George Pencz.* Trans. A. Paul. Milano: Salamon e Agustoni.

Leistra, J. E. P. 1997. Adraien van der Werff. *Dictionary of art*, vol. 33. Ed. J. Turner. New York: Grove Dictionaries.

Lewalski, Barbara Kiefer. 1979. *Protestant poetics and the seventeenth-century religious lyrics.* Princeton: Princeton University Press.

Van Lier, Jan. 1995. Door rivaliteit getekend. Het beeld van Hagar in kunst en kathechese, vol. 28. *Jota: Uitleg van bijbelteksten met het oog op katechese en liturgie.*

Loughman, John, and John Michael Montias. 2000. *Public and private spaces: Works of art in seventeenth-century Dutch houses.* Zwolle: Waanders.

Luijtens, Ger. 1997. Gerrit Claesz Bleker: Milkmaid 1643. In *Mirror of everyday life: Genreprints in the Netherlands, 1550–1700.* Ed. E. de Jongh, G. Luijten. Ghent: Rijksmuseum Amsterdam/Snoeck-Ducaju & Zoon.

Luther, Martin. (1483–1546). *Luther's works.* Ed. and trans. Jaroslav Pelikan. 55 vols. St. Louis: Concordia Publishing House, 1955–86.

Luyken, Jan. 1736. *Goddelyke Liefde-Vlammen of vervolg van Jesus en de Ziele. Handelende van een Botvaerdige, Geheiligde, Liefhebbende, en haar zelfstervende Ziele.*

In drie deelen met Koopere Afbeeldingen verciert. Nevens haar vaarsen, aanmerkingen, en zielzughtingen. Amsterdam: de Veryheydens.

Lyserus, Johannes. 1675. *Politisch Discours tusschen monogamo en polygamo, van de Polygamia ofte veelwyvery, opgestelde en met 300 argumenten verklaert uyt het Latijn en Hoogduyts vertaalt, en nu in 't Nederduyts overgeset, door Johannes Lyserus.* Freiburg. Translator and publisher unknown.

De Mare, Heidi, and Anna Vos, eds. 1993. *Urban rituals in Italy and the Netherlands.* Assen: Van Gorcum.

Magurn, Ruth Saunders, ed. and trans. 1955. *The letters of Peter Paul Rubens.* Cambridge, MA: Harvard University Press.

Manuth, Volker. 1993–94. Denomination and iconography: The choice of subject matter in the biblical painting of the Rembrandt circle. *Simiolus: Netherlands Quarterly for the History of Art* 22:235–52.

McGrath, Susan. 1997. *Rubens: Subjects from history.* Ed. A. Balis. 2 vols. Corpus Rubenianum Ludwig Burchard, pt. 13. London: Harvey Miller.

———. 1994. River-gods, sources and the mystery of the Nile: Rubens's *Four Rivers* in Vienna. In *Die Malerei Antwerpens—Gattungen, Meister, Wirkungen. Studien zur flämischen Kunst des 16. und 17. Jahrhunderts. Internationales Kolloquium, Vienna, 1993.* Ed. C. Stukenbrock. Köln: Locher.

———. 1984. Rubens's "Susanna and the Elders" and moralizing inscriptions on prints. In *Wort und Bild in der Niederlanden: Kunst und Literatur des 16 und 17 Jahrhunderts.* Ed. Hans Vekeman. Erftstadt: Lukassen.

Mees, Gregorius. 1673. *Hagars Dienst onder de Vrye Sara; Verdedigende het vorrecht van Godts genade boven de Wet om tot God te naken. Nevens de oorsprongh, aerdt, order, kracht, eygenschappen, werckingen, oogemerck, vruchten &c. der Vermaningen, en aengeknopte Beloften Godts.* Groningen: Dominicus Lens.

Mellinkoff, Ruth. 2005. Two erotic women warriors: Sexy, violent, and lethal. In *Studies in illuminated manuscripts: A tribute to Lucy Freeman Sandler.* London: Harvey Miller.

———. 1998. Sarah and Hagar: Laughter and tears. In *Illuminating the book: Makers and interpreters.* Ed. Michelle P. Brown and Scott McKendrick. London: British Library.

Mijnhardt, Wijnand, and Joost Kloek. 2001. *1800: Blauwdrukken voor een Samenleving.* Den Haag: Sdu Uitgevers.

Miller, Debra. 1992. The word of Calvin in the art of Jan Victors. *Konsthistorisk Tidskrift* 61, 3:99–105.

Miller, Leo. 1974. *John Milton among the polygamophiles.* New York: Loewenthal Press.

Molhuysen, P. C., Blok, J. P., eds. 1912. *Nieuw Nederlandsch Biografisch Woordenboek.* 10 vols. Leiden: A. W. Sijthoff's Uitgevers-Maatschappij.

Von Moltke, Joachim Wolfgang. 1997. Salomon de Bray. In *Dictionary of art*, vol. 4. Ed. J. Turner.

———. 1994. *Arent de Gelder. Dordrecht 1645–1727.* Doornspijk: Davaco.

———. 1938–39. Salomon de Bray. In *Marburger Jahrbuch für Kunstwissenschaft* 11–12:342–43.

Montias, John Michael. 1991. Works of art in seventeenth-century Amsterdam. In *Art in history, history in art: Studies in seventeenth-century Dutch culture.* Ed. David Freedberg and Jan de Vries. Issues and Debates 1. Santa Monica, CA: Getty Center for the History of Art.

Moxey, Keith. 1977. *Pieter Aertsen, Joachim Beuckelaer, and secular painting in the Reformation.* New York: Garland Publishing.

Muller, Sheila D. 1985. *Charity in the Dutch Republic: Pictures of rich and poor for charitable institutions.* Diss., University of California, Berkeley. Ann Arbor: UMI Research Press.

Myers, Allen C., ed. 1987. *Eerdmans Bible dictionary.* Grand Rapids: Eerdmans.

Nicolson, Benedict. 1977. Stomer brought up-to-date. *Burlington Magazine* 119, 1:230–45.

Nieuwstraten, J. 1998. Het Werkelijke Onderwerp van Aert de Gelders "Heiligie Familie" te Berlijn. *Oud Holland* 1, 2–3:157–67.

North, Michael. 1997. *Art and commerce in the Dutch Golden Age.* New Haven: Yale University Press.

Offerhaus, J. 1962. *De Betekenis van Francesco Cozza's Hagar en Ismaël.* Bulletin van het Rijksmuseum, 5–15.

Panhuysen, Luc. 2000. *De beloofde stad. Opkomst en ondergang van het koninkrijk der wederdopers.* Amsterdam: Atlas.

Parshall, Peter. 1978. Lucas van Leyden's narrative style. In *Nederlands Kunsthistorisch Jaarboek: Netherlands Yearbook for the History of Art,* 29:185–237.

Van der Passe, Crispijn (the elder). 1616. *Liber Genesis.* 2nd ed.

Van der Passe, Crispijn (the younger). 1630. *Le Miroir des Plus Belles Courtisannes de ce Temps.*

Pauwels, C. H. 1953. De Schilder Matthias Stomer. *Gentse Bijdragen tot de Kunstgeschiedenis* 14:139–92.

Pelzer, Rupert Arthur. 1913–14. Lambert Sustris von Amsterdam. *Jahrbuch der kunsthistorischen Sammlungen des Allerhöchsten Kaiserhauses.* Wien: A. Schroll, 31:221–46.

Pepper, Stephen. 1984. *The Bob Jones University collection of religious art.* Greenville, SC: Bob Jones University.

Perkins, Wilhelm. 1662. *Een verklaringe over de vijf eerste Capittels van den Zend-Brief Galaters.* Amsterdam: Iohannes van Someren.

———. 1659. *Alle de werken van Mr. Wilhelm Perkins, vermaarde Ghodgheleerde in Engelandt.* 3 vols. Amsterdam: Iohannes van Someren.

———. 1606. *De Gulden Keten, Ofte eene bescrijvinghe van de gantsche Theologie inhoudende ende verclarende het vervolch vande oorsaken der salicheyt ende der verdoemenisse der menschen, uyt ende nae den woorde Gods. Hier is noch een sturcken van Theodorvs Beza, om de vedroefde ghewissen te troosten. Alles ghetrouwelijck uyt het Latijn in Nederlantsche sprake overgheset door Philippvm Rvyl, Alcamarianvm, Dienaer Jesu Christi tot Sevenhoben. Gedruct t' Haerlem, by Gillis Rooman. Door Jan Evertz Cloppenburch, Amsterdam.* Haarlem: Gillis Rooman.

Perlove, Shelly. 1996. Awaiting the Messiah: Christians, Jews, and Muslims in the Late Work of Rembrant. *Bulletin: The University of Michigan Museums of Art and Archaeology* 11:84–113.

Pietersz, Roelof. 1632. *Lof van onses heeren Jesu Christ.* 8th ed. Amsterdam: M. J. Brandt.

———. 1629. *T. Lof der Kercke ende Gemeynte Jesus Christi. Dat is: Korte Verklaringe van eenige voorneme Figuren, Gelijckenissen, Ciernamen / Privilegien / Heerlijckheden / enden Eygenschappen die der Kercke Jesus Christi in het Oudte ende Nieuwe Testament gegeven worden. Aen de Actbare, Wyse, Voorsienige, Seer discrete Heeren, de Heeren Bewinthebberen der Geoctroyeerde West-Indische Compagnie ter Camere binnen Amstelredam.* Amstelredam: Hendrick Laurentsz, 1629.

Pigler, Andor. 1974. *Barockthemen: Eine Auswahl von Verzeichnissen zur Ikonographie des 17. und 18. Jahrhunderts.* 3 vols. Budapest: Académie Kiadó.

van de Pol, Lotte C. 1994. The lure of the big city: Female migration to Amsterdam. In *Women of the Golden Age: An international debate on women in seventeenth-century Holland, England, and Italy.* Ed. Els Kloek, Nicole Teeuwen, and Marijke Huisman. Hilversum: Verloren.

———. 1988. Beeld en Werkelijkheid van de Prostitutie in de Zeventiende Eeuw. In *Soete minne en helsche boosheit: Seksuele voorstellingen in Nederland, 1300–1850.* Ed. Gert Hekma and Herman Roodenburg. Nijmegen: Sun.

Pollman, Judith. 2000. Women and religion in the Dutch Golden Age. *Dutch Crossing: A Journal of Low Countries Studies* 24, 2:162–82.

Poortman, Wilco C. *Bijbel en Prent.* 's-Gravenhage: Boekencentrum, 1983–86.

Puckett, D. L. 1995. *John Calvin's exegesis of the Old Testament.* Louisville, KY: Westminster John Knox.

Ruether, Rosemary Radford. 1974. *Religion and sexism: Images of woman in the Jewish and Christian traditions.* New York: Simon & Shuster.

Ridderus, Franciscus. 1657. *Onlangs Godtsaelighe, en nu Zalige, Sara, voorgestelt aan de dochteren Zions van Rotterdam.* Rotterdam: Johannes Vishoeck.

Rijksbureau voor Kunsthistorische Documentatie, Netherlands. 1968. *Decimal index of the art of the Low Countries.* D.I.A.L. Den Haag: Rijksbureau voor Kunsthistorische Documentatie.

Ripa, Cesare. 1779. *Iconologia.* Repr. of the edition by G. Scott of London. Ed. Stephen Orgel. 2 vols. New York: Garland Publications, 1979.

Robbins, Bruce. 1986. *The servant's hand: English fiction from below.* New York: Columbia University Press.

Roberts, Helene, ed. 1987. *Iconographic index to Old Testament subjects represented in photographs and slides of paintings in the visual collections, Fine Arts Library, Harvard University.* New York: Garland Publications.

Robinson, F. W. 1974. *Gabriel Metsu: A study of his place in Dutch genre painting of the Golden Age.* New York: A. Schram.

Robinson, Franklin W., and William H. Wilson. 1980. *Catalogue of the Flemish and Dutch paintings, 1400–1900.* Sarasota, FL: John and Mable Ringling Museum of Art.

Robinson, William W. 1987. The eavesdropper and related paintings by Nicolaes Maes. In *Holländische Genremalerei im 17. Jahrhunder, Symposium Berlin, 1984,* vol. 4. Ed. Henning Bock and Thomas W. Gaehtgens. Berlin: Jahrbuch Preußischer Kulturbesitz.

Roethlisberger, Marcel G. 1993. *Abraham Bloemaert and his sons: Paintings and prints.* 2 vols. Doornspijk: Davaco.

———. 1981. *Bartholomeus Breenbergh: The paintings.* Berlin/New York: Walter de Gruyter.

Rouwen, Herbert H. 1990. *The princes of Orange: The stadholders in the Dutch Republic.* New York: Cambridge University Press.

Roy, Alain. 1992. *Gérard de Lairesse 1640–1711.* Paris: Arthena.

Rubens, Peter Paul, Sir. 1887–1909. *Correspondance de Rubens et documents épistolaires concernant sa vie et ses oeuvres, publiés, traduits.* Ed. M. Rooses and C. Ruelens. Anvers: Veuve de Backer.

Rupprecht, Bernhard. 1992. Die faule Hausmaid. Schwank und Bild. In *Jahrbuch für Fränkische Landeforschung.* Ed. Jürgen Schneider and Gerhard

Rechter. Neustadt: Institut für Fränkische Landesforschung.

Rybczynski, Witold. 1986. *Home: The short history of an idea.* New York: Viking.

Salomon, Nanette. 1987. Jan Steen's formulation of the dissolute household, sources and meanings. *Holländische Genremalerei im 17. Jahrhunder, Symposium Berlin, 1984*, vol. 4. Ed. Henning Bock and Thomas W. Gaehtgens. Berlin: Jahrbuch Preußischer Kulturbesitz.

De Saluste, Guillaume, Sieur du Bartas. 1605. *The divine weeks and works of Guillaume de Saluste Sieur du Bartas.* Ed. Susan Snyder. Trans. Joshuah Sylvester. Oxford: Clarendon Press, 1979.

Sánchez, Alfonso E. Pérez. 1997. "Jusepe de Ribera." In *Dictionary of Art*, vol. 26. Ed. J. Turner. New York: Grove Dictionaries.

Schabaelje, J. P. 1654. *De Grooten Emblem Sacrae.* With reprints of 1588 engravings by Pieter van der Borcht. Amsterdam.

Schama, Simon. 1988. *The embarrassment of riches: An interpretation of Dutch culture in the Golden Age.* Berkeley: University of California Press.

————. 1980. Wives and wantons: Versions of womanhood in the Dutch seventeenth century. *Oxford Art Journal* (April): 5–13.

Schapiro, Meyer. 1963. The Bowman and the Bird on the Ruthwell Cross and Other Works: The Interpretation of Secular Themes in Early Mediaeval Religious Art. *Art Bulletin* 45:351–57.

Schmidt, Philipp. 1962. *Die Illustration der Lutherbibel, 1522–1700; ein Stück abendlandische Kultur- und Kirchengeschichte mit Verzeichnissen der Bibeln, Bilder und Künstler.* Basel: F. Reinhardt.

Schott, Elizabeth Ann. 2000. *Representing the body in the seventeenth-century Netherlands: Rembrandt's nudes reconsidered.* Diss., University of California, Berkeley.

Schwartz, Gary. 1998. The shape, size and destiny of the Dutch market for paintings at the end of the Eighty Years War. In *1648, War and Peace in Europe.* Ed. Klaus Bussman and Heinz Schilling. Trans. David Allison. Münster: Westfalisches Landesmuseum.

————. 1985. *Rembrandt, his life, his paintings: A new biography with all accessible paintings illustrated in colour.* New York: Viking.

Schweers, Hans F., ed. 1994. *Gemälde in Deutschen Museen: Katalog der ausgestellten und depotgelagerten werke.* 10 vols. München: New Providence.

Sellin, Johan Thorsten. 1944. *Pioneering in penology: The Amsterdam houses in the sixteenth and seventeenth centuries.* Philadelphia: University of Pennsylvania Press.

Sellin, Paul R. 1988. *So doth, so is religion: John Donne and diplomatic contexts in the Reformed Netherlands, 1619–1620.* Columbia: University of Missouri Press.

————. 1984. Lieuwe van Aitzema and the Dutch translation of Milton on divorce. In *Papers from the Second Interdisciplinary Conference on Netherlandic Studies*, Ed. W. H. Fletcher. Publications for the American Association for Netherlandic Studies. New York: Lanham University Press of America.

Sibersma, Hero. 1715. *De Tente van Hagar en Sara, dat is, de dienstbare gemeente onder Moses; en de vrye onder de Messais en Hoe daar in den Hemel nederdaaldt op aarden, en de inwooners van die Tente die Messianen of Christenen zyn, en also het Israel na den Geest.* Amsterdam: Jacobus Borstius.

Silver, Larry. 1983. Forest primeval: Albrecht Altdorfer and the German wilderness landscape. *Simiolus: Netherlands Quarterly for the History of Art* 13, 1:4–43.

Slatke, Leonard. 1997. Mathias Stomer. *Dictionary of art*, vol. 29. Ed. J. Turner.

Slatter, Eugene. 1950. *1950 Exhibition of Dutch and Flemish masters.* London: Eugene Slatter Gallery.

Slive, Seymour. 1995. *Dutch painting, 1600–1800.* New Haven and London: Yale University Press.

Sluijter, Eric Jan. 2001. "Horrible nature, incomparable art": Rembrandt and the depiction of the female nude. In *Rembrandt's Women.* Ed. J. Williams et al. Edinburh: Trustees of the National Galleries of Scotland.

————. 1998. Rembrandt's Bathsheba and the conventions of a seductive theme. In *Rembrandt's Bathsheba reading King David's letter.* Ed. Anne Jensen Adams. Cambridge: Cambridge University Press.

Smith, Susan. 1995. *The power of women: A* Topos *in medieval art and literature.* Philadelphia: University of Pennsylvania Press.

Snoep, D. P., and C. Thiels. 1973. *Adriaen van der Werff; Karlingen 1659, 1722 Rotterdam.* Rotterdam: Historisch Museum Rotterdam.

Stevenson, Kay Gilliland. 1995. Emblematic and incremental imagery: Rabelais, Spenser, Milton, Herbert, Cats. In *George Herbert: Sacred and profane*, vol. 2. Ed. Richard Todd and Helen Wilcox. Amsterdam: VU University Press.

Stewart, Alison. 1977. *Unequal lovers: A study of unequal couples in northern art.* New York: Abaris Books.

Sumowski, Werner. 1996. Ein Gemälde von Carel Fabritius. *Pantheon* 54:77–84.

———. 1983. *Die Gemälde der Rembrandt-Schüler.* 6 vols. Landau: Edition PVA.

Sutton, Peter C. 1998. *Pieter de Hooch, 1629–1684.* New Haven and London: Wadsworth/Atheneum with Yale University Press.

———. 1986. *Dutch art in America.* Grand Rapids: Eerdmans; Kampen: Kok.

———. 1984. *Masters of seventeenth-century Dutch genre painting.* Philadelphia: Philadelphia Museum of Art.

———. 1980. *Pieter de Hooch: Complete edition with a catalog raisonne.* Oxford: Phaidon Press.

Van Tatenhove, J. 1994. Een ets van Jan de Bisschop en een schilderstuk van Karel Dujardin. *Delineavit et Sculpsit: Tijdschrift voor Nederlandse prent— en tekenkunst tot omstreeks 1850* (April): 46–48.

Teubal, Savina J. 1990. *Hagar the Egyptian: The lost tradition of the matriarchs.* New York: Harper Collins, Harper San Francisco.

Thieme, Ulrich, and Felix Becker. 1913. *Allgemeines Lexikon der bildenden Künstler von der Antike bis zur Gegenwart.* 37 vols. Liepzig: Verlag von E. A. Seeman.

Thompson, John L. 2001. *Writing the wrongs: Women of the Old Testament among biblical commentators from Philo through the Reformation.* New York: Oxford University Press.

———. 2000. Calvin's exegetical legacy: His reception and transmission of text and tradition. In *The legacy of John Calvin: Papers presented at the 12th colloquium of the Calvin Studies Society Papers, 1999.* Ed. David Foxgrover. Grand Rapids: CRC Product Services.

———. 1997. Hagar, victim or villain? Three sixteenth-century views. *Catholic Biblical Quarterly* 59:213–33.

———. 1994. Patriarchs, polygamy, and private resistance: John Calvin and others on breaking God's rules. *Sixteenth-Century Journal* 15, 1:3–27.

———. 1992. *John Calvin and the daughters of Sarah: Women in regular and exceptional roles in the exegesis of Calvin, his predecessors, and his contemporaries.* Geneva: Library Droz S.A.

———. 1991. The immoralities of the patriarchs in the history of exegesis: A reappraisal of Calvin's position. *Calvin Theological Journal* 26, 1:9–46.

Tillotson, Johannes. 1695. *De Verkore Godsdienst Binnens Huys geoeffent: en d'Opvoeding der Kinderen in de selve; met de voordeelen van een vroegen Godzaligheyd verhandeld in ses Predicatien door Dr. Johannes Tillotson.* Trans. Salomon Bor. Utrecht: Willem Broedelet.

Trible, Phyllis. 1984. *Texts of terror*. Philadelphia: Fortress.

Tümpel, Astrid, and Peter Schatborn. 1991. *Pieter Lastman: The man who taught Rembrandt*. Zwolle/Amsterdam: Waanders Uitgevers/Museum Het Rembrandthuis.

Tümpel, Astrid. 1974. Claes Cornelisz. Moeyaert. *Oud Holland* 88,1–2:1–163.

Tümpel, Astrid, and Christian Tümpel. 1974. *The Pre-Rembrandtists*. Sacramento: E. B. Crocker Art Gallery.

Tümpel, Christian. 1991. *Het Oude Testament in de Schilderkunst van de Gouden Eeuw*. Zwolle: Waanders Uitgevers.

———. 1983. Die Reformation und die Kunst der Niederlande. In *Luther und die Folgen für die Kunst*. Ed. Werner Hoffman. München: Prestel-Verlag.

———. 1980. Religious history painting. In *Gods, saints, and heroes: Dutch painting in the age of Rembrandt*. Washington: National Gallery of Art.

———. 1970. *Rembrandt legt die Bibel aus. Zeichnungen und Radierungen aus dem Kupferstichkabinett der Staatlichen Museen Preußischer Klturbesitz*. Berlin: Verlag Bruno Hessling.

Twisk, Pieter Jansz. 1632. *Bybelsche naem- ende Chronijck-boek wesende Het tweede deel der Concordatie der Heylieger Schrifture*. Hoorn: Sacharias Cornelisz.

Utrecht Centraal Museum. 1952. *Catalogus der Schilderijen*. Utrecht: Utrecht Centraal Museum.

Veldman, Ilja M. 2002. *Profit and pleasure: Print books by Crispijn de Passe*. Studies in Prints and Printmaking 4. Rotterdam: Sound and Vision Publishers.

———. 2001. *Crispijn de Passe and his progeny (1564–1670): A century of print production*. Studies in Prints and Printmaking 3. Rotterdam: Sound and Vision Publishers.

Verdi, Richard. 1999. *Matthias Stom: Isaac blessing Jacob*. University of Birmingham: Edward Fox & Son Ltd.

Vertova, Luisa. 1979. *Caravaggism in Europe*. Oxford, Phaidon Press Ltd.

Verwijs, E., and J. Verdam. 1885–1952. *MiddelNederlandsch Woordenboek*. S'Gravenhage: Martinus Nijhoff.

Van den Vondel, Joost. 1986. *Vondel: Volledige Dichtwerken en Oorspronkelyk Proza verzorgt door Albert Verwey*. Ed. Mieke B. Smits-Veldt and Marijke Spies. Amsterdam: H. J. W. Becht.

Voss, Hermann. 1924. *Die Malerei des Barock in Rom.* Berlin: Ullsteinhaus.

De Vries, A. D, and A. Bredius. 1885. *Catalogus der Schilderijen in het Museum Kunstliefde te Utrecht.* Utrecht: J. L. Beijers.

De Vries, Lyckle. 1990. Portraits of people at work. In *Opstellen voor Hans Locher.* Ed. J. de Jong et al. Groningen: Instituut voor Kunstgeschiedenis, Rijksuniversiteit Groningen.

Van de Waal, H. 1973–83. *Iconoclass: An iconographic classification system,* pt. 1. Ed. L. D. Couprie, R. H. Fuchs, and E. Tholen. 9 vols. Amsterdam: North Holland Publishing Company.

———. 1974. "Hagar in the Wilderness by Rembrandt and His School." In *Steps toward Rembrandt: Collected articles, 1937–1972.* Ed. R. H. Fuchs. Trans. P. Wardle and A. Griffiths. Amsterdam: North Holland Publishing Company.

Walsh, John. 1972. The earliest dated painting by Nicolaes Maes. *Metropolitan Museum Journal* 6:105–14.

Weems, Renita J. 1988. *Just a sister away: A womanist vision of women's relationships in the Bible.* San Diego: LuraMeida.

Weller, Dennis P. 1998. *Sinners and saints, darkness and light: Caravaggio and his Dutch and Flemish followers.* Raleigh, NC: North Carolina Museum of Art.

Wieseman, Marjorie Elizabeth. 2002. *Casper Netscher and late seventeenth-century Dutch painting.* Doornspijk, the Netherlands, Davaco.

———. 1991. *Caspar Netscher and late-seventeenth-century Dutch painting.* Diss., Columbia University. Ann Arbor: UMI Research Press.

Wiesner, Merry E. 1998. Spinning out capital: Women's work in preindustrial Europe, 1350–1750. In *Becoming visible: Women in European history.* 3rd. ed. Ed. E. Bridenthal, S. Mosher Stuard, and M. E. Wiesner. Boston/New York: Houghton Mifflin.

Wilberg-Schuurman, Thea Vignau. 1983. *Hoofse minne en burgerlijke liefde in de prentkunst rond 1500.* Leiden: Uitgeverij Martinus Nijhoff.

Williams, Delores S. 1993. *Sisters in the wilderness: The challenge of womanist God-talk.* Maryknoll: Orbis.

De Winkel, Marieke. 2001. Fashion or fancy? Some interpretations of the dress of Rembrandt's women re-evaluated. In *Rembrandt's women.* Ed. J. L. Williams et al. Munich/London/New York: Prestel.

Wolf, Peter et al. 2003. *Der Winterkönig, Friedrich von der Pfalz: Bayern und Europa im Zeitalter des Drießigjährigen Krieges.* Stuttgart: Konrad Theiss Verlag.

Wolfthal, Diane. 1999. *Images of rape: The "heroic" tradition and its alternatives.* Cambridge: Cambridge University Press.

Woods-Marsden, Joanna. 2001. Portrait of the lady, 1430–1520. In *Virtue and beauty: Leonardo's Ginevra de' Benci and Renaissance portraits of women.* Ed. D. A. Brown et al. Princeton: Princeton University Press.

Wright, Christopher, ed. 1992. *The world's master paintings from the early Renaissance to the present day.* London: Routledge.

Zijlstra, S. 2000. *Om de ware gemeente en de oude gronden. Geschiedenis van de dopersen in de Nederlanden, 1531–1675.* Hilversum: Verloren.

INDEX